ALSO BY STACY DeBROFF

The Mom Book: 4,278 of Mom Central's Tips . . . for Moms, from Moms

Sign Me Up! The Parents' Complete Guide to Sports, Activities, Music Lessons, Dance Classes, and Other Extracurriculars

Mom Central: The Ultimate Family Organizer (with Marsha Feinberg)

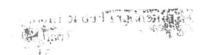

The M☮M Book Goes to School

Insider Tips to Ensure Your Child Thrives in Elementary and Middle School

Stacy DeBroff

FREE PRESS

New York   London   Toronto   Sydney

/ P

FREE PRESS
A Division of Simon & Schuster, Inc.
1230 Avenue of the Americas
New York, NY 10020

First FREE PRESS trade paperback edition 2005

FREE PRESS and colophon are trademarks of Simon & Schuster, Inc.

Mom Central is a trademark of Mom Central, Inc.

For information about special discounts for bulk purchases,
please contact Simon & Schuster Special Sales:
1-800-456-6798 or business@simonandschuster.com

Designed by Charles Kreloff

Manufactured in the United States of America

10   9   8   7   6   5   4   3   2

Library of Congress Cataloging-in-Publication Data

DeBroff, Stacy M.
   The Mom book goes to school: insider tips to ensure your child
thrives in elementary and middle school / Stacy DeBroff.—
1st Free Press trade pbk. ed.
      p. cm.
"Mom Central."
Includes bibliographical references and index.
1. Education, Elementary—Parent participation. 2. Middle school education—
Parent participation. 3. Mother and child. I. DeBroff, Stacy M. Mom central. II. Title.

LB1048.5.D43 2005
372.119'2—dc22
                                                                              2005040088

ISBN-13: 978-0-7432-5754-1

Acknowledgments

Writing this book would have been impossible without the hundreds of teachers and parents who participated in in-depth interviews, shared their insights, and gave so generously of their time. In addition, a group of profoundly talented editorial associates helped me with the extensive research that went into the content. Lisa Logerfo served as my fabulous senior in-house editor on this book, and her exceptional writing and editorial skills, dedication to detail, and coordination of efforts made the writing resonate and the logistics seamless. Karen Bukowick also played a critical and vastly appreciated senior role in the book, from the initial research to the final editorial touches. And my profound thanks to the rest of my editorial interns who devoted many long hours of research, incredible attention to detail, countless hours culling information from interviews, editorial finesse, and a tremendous spirit that infused this book with passion: Ali Ballard, Isabel Kunkle, Elizabeth Furbish, Catherine Ellinwood, Eliza Xenakis, Mairead Ridge, Eliza Lane, and Dana Keenholtz. To these Treehouse Interns—you are simply the best! My talented illustrators used their artistic talent to doodle dozens of wondrous school images: to my daughter Kyle Remy, her fabulous art teacher Alexandra Gelles, and my former intern Stephanie James—thanks for bringing the text to life! This book developed during a changing of my editorial guard at the Free Press, as it started under the attentive, nurturing care of Andrea Au who has many times over earned from me the nickname of Editorial Goddess. This book has been brought to print under Wylie O'Sullivan who has proved herself a magnificent inheritor of the editorial throne, so smart, compassionate, and fun to work with! And I have to thank Mimi Doe, spiritual parenting guru, for being my author comrade-in-arms through the often ludicrous situations of getting a nonfiction book published. Lastly, I thank my awesome kids, Kyle and Brooks, for giving me lots of real-life school situations to learn from and for just making being a Mom so profoundly fulfilling, and my husband Ron for his endless support, encouragement, and love.

—*Stacy DeBroff*

Contents

Part I. At School

Part II. On the Home Front

The MOM Book Goes to School

Introduction

The Big Picture

Long gone are the days of the one-room schoolhouse in which a teacher had virtually autonomous control over curriculum. Over the last 200 years, the education of American children has changed drastically. The national school system has ballooned into a bureaucratic structure of gigantic proportions, entangling millions of kids in a web of often opposing interests, from teachers' unions to governmental agencies to parents who just want to ensure their children receive the highest-quality education available.

During his first term in office, President George W. Bush and his cabinet urged Congress to pass the No Child Left Behind Act (NCLB), a sweeping educational plan with the goal that no child—regardless of ethnicity, gender, or family income—be disadvantaged in life due to the lack of a proper education. The program

1

relies on strengthening public elementary and secondary schools across the nation by periodically assessing all students through standardized testing, and has been somewhat successful in developing better quality schools in neighborhoods with high concentrations of struggling, disabled, poor, and minority students. However, NCLB has yet to be adequately funded and primarily focuses on salvaging the students languishing at the very bottom. There are virtually no innovative strategies included in the act for improving the educational experience of the majority: kids who are just slightly behind where they should be, average kids, and exceptional kids.

Increasingly, teachers are turning to cookie-cutter curriculums in an effort to teach to the standardized tests that form the benchmark of NCLB reforms. All too often, this pressure means dropping fun and interactive activities because they prove too time-consuming to fit into an already packed day. Instead of raising children who love to learn and solve problems creatively, we are raising a generation of terrific test takers. The end result is bored children who are dispassionate about school and trained to believe that the most important reason to learn is to receive the highest marks on a standardized test or a report card. Discouraged teachers long for the ability to be creative and embellish their curriculum to meet the unique interests and needs of their classrooms, and frustrated parents find themselves dealing with stressed-out kids and overextended educators.

We are raising kids in an era filled with debate, but not much agreement, about what it takes to ensure they succeed in school. A critical part of the formula is the vital role of parents—often the missing component in sweeping educational reform plans.

In an era of school budget cuts, overcrowded classrooms, constant testing, and highly competitive admissions processes to private schools and colleges, parents need to be hands-on intermediaries and strategic problem solvers for their children when issues arise. To be an effective advocate for your child, you need to take a proactive and sophisticated approach in communicating with your child's teachers, specialists, and principal. You also need to be aware of how peer relationships impact your child's school performance, from bullies to cliques to problematic classroom behavior. It all boils down to a single concern: *How can you make sure your child succeeds at school without becoming an overly involved parent?*

At points during your child's educational experience, you will find yourself wondering what it will take to vault him out of a current educational snag and prevent a downward spiral for the rest of the academic year. How can you ensure that you serve as a coach instead of a homework partner, an enabler rather than a controller, a facilitator over a meddler? It's easy to feel discouraged and baffled when your child suddenly brings home nosediving grades, disconnects from a teacher, or starts acting out. I've listened to innumerable parents ruminate about how best to cultivate their children's academic gifts and help them find a niche in which they flourish. In the midst of this frenzy, like many parents, I have felt the tremendous burden of helping my children make thoughtful, strategic choices to prepare them for a future of academic success.

Recent studies show that effectively engaging parents in their children's education creates more change than any educational reform. Children with parents who are actively involved in their education achieve higher grades and standardized test scores, behave better in class, have more self-confidence, and tend to enjoy continuing success throughout their lives. Moreover, involved parents are better able to recognize subtle signs of problems and intervene before they become critical. This has been found to be true for all ages and ability ranges. Indeed, the extent to which parents are involved in their children's education is the single most important factor in each child's level of achievement; school quality, family income, race, and parents' education level are all of secondary importance.

The Mom Book Goes to School serves as a guide for parents who know they need to roll up their sleeves and help their children succeed in school, but are unsure about how to approach this most effectively. Hard pressed to determine what our exact roles should be vis-à-vis school, we find it difficult to strike the fine balance of advocating for our children in an informed, strategic manner without micromanaging details to the point where our children lack the confidence to tackle problems independently. The answer lies somewhere between building our children's science projects for them and throwing our hands up in frustration vowing to never, ever help them with homework again!

A poignant example of the issues parents face surfaced in my own life when a good friend called with a school-success crisis of her own. Her ninth-grade daughter, usually a brilliant student, came to her with a midterm summary from her math teacher, indicating she had received C's on the past three quizzes. My friend suddenly learned that her child, who had formerly earned all A's and breezed through her classes, had become disheartened in math as the result of a teacher who had disparaged her math skills and refused to place her in the highest math track that spring, lumping her instead with the average class. This frustration turned into rebellion, and she let her math grades slide without telling her parents. My friend felt shocked, dismayed, and angry. How could she not have known her daughter was struggling academically? Why didn't her daughter seek help? How should she respond as a parent?

This incident captures the tough dilemmas all parents invariably face at some point during a child's school years and reinforces our need for vigilance in watching for surfacing problems. Because of the overwhelming number of students in many classrooms, we often need to fight for schools to meet the individual needs of our children—whether they are learning disabled, gifted, struggling with reading, or acting out in class. With the emergence of competing resources inside and outside of school, we face myriad decisions when our children encounter problems:

should we test for learning disorders inside or outside of school, hire a tutor or try to finagle extra teacher attention for academic issues, send our children to in-school specialists or outside learning centers, or opt for private school over public school?

In my friend's case, she had a heartfelt discussion with her disillusioned daughter about the underlying reasons for her slide in academic performance, her neglect of the problem, and her parents' dismay at not having been informed. My friend arranged a meeting to talk directly with the teacher and created an achievement plan to facilitate her daughter's goal of getting into the accelerated math class. She challenged her daughter to prove herself to the teacher by raising her grade to a B by the semester's end or else taking a summer math class and engaging the help of a math tutor come fall. Back in synergy, mom and daughter formed a team focused on the same goals: getting past the hurdle of a recalcitrant teacher and rekindling her passion for math.

Also embedded in this story is how, in our society, average has become a pejorative. We ultimately want our children to be better than run-of-the-mill students, and secretly hope for them to emerge as A+ students with glowing recommendations from every teacher. We fear that otherwise they will be vulnerable, lacking skills essential to thrive in a highly educated, success-oriented culture. We don't want an average kid but an extraordinary one—so much for the bell curve! But we are utterly unsure about to how to invest our energy. Should we spend 90% of it helping with homework? Scramble to find tutoring? Move to a private school? Set up frequent meetings with teachers in hopes of getting more individualized attention for our children?

Navigating the sometimes hostile and always complex school environment has become so nuanced that we need to get up to speed on how best to assume our varying roles, from sophisticated advocate to intermediary, from disciplinarian to homework editor. When school issues arise, it's crucial to be as informed as possible with insights and advice on what methods prove most effective when stepping into this complicated fray to help our children.

A huge parental fear lurking in the background is that our children will fall behind academically if we don't push and stay on top of the details. In our more anxious moments, we worry that our children's untapped potential will be lost forever and a tidal wave of mediocrity will sweep them into adulthood. If our children are not top students by second grade, we fear they have already fallen behind the students against whom they will eventually compete for college admissions. Ultimately, we spend so much time preparing our children for the challenges they will face in their academic future that we lose sight of raising children who love to learn.

In response to parental fears and expectations, the academic curriculum in most schools has become more rigorous and the homework more difficult. Education reforms in recent years have lead to longer school days, more academic intensity, and homework starting as early as kindergarten. You may find yourself shaking your head in bewilderment as you compare your second grader's schedule and assignments to what you remember from your own elementary school experience.

Given this new educational paradigm, the best way to help your child become an impassioned student who thrives in school is to become closely involved in his education and remain steadfast in that commitment. The average child spends 180 days a year in school for approximately seven hours a day, totaling 1,260 hours a year. While this time is vital to student learning, consider the 7,500 hours a year your child does not spend in school. How he spends his time outside of the classroom deeply impacts his quality of learning. Your challenge is to make the most of your child's education away from school.

Not only have school hours increased for kids, but parents now face the new part-time job of ensuring that piles of homework get completed correctly and our children's particular academic, social, and behavioral issues are addressed quickly and effectively. While parents view global issues of school reform as important, at the end of the day we care most deeply about meeting the needs of our individual child and figuring out how to get him to perform in the uppermost echelon of his class. It used to be that only high school grades mattered, but academic tracking, high-stakes testing, and gifted programs have brought this competitive focus down to the elementary and middle school levels.

School administrators often fear increased parental vigilance because it so often conflicts with the schools' overall needs. Many teachers would prefer to shut their classroom doors to keep parents away from school-related decisions rather than be overwhelmed by criticism, demands, incessant meddling, and complaints to the principal. Add to this the constant public scrutiny of test results, and teachers, principals, and administrators all feel the heat of microscopic attention focused on their performance—not just compared to other local schools, but schools across the nation as well. Moreover, with increased school violence and more media coverage of cliques and gangs of bullies, parents are demanding a military-type, zero tolerance shutdown of any problematic social behavior. The intense focus on these issues, while important, distracts energy and funding from academics.

Not having a dozen kids, most parents lack the experience with the system a repeat player would develop. The unique research platform of *The Mom Book Goes to School* draws on the collective wisdom of hundreds of teachers and specialists, as well as experienced parents, on how best to navigate the complexities of a child's elementary and middle school years. Because teachers who have spent years in the trenches are rarely asked to be candid about how parents can most effectively augment and support a child's classroom experience, they were thrilled to have a forum to share their opinions and insights. In turn, their advice provides you with a repeat player's framework with which to address your children's school and learning issues.

The teachers whose in-depth interviews augmented my research for this book come from diverse school backgrounds from Yakima, Washington, to Fort Myers, Florida. I spoke to first-year teachers, full of questions themselves but armed with fresh, bright perspectives on their profession, as well as truly seasoned veterans, retired after decades of classroom experience. Those interviewed come from inner-city schools with forty-five children in a classroom to rural towns with classrooms of only ten, from public schools and private, from preschools and high schools, and from schools valuing the oldest teaching traditions as well as those innovating and experimenting with modern approaches. These teachers guided me through the inner workings of a complicated, tangled education system so caught up in politics and red tape that its true purpose frequently gets overlooked: educating young minds and raising curious, engaged, successful learners. Their insider expertise has truly been the driving force in shaping this book, and has dramatically shifted how I view my own role in my children's education.

Throughout the interview process, I concentrated on teachers instead of principals or other members of the educational system. Teachers are the most actively engaged with your child while he is at school, and they are the individuals with whom you are most likely to interact. They serve as a powerful influence on your children in their classrooms and even within a standardized curriculum determine the tone, structure, and teaching methods. In contrast, principals are more involved with setting the overall school philosophy, managing the staff, and dealing with serious student behavioral and learning issues.

In Part I of *The Mom Book Goes to School,* I focus on classroom experiences and bolstering your child's relationship with his teacher, which can make or break the school year. Part II of the book concentrates on routines you can set up at home to create a nurturing academic environment, and ways to instill in your child the organizational, homework, studying, test-taking, and time-management skills so crucial to academic success.

Throughout this book, I have used *parent* to include any adults who have the primary responsibility of raising a child. Furthermore, I identify teachers as female and students as male simply for convenience, except in certain cases; for instance, cliques tend to involve mostly girls. By no means do I intend to promote gender stereotypes.

Extracurriculars now have a huge impact on a child's school experience and success. Lessons and practices get stacked upon each other in after-school hours, leaving kids tired, stressed out, and staying up late to finish homework. Because I address these issues in my last book, *Sign Me Up! The Parents' Complete Guide to Sports, Activities, Music Lessons, Dance Classes, and Other Extracurriculars* (Free Press, 2003), I have chosen not to focus on them here.

More important than pushing your child to receive good grades is helping him realize his own potential for success and encouraging him to come alive with intellectual curiosity and passion. Create realistic expectations with respect to your child's strengths and find a balance that encourages your child to strive for his best work without making him strain to succeed beyond reasonable goals. Rethink your own definition of academic success and embrace the philosophy that learning is a process of mastery, maturation, and the development of problem-solving skills, not just an end result of facts memorized or questions answered correctly. Enjoy *The Mom Book Goes to School*—use it to tackle difficult school-related issues and embrace your crucial role in enabling your child to not only thrive in school but also to become a passionate, lifelong learner. Your child's school will dramatically benefit from your increased support and willingness to help out with time and resources, and you will find yourself similarly gratified to realize how much of a difference you can make in your child's school experience.

Part I

At
School

Parent-Teacher Relationship

How Can I Establish an Ongoing Rapport with My Child's Teacher?

Forging a strong parent-teacher relationship early in the academic year will make it much easier for you if a problem arises later in the year. Frequent communication can stop small issues from growing into larger obstacles and provide new insights into your child's learning style and interpersonal dynamics. Limiting your involvement to troubleshooting when a problem arises diminishes the positive impact you have on your child's learning process and overall school experience.

Trust is one of the most important components of any parent-teacher relationship. When the teacher knows and trusts you as a parent who respects her skills in the classroom, she will be more likely to keep you informed because she can be honest with you without worrying about your reaction.

⊚ Take advantage of everything your child's school offers, including open houses and Back-to-School Nights. While there is little to no one-on-one time with the teacher at these larger events, you will still have the opportunity to introduce yourself warmly and make a good impression without monopolizing her time. Especially in elementary school, teachers spend a lot of time setting up the classroom to create an inviting and intellectually stimulating atmosphere for their students. Complimenting the room your child's teacher put together is a great way to start a conversation.

⊚ Besides attending the open house, contact your child's teacher and set up a one-on-one meeting early in the school year. Let her know about any special needs or learning problems your child has, his strengths, habits to watch out for, and skills she needs to work on.

⊚ Ask your child's teacher what you can do at home to emphasize material taught in class, how you can help in the classroom, and what you can do to help with projects or school events.

⊚ Let the teacher know you want to stay in touch with her throughout the year. Ask her to keep you informed when both good and bad situations arise.

⊚ Give her your home and work telephone numbers as well as any other contact information you might want her to have, such as a cell phone or fax number.

⊚ If you walk or drive your child to school in the morning, short and spontaneous visits to his classroom are best for a friendly hello with the teacher.

⊚ Send a thank-you note to your child's teacher after the first week of class. Say something like, "Thank you for making the transition from grade school to middle school such an easy one for Kyle. I really appreciate all of your efforts during one of the most difficult weeks of the year."

⊚ If you are willing to go out of your way for your child's teacher, she is more likely to do the same in return. If she is comfortable with you, she will be more apt to call you when she has general issues or concerns—such as when your child is hanging out with someone who seems to be a bad peer influence.

◉ Touch base with your child's teaching specialists—from music teachers to art instructors to physical education coaches. Specialists often see a different attitude in your child than he exhibits in his regular classroom. For example, he might be more competitive or more standoffish in a physical education class. These specialists get fewer phone calls than regular classroom teachers, and may have special insights on your child because of the unique settings in which they see him.

◉ Recognize the unique and often difficult job of teachers—they are expected to follow a complex curriculum that both enriches the lives of their students and addresses each child's individual needs, while also preparing them for the annual standardized tests. Providing children with a solid academic experience while at the same time accommodating learning disorders, keeping the class disciplined, providing emotional support for children with difficult family situations, and working on the academic development of those who lag behind requires a continual, delicate balancing act on the part of teachers.

If there's an ongoing relationship with the teacher, parents won't feel like they're being called onto the carpet when a problem comes up. Parents who constantly talk to us when things are going well make it feel like a problem is just part of the ongoing dialogue.
—*Chris Grimm, 7th grade social studies teacher for 3 years, Ventura, California*

Teachers really appreciate the insight parents can provide. With 20 kids in the classroom, it's hard for the teacher to get to know each kid's quirks. Give the teachers as much helpful information as possible and stay in touch with them throughout the year. Making the most of the partnership with the teachers is really important.
—*Vinca LaFleur, mom of Jackson, 6, and Evan, 4, Washington, D.C.*

Meet your child's teacher and have a conversation with her at the start of the year. First impressions matter for both the teacher and the parent. That way, if something comes up during the year, both you and the teacher will know to whom they are talking.
—*Steve Shadle, middle school guidance counselor for 29 years, South Sioux City, Nebraska*

I try to set up a meeting with the teachers within the first two weeks of school, because if you wait for the first official parent-teacher conferences, you've missed a quarter of the school year. I go in to discuss issues I want the teacher to keep an eye on. Lots of teachers want to figure out how to handle problems themselves, but I like to put the thought in the back of their minds.
—*Jennifer O'Gorman, mom of Olivia, 11, Jake, 9, Sam, 7, Annabelle, 4, Luke, 2, and Eleanor, 1, Lebanon, Maine*

Introduce yourself to the secretary and custodian, because those are the two people who can get you in to see anybody, get you anywhere you need to go, and have keys to absolutely everywhere.
—*Kathleen Spinale, mom of Joey, 9, and Peter, 4, Ipswich, Massachusetts*

You need a good working relationship with the teacher, established at the beginning of the school year, so you can bounce things back and forth and work together for your child's benefit. Parents want the same things as teachers do: good grades, success, and to be able to work together to help a child achieve to his maximum potential. Remember that we are in the same court.
—*Martha Ann Chandler, 3rd to 6th grade teacher for 14 years, Florence, South Carolina*

Let the teachers know at the start of the school year all about your child and his character traits. Is he sensitive, shy, aggressive, or talkative, or does he have poor self-esteem? Discuss expectations—what the teacher expects from your child and what you expect your child to achieve.

Keep in close touch with your child's teacher. Not only do you need to know when your child's academic work needs improvement, but you should also be aware when your child's attitude or behavior changes, which can be an indication of emotional problems. Also, ask the teacher to let you know when your child does something exceptionally well, such as when he improves in a certain subject area, or accomplishes something he has been working toward.
—*Beverly Hammond, kindergarten to 4th grade teacher for 31 years, West Point, Virginia*

Teacher-parent communication is vital to the school year. It's important to get to know the teacher—the better you know her, the better the year will be.
—*Nickey Langford, 2nd and 3rd grade teacher for 3 years, Birmingham, Alabama*

Parents who assume all is well if they don't hear from the teacher are making a mistake. Stay on top of communication with the teacher at all times. Otherwise, parents come to an Open House or get a call with different information. Don't assume everything is okay unless you are told otherwise.
—*Paul O'Brien, 7th to 12th grade math and science teacher for 27 years, Sheffield, Massachusetts*

How Can I Best Use Email and Other Technology to Facilitate Communication?

◎ Email is a great way to maintain open communication with your child's teacher. It is much easier for her to respond to a slew of emails on her own time than to contact parents with a dozen follow-up phone calls.

◎ Ask your child's teacher whether she prefers online communication and if she does, exchange email addresses. Call your child's teacher or send short email messages to catch up between conferences. Either form of communication is a great way to stay informed about classroom issues.

◎ If there is a specific issue you feel strongly about and want to discuss with your child's teacher via email, avoid confrontational and brutally honest statements you would not make if you were speaking on the phone or in person.

◉ Find out if it's okay for your child to email his teacher directly. If it is, your child has a great opportunity for supplemental learning, as he can ask questions about homework and class material.

◉ School websites are great resources and provide a broad range of useful information: faculty and staff contact information, school rules and general policies, student activities, and parent committees.

◉ Faxing is another great communication option. Zipping a quick fax over to the appropriate school office can save you a trip to school if your child forgets an important document, such as a permission slip or homework assignment.

The most convenient type of conference for me has become an e-conference. For parents who might not have time to hold a conference with the teacher, email can get problems settled in a few minutes—it's one of the most efficient uses of time I can think of. Email also gives you much better control when you're angry, and that can really make a big difference! Plus with email, you often get a quicker response than you would if you left a message on the teacher's answering machine.
—Angela McNutt, 6th to 12th grade Spanish teacher for 1 year, Glade Spring, Virginia

◉

Email is so much easier than playing phone tag. I hate leaving phone messages; some middle schoolers will simply delete my message right off the answering machine! It makes communication more convenient given most families have two working parents who aren't available for a lengthy phone call or a visit to the school during traditional school hours.
—Amy Watson, 7th to 12th grade teacher for 5 years, Oyster Bay, New York

◉

Email makes it much easier for teachers and parents to contact one another. In the state of Maine, we now have a laptop initiative, so every student in the 7th and 8th grades has a laptop and has access to his teachers' web pages and email addresses. Parents also have access to notes on projects, homework links, and an email section with an additional parent email address, so they can easily let the appropriate teacher know of concerns. It's hard for teachers to call or meet with parents, but email facilitates communication and lets the kid know his parents have access to his teachers.

—*Laurie Olmstead, 7th and 8th grade math and science teacher for 4 years, Union, Maine*

At the beginning of the school year, I asked my son's teacher, "For future reference, do you prefer email or voicemail?" This year, his teacher tended to return phone calls at 9:30 at night, so I made sure to respect that and be home then if I needed to talk to her. You have to make the effort and gesture because if you don't, the teacher won't either.

—*Kathleen Spinale, mom of Joey, 9, and Peter, 4, Ipswich, Massachusetts*

I love faxing documents to my children's school. I fax in a note instead of trying to call the teacher I want to contact. On my note I'll include my schedule, the best times to reach me, and the issues I need to talk to the teacher about. I also fax the school if someone other than the kids' grandmother will be picking my children up at the end of the day. This way I know the secretary of the school has the last-minute change in her hand, and that will ensure my message reaches my kids and their respective teachers.

—*Shannon McDermott, mom of Catherine, 13, Matthew, 11, and Joshua, 7, Lemont, Illinois*

Email makes keeping an open dialog throughout the year with my kids' teachers so easy. Almost all the teachers have email and check it daily. This way they can answer questions I have as we go along.

—*Whitney Caudill, mom of Caitlyn, 9, and Parker, 8, Louisville, Kentucky*

Why Does Putting Up a United Front with My Child's Teacher Matter So Much?

When you and your child's teacher form a partnership and work as a team, you become a dynamic force that can truly effect change. Not only will collaboration foster a tighter bond between you and the teacher but you will also become accountable to each other and will likely work harder to meet each other's expectations.

Speaking highly of your child's teacher is especially challenging when you dislike her personal style or disagree with her teaching methods, so handle disagreements with her discreetly. Sending negative messages to your child about his teacher or school will only confuse and dishearten him. Allow him to express his feelings about school and his teachers even if you don't agree, and respond with neutral comments to encourage him to continue the conversation. Besides lowering your child's motivation levels, implications of disrespect create a conflict in his mind between you and his teacher, both of whom he should trust.

Voicing your disapproval of the teacher in front of your child essentially encourages him to show his dissatisfaction or disdain for the teacher as well.

Be aware of what you say on the phone and to a spouse, friend, or the teacher, when your child is within earshot. Children are exceptionally good at tuning into the more private things adults say, especially when they think they are the subjects of discussion. Even when you think he isn't listening, your child might interpret what you say once as representative of how you truly feel.

Don't pass negative feelings about your own school experience along to your child. Instead, let him know certain subjects may have been difficult for you, but that you stuck with them and still use the skills you learned today. He will listen more to stories about your life than to lectures, so share examples of things you did in school that were fun or at which you excelled.

At times, school rules can seem strict, but keep in mind the huge weight of responsibility that goes along with caring for the safety of all the children at the school. Sympathize with your child when he complains, but point out the administration's perspective, and concern for his personal safety.

The parent and teacher relationship is a marriage of sorts—a partnership—and it won't work unless both partners are fully engaged and working together for the benefit of everyone involved.
—*Niambi Muhammad, 1st and 2nd grade teacher for 4 years, Chicago, Illinois*

Teachers often feel as if they are an extension of your family and parents are an extension of their classrooms.
—*Laura N., 4th grade teacher for over 20 years, Boston, Massachusetts*

I had one student who said he was going to get his parents to sue me, so I called his mother right in the middle of class and had him speak to her on the phone. The child learned a wonderful life lesson, as did all those in the class who were watching. Support from parents when a child does an outrageous thing is wonderful. Children do things that surprise us—teachers and parents alike—things we're not proud of. Parents and teachers need to work together, as a team, to make these negative experiences positive. Parents who have this goal for transforming their child's behavior help their children grow into wonderful adults.

When I was a child, I had an absolutely horrible teacher one year, and I didn't find out until college my parents talked to that teacher every week and were as angry with the teacher as I was. There's a fine line between letting students in and sharing with them adult issues they are not ready to handle. You can be supportive and understanding, but if you agree with them that the teacher is a witch, it's not helpful to the child. Don't tell your child about negative school experiences! I always cringe when the parents sitting in a conference to talk about their child's problems say they weren't good at a certain subject either or hated that grade, too. Tell your child you know this can be difficult, instead of giving him the idea he's excused from all behavior because you had a hard time, too.
—*Claudia Flanders, kindergarten to 8th grade teacher for 34 years, Santa Monica, California*

To portray the right image to teachers, it is important to communicate with them and give them positive feedback instead of merely criticizing them to the point where the relation-

ship goes bad. If you don't embrace the teacher, it's not going to work.
—*Alesha Worra, mom of Brandon, 12, and Travis, 11, Greer, South Carolina*

There are some parents who I know I can call on if I need something, and who will support me if there are questions or problems in the classroom. They are the parents who have established a rapport with me up front. The parents who show up to meetings ranting and raving are usually the parents I don't hear from until there's a problem.
—*Nickey Langford, 2nd and 3rd grade teacher for 3 years, Birmingham, Alabama*

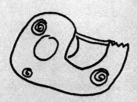

Teachers want parents to be as involved as possible without interfering, and they want to feel like parents are part of one united team, instead of one party teaming up against the other. It's also important not to take your child's academic problems or school difficulties personally. If your child has a learning problem, it's not your fault. So many parents today are too sensitive about what others think of them.
—*Kay Symons, special education and kindergarten to 8th grade teacher for 27 years, South Georgia*

I've handled things I thought weren't proper on a teacher's part, but overall I tend to side with the teacher. After all, it's her classroom, and even if she dealt out a punishment in which my kid thought he was wrongly included, I assume she did it for a reason. You need to be supportive of that. I might be biased because both my parents were schoolteachers, and they never sided with me! I would never openly disagree with something a teacher had done. Instead, I would go to the teacher and try to work out the problem with her. Disagreeing with your child's teacher in front of him ends up being a problem for everyone in the classroom because the kids then think they have the right to disrespect the teacher, too.
—*Jennifer O'Gorman, mom of Olivia, 11, Jake, 9, Sam, 7, Annabelle, 4, Luke, 2, and Eleanor, 1, Lebanon, Maine*

Speak to your child's teacher about any issues you are concerned about, but take a team-work approach to problems, not a confrontational one.

—*Keith Averell, 3rd grade teacher for 27 years, Pleasanton, California*

If a teacher brings a problem up, that's a good sign you should take the issue seriously. Teachers are experts, and they're going to see most problems before parents do.

—*Erika Bare, 6th to 8th grade special education teacher for 3 years, West Linn, Oregon*

One of very first things I tell parents is that we need to be on the same page. I even sign a little contract with each set of parents and their child. I ask the parents how they would like to see their child grow during the year, and I ask the child what he would like to learn. Together, we set specific goals based on these aims.

—*Libby Anne Inabinet, kindergarten, 1st grade, reading, and gifted and talented teacher for 15 years, Columbia, South Carolina*

When you talk to your friends negatively about a teacher, your child will likely overhear you. If you have a conflict with the teacher, you need to approach the teacher away from your child. Showing your children a united front with teachers gives them the confidence they need to be the best they can be.

—*Joy Pumphrey, 2nd and 3rd grade teacher for 12 years, Clearwater, Florida*

If you need to talk to the teacher about something, don't do it in front of your child. If a child hears his parent tell the teacher, "He's very shy," the child then thinks, "Oh, I'm very shy."

—*Kathy Carabine, 3rd grade and pre-k teacher for 16 years, Boston, Massachusetts*

Always say positive things about school, teachers, and learning. If you have a concern or complaint, take that up with the teacher or administrator. Don't discuss it in front of your child. Schools and teachers need your support.

—*Beverly Hammond, kindergarten to 4th grade teacher for 31 years, West Point, Virginia*

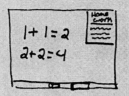

It's the discussion that takes place at the dinner table that really matters. If parents talk about how terrible their child's teacher is, where does the child get his opinions? The child can only see the negatives then, even if the teacher tries to turn it around. Sometimes parents have to not be so knee-jerk. In life you run into all kinds of people and learning to deal with an occasional tough personality in a teacher helps kids become more grounded as they grow up.
—*Edward Sapienza, 9th to 12th grade science, math, and computer teacher for 31 years, North Reading, Massachusetts*

I find when a child goes home, tells a parent about his day, and listens to his parent attack his teacher over an event that occurred, the relationship between the child and teacher suffers. I encourage the parents of children in my classroom to call me before jumping to conclusions—and I tell them I'll believe 10% of what I hear about them at home if they believe 10% of what they hear about our classroom.
—*Amie Parker, 1st and 2nd grade teacher for 7 years, Lynnwood, Washington*

How Do I Avoid Being Perceived as the Notorious Difficult Parent?

While it is always your prerogative to let a teacher know when you disagree with her decisions or have concerns about your child's classroom performance, recognize that she is responsible for satisfying many other parents besides you. Be willing to forgive if your child's teacher makes a mistake or fails to devote full attention to your specific issue. Move on to the new challenge you face together, but consider how you can best approach the next situation with her.

Although it's tempting to emphasize your child's skills and strengths, hoping to impress the teacher and put your child in a favorable light, let him demonstrate his talents to the teacher himself.

◎ If you constantly barrage your child's teacher with questions about minor issues and requests for conferences, she will quickly feel harassed and annoyed, and become increasingly evasive.

◎ Angrily storming into a meeting with your child's teacher when you have already developed your own assumptions about an issue puts you at risk for developing a negative reputation with not only the teacher involved, but also all the teachers at your child's school. Once you attain a reputation as a pushy and demanding or overly dramatic parent, teachers are far less willing to take you and your concerns seriously.

◎ Teachers are partial to parents who follow through on their promises, who keep private conversations confidential, and who do not participate in gossip with other parents. If you approach your child's teacher in a focused, honest, and tactful way, you will gain the reputation of being a helpful parent, and the teacher will be more willing to help you and respect your opinion.

◎ Keep in mind that teachers need to talk with one another for their own sanity, and the information they share about parents can label you for the rest of your child's career at school. Some common negative stereotypes include:

❋ *Complainer:* This parent frequently calls the teacher or drops in on the classroom to gripe about minor details. She complains about anything and everything, and is still not content, even when her demands are implemented.

❋ *Confrontational:* This parent constantly pesters the teacher and is unwilling to listen to feedback and suggestions. Teachers take confrontational exchanges with parents as a sign of profound lack of respect and often respond to this type of aggression by withdrawing and becoming defensive.

❋ *Meddler:* This parent typically micromanages every detail of her child's education and personal life.

❋ *Needy:* This parent is one whose hand the teacher has to hold through every step of the child's education. This parent constantly calls the teacher just to check up on things.

❋ *Nowhere-to-be-found:* This parent is almost impossible to track down and is never available when teachers need to meet with her.

❋ *Overreacting:* This parent's first instinct is to barge into the school highly agitated, emotional, and irrational. She is prone to overreacting and quickly becomes enraged over trivial matters.

✸ *Overachiever:* This parent lives vicariously through the high standards she sets for her child and the success that child achieves.

✸ *Overstressed and overworked:* This parent constantly feels stressed and overcommitted, yet continues to commit to activities. She feels guilty about her lack of involvement and wishes she had time to be more invested in her child's education, but is unreliable.

✸ *Parent Spy:* This parent volunteers in the classroom to keep an eye on the teacher and reports back to other parents, the PTA, or the principal.

✸ *Passive-aggressive:* This parent hides behind nasty notes but will not tackle an issue with a teacher face-to-face. When a teacher approaches a passive-aggressive parent in person, the parent takes on a much friendlier persona.

✸ *Well-intentioned but completely unreliable:* This parent wants to be involved, but makes promises she never follows up on.

◉ Positive stereotypes include:

✸ *Behind the scenes:* This parent is rarely visible around the school, but will help from home in thoughtful ways.

✸ *Worker bee:* This parent is the ultimate "I'll do anything" volunteer around the school who supports the teacher and her child.

I had a problem with parents constantly questioning everything I did, instead of just letting me be the teacher. Teachers can't do their job if parents are too involved. It hurts the child, because he won't trust the teacher or will think she doesn't know what she's doing due to his parents' attitude.
—Nickey Langford, 2nd and 3rd grade teacher for 3 years, Birmingham, Alabama

Most teachers like a parent who is involved, but not overly so. Everyone knows faculty lounge talk does take place, and teachers will say things like, "Watch out for his parents!" But if you come to teachers in a nonthreatening way, you don't need to worry about this. Watch your language as a parent, not in terms of profanity, but in terms of saying things like, "Well, my child's never had this trouble before! She hates your class; she always got A's until now." Comments like this put teachers on the defensive. Most teachers will take it one conversation at a time, and are usually pretty decent at giving even the toughest parent another chance.
—Ken Pauly, high school social studies teacher for 13 years, St. Louis Park, Minnesota

One day I walked into my classroom an hour before school and found a cake wrapped in foil and some napkins and plates, but no note. A mom had dropped it off for her child's birthday, but hadn't run it by me first or asked my permission. The teacher next door said the mom had asked if I could serve the kids cake. A great way to irritate teachers is by assuming they will do something for you without asking.
—Kallie Leyba, 1st and 2nd grade teacher for 2 years and mom of Lauren, 11, Lucas, 8, and
   Samson, 4, Highlands Ranch, Colorado

What Kind of Positive Feedback Do Teachers Care About Most?

◉ Although gift giving is a great way to say thank you to your child's teacher, something as simple as a note or personal phone call really goes a long way in furthering your relationship. Just as parents enjoy hearing about their child's progress and academic successes, teachers feel personally vested in their students' emotional and intellectual development and are grateful for your recognition.

◉ A note is the perfect way to thank a teacher when your child comes home bubbling about something exciting he learned in school or brings home an assignment you think is really creative and fun. Let the teacher know if you notice a new intellectual interest she has sparked in your child, or if he raves about a remarkable skill or personal quality she demonstrates in the classroom. The short time you spend writing this note will mean an extraordinary amount to the teacher, and the gesture will surely strengthen your relationship.

⊙   Instead of just signing your child's homework folder, add a note. Even if nothing important is happening, just saying, "Thanks for your hard work!" goes a long way.

⊙   Write a letter at the end of the year thanking your child's teacher for the role she played, leaving space for your child to add his thoughts.

⊙   For a truly fabulous teacher, write a letter with specific examples of how she touched your child's life and forward it to the principal. Everyone appreciates having positive feedback shared with their supervisor.

Parents who remember their child's teacher during holidays with just a little card, like "#1 Teacher" or "We remember you on this holiday," make teachers feel appreciated. Your child can even make a card: "Thanks for a special year." Knowing the parents and my students remembered me was always so important.
—Holly Parker, teacher of deaf students for 10 years, Colorado Springs, Colorado

When parents tell me little stories about how I touched their child's life, those are the most rewarding moments for me as a teacher. That makes me feel like, "Oh, wow!"
—Niambi Muhammad, 1st and 2nd grade teacher for 4 years, Chicago, Illinois

I always appreciate a note even more than a phone call. There are days after work when I go home wanting to rip my hair out, and I pull out those notes to look through them. Even though teaching's a hard job, it's so worth it!
—Kathy Carabine, pre-k and 3rd grade teacher for 16 years, Boston, Massachusetts

To me, the best gift is a compliment, a thank you for helping—something specific I did that was appreciated. It's a very high form of praise for a teacher, because in teaching we receive so little of that today. You feel parents really recognize what you're doing for their child.
—*Kay Symons, special education and kindergarten to 8th grade teacher for 27 years,*
  South Georgia

Throughout the school year, when my kids tell me about something special that happened on a particular day at school, I send a card in to the teacher telling her how much I appreciate what she did, or how great she is at working with my kids all day.
—*Whitney Caudill, mom of Caitlyn, 9, and Parker, 8, Louisville, Kentucky*

When parents write positive, thankful letters to an administrator appreciating a teacher's work and classroom performance, it absolutely makes a difference.
—*Amy Watson, 7th to 12th grade teacher for 5 years, Oyster Bay, New York*

Getting words of appreciation from a parent for what I've done for their child is better than any gift. I keep a file of letters from parents that I call my "happy file." When a parent berates me, I take out the file and I know I'm not doing such a bad job. I still have all of them today. I had a parent write a letter to my principal praising me, and he made a copy for me with a note saying, "Keep up the good work," and I saved that, too!
—*Joy Pumphrey, 2nd and 3rd grade teacher for 12 years, Clearwater, Florida*

Which Gifts Do Teachers Appreciate Most?

The teacher's job doesn't end when the dismissal bell rings. Teachers spend countless hours after school volunteering at school functions, arranging social events, and putting energy into everything from planning special projects to coordinating field trips. As school budgets continue to drop, more and more teachers dip into their own pockets to provide materials students would not receive otherwise.

Teachers especially appreciate gifts they can use in the classroom. Ask the teacher about supplies you can provide like poster board, extra tissues, or glitter. A gift certificate to a bookstore or an office supply store is always useful, as teachers will happily put it toward paying for all those extra learning materials. Or, fill out a classroom subscription for a fun and educational periodical.

During the year, send your child's teacher occasional tokens of appreciation. Delicious treats you bake with your child are always a good idea: homemade fudge, biscotti, gingerbread men, or chocolate-dipped anything. Put them in a cute container like a Chinese take-out box or oversized coffee mug. Take a picture of your child creating the gift to use as a cover for the thank you note. You can also send a homemade coupon for an hour or two you are willing to volunteer in the classroom.

Send an oversized mug filled with herbal teas, flavored coffee beans, or gourmet cocoa wrapped in colored cellophane. Pamper your child's teacher with a basket of lotions, soaps, bath oils, scented candles, or a spa gift certificate.

Personalize gifts as much as possible. Monogrammed stationery, pens, pencils, and tote bags are not only great gifts but also extremely practical.

Another great idea is to send in rolls of film with a gift certificate for developing the photos.

Make a donation to a good cause your child or his class supports and let the organization know you are donating on her behalf. Ask them to send her a confirmation letter applauding her efforts.

◉ Pool your resources with other parents and decide on a present from the entire class. Start planning early before other parents purchase their own gifts. Or, mobilize the classroom to prepare a gift to which all the children can contribute. Obtain samples of the students' work from their parents and compile a collection booklet to give the teacher at the end of the year. Ask the students to write a short essay on what they liked best about the teacher and what they will remember about her.

I had one student who covered a box for me to keep paperclips in—it was so bright and shiny when she brought it in. Another student brought in fresh-squeezed carrot juice in a Tupperware container when I was pregnant. Presents like this make the teacher feel like extended family. Even small stuff makes the teacher feel supported by the parents. One family in particular stands out in my mind. I had their daughter for 1st and 2nd grade. They were from Lebanon and their culture really respects teachers, so they invited me over for dinner as a guest of honor. They also helped me set up my classroom the first few days before school started and even helped me paint. They bought me storage containers because they could tell I needed them for the classroom and we sent notes back and forth all year long. A family's support is so important.
—*Kallie Leyba, 1st and 2nd grade teacher for 2 years and mom of Lauren, 11, Lucas, 8, and Samson, 4, Highlands Ranch, Colorado*

My teachers love the generic mall certificates for restaurants, day salons, or bookstores, and since the certificates are available in different denominations, they fit all budgets.
—*Susan Fochtmann, mom of William, 11, and Thomas, 8, Atlanta, Georgia*

A teacher can only get so many mugs! They're nice, but I would rather get things for my classroom, such as boxes of Kleenex, baby wipes for hand-wiping and spills, chalk, and dry-erase markers. A gift certificate to Wal-Mart or Target is great because the teacher can get what she wants for her classroom. At the beginning of the school year, if you know your teacher is new, give a new teacher shower with stuff to fill a basket, such as pens, papers, and scissors. Teachers use all of that stuff. If you know your child's teacher has a student teacher who will be moving on to her own classroom the next year, do the same at the end of the year for the student teacher.
—*Nickey Langford, 2nd and 3rd grade teacher for 3 years, Birmingham, Alabama*

Be thoughtful to the teacher as a whole person. One of my children's teachers was moving, and all the moms got together and made her dinner to help her get through the stressful time. If a teacher is stressed, she won't teach well, so you need to think about what you can do for her instead of just what she can do for you.
—*Pam Fierro, mom of twins Meredith and Lauren, 8, and parenting multiples guide at www.multiples.about.com, Virginia Beach, Virginia*

I've sent teachers and the school office flowers for no reason other than I want to let them know how much I appreciate their help. For the end of the year, the kids make something as a gift: like painting their own ceramic bowl or bookends.
—*Kelly Levinson, mom of David, 14, Zachary, 10, Michael, 9, Shaina, 8, and Amanda, 5, Guilford, Connecticut*

Meetings and Conferences

When Is It Appropriate to Approach the Teacher About a Problem?

◉ Every teacher has quirks students will find annoying at times, and every child will occasionally complain. However, if your child repeatedly tells you he dislikes school, does not feel challenged by the curriculum, or is frequently ignored by the teacher in class, step in and take action. Remember to approach the teacher respectfully.

◉ Don't feel intimidated by the prospect of notifying your child's school or teacher if you feel something has gone awry. If you notice a significant change in your child's behavior, school performance, or attitude, contact his teacher as soon as possible. Don't wait until his report card arrives to talk to the teacher about a potential problem with his schoolwork; act quickly to prevent small problems from mushrooming into huge obstacles. Schools and teachers depend on parents to alert them when specific issues arise.

◉ When trying to gauge the severity of a problem, ask your child how he feels and whether or not he wants you to get involved. But while you should do your best to respect his ideas and wishes, there may be times when you need to override his preferences and involve yourself in the problem.

With teaching teams, each involved teacher only sees a part of your child's academic experience: reading skills here, math there, and so on. Each observes your child in a completely different environment than the others and focuses on developing a unique set of academic skills. As classmates may vary from subject to subject, your child's patterns of academic engagement, participation, and social interaction can shift completely based on classroom dynamics. Request a team meeting at the beginning of the year to discuss your child's education, especially if you have a particular concern, such as if your child is gifted, learning disabled, or has had past behavioral problems. Getting the entire team together to hold a group discussion and brainstorming session will generate a range of ideas, options, and action plans, streamline different approaches and perspectives, and save you the legwork of meeting with each teacher individually.

Always—without hesitation—contact the teacher to address all concerns.
—David Lancucki, 3rd to 7th grade teacher for 23 years, King William County, Virginia

If you have a concern about your child's performance, talk to the teacher about it right away and see if you can get to the root of the problem together. Start the conversation off by saying something like, "I can see my child is struggling with instructions when he brings his homework home; is this something you see in the classroom? Does my child need extra help in this area?" The first step is to be respectful of the chain of command; go first to the teachers, because nine times out of ten, they will help.
—Julie Kirkpatrick Carroll, 4th grade teacher for 6 years, Benson, Minnesota

Teachers are collaborators by nature. Solving a problem in tandem with the parents is the first strategy a teacher will employ. Sometimes parents have information about kids that teachers don't have that can give a broader insight into their children.
—*Sue Abrams, elementary school principal and former 1st to 5th grade teacher for 22 years, Natick, Massachusetts*

It's very helpful to get feedback from parents, especially if there is a particular concern demanding attention. If a child is bullied, the teacher can help deal with this problem. If a child has problems with math, the teacher can help counteract any resulting dislike of the subject, and make the student feel more comfortable around it and even grow to like it. There are some personal situations where it's very comforting and helpful to let the teacher know, like when the child is dealing with a death in the family, because such information may be helpful in the classroom.
—*Kathy Traficanti, 4th to 6th grade teacher for 9 years, Brighton, Massachusetts*

Teachers especially appreciate parents who clue them into their child's concerns and who want to be apprised of problems in the classroom.
—*Deborah Berris, 3rd, 5th, and 8th grade teacher for 5 years*

Most teaching teams have regular group meetings to discuss kids with problems. If you have concerns, it's worth holding a team meeting to hear from all the teachers how your child is doing. Sometimes personalities just clash, so if your child is doing well in all classes but one, then you have the root of the problem.
—*Amy Watson, 7th to 12th grade teacher for 5 years, Oyster Bay, New York*

How Much Personal Information Should I Divulge to the Teacher?

◉ Just as it is important for you to know how your child is doing in class, it's valuable to inform his teacher about any situations or conditions that may adversely affect his schoolwork or behavior, like learning disorders, sensory or perception problems, and health issues. By sharing this information, you can work with your child's teacher to head off potential problems. It will help her contextualize her impressions of him and frame mutual goals. Things to discuss include:

✦ Reflections your child shares about school and concerns he expresses about his relationship with the teacher.

✦ Your observations of significant changes in his behavior about which the teacher might have some perspective.

✦ Extracurricular activities in which your child participates, so the teacher has a well-rounded sense of what he does outside of school.

◉ While you don't have to divulge the details of private family issues, you may want to let his teacher know about serious difficulties or events like a new baby, a divorce, a remarriage, or a death. When your child is dealing with major stressors, he will be more sensitive to his teacher's harsh words and the threat of discipline. Update the teacher on any changes throughout the year, so she can help your child through these situations and make allowances for changes in work habits or behavior. When the teacher knows about major events going on in your child's life, she can help provide the support and sense of safety he needs to transition through tough times.

◉ Your elementary school child won't necessarily understand the line between what should be shared at school and what should stay within your family. He is likely to give a detailed commentary on any trouble at home, or other private and potentially embarrassing stories. Despite your efforts to teach him to distinguish between what needs to stay private and what can be shared with others, understand that information may slip out. Teachers are sometimes put in the uncomfortable position of knowing your personal family issues without your having brought them to their attention.

The teacher is vital to your child's life. Children are with the teacher for so much time—often more than they are with a parent—so if there is something going on, it's critical for the teacher to know. Problems at home can affect a child's schoolwork, and there are resources to draw on at school, such as the guidance counselor, a social worker, or support groups, to help a child if needed. For example, last year I had five students whose parents were going through divorce and one whose parent was dying of cancer. People often get caught up in solving their own marital problems or grief and forget it is affecting their children. Children absorb so much more than parents realize.

—*Joy Pumphrey, 2nd and 3rd grade teacher for 12 years, Clearwater, Florida*

I try to get in touch with parents, and hold a meeting to go over any concerns. I really want to know whether something has happened at home that I should be aware of, so the child and I can deal with the situation better together. Sometimes parents open up and sometimes they don't. I prefer that they do. One especially important thing to let a teacher know about is a parental argument that has been overheard by a child. When my husband and I separated, we immediately notified our son's school so they could help him cope, if need be. Schools and teachers have to deal with these issues quickly.

—*Ruth Anne Manroe, kindergarten to 6th grade teacher for 27 years, Golden, Colorado*

Anything you tell the teacher is useful information, especially if it impacts your child's school performance. It's better for the teacher to know what's going on than to have to guess. If the teacher is not aware of the root of a problem, she will constantly be casting about for strategies to address it yet won't be able to fix the situation.

—*Sue Abrams, elementary school principal and former 1st to 5th grade teacher for 22 years, Natick, Massachusetts*

If you notice a behavior change in your child, point it out to the teacher, because she simply may not be aware of it. Parent contact keeps my eyes open to a change in children's behavior at school.

—*Julie Kirkpatrick Carroll, 4th grade teacher for 6 years, Benson, Minnesota*

I find that when I'm honest and up front with teachers about stressful things going on at home, they're better able to help when my kids misbehave.
—*Kymme Simchak, mom of Brandi, 19, Courtney, 13, and Colleen, 10, Seguin, Texas*

In most cases, teachers are highly appreciative of parents letting them know if there is something going on in the life of a child. Sometimes, as a teacher, you pick up on things but you don't know what's causing them. Last year I had a child who was struggling with the death of a grandparent, and the parents shared that information with me and let me know how I could be helpful and supportive. It's a teacher's job to reach out and help a child in any way she can, and in order to do so she must know what's going on.
—*Kathy Traficanti, 4th to 6th grade teacher for 9 years, Brighton, Massachusetts*

Why Do Teachers Hate Being Approached on the Fly?

☺ Don't call and say, "I need to talk to you immediately!" or drop in spontaneously when you drop your child off at school, even if you feel incredibly upset about something that happened the day before. Teachers appreciate and depend on advance notice in order to reflect on what you want to discuss and to be prepared to speak about it in detail with the benefit of thoughtful consideration. Whenever possible, make an appointment to talk with your child's teacher, as you will not get the same kind of attention just dropping by.

☺ If the teacher knows beforehand, she can be prepared with a thoughtful and nondefensive response. If you come in acting accusatory and put the teacher on the spot, she has no time to reflect on when and why something happened. You both need to process the situation. Drop the teacher a note or leave her a voicemail or email asking to talk with her after school.

☺ When setting up a meeting with your child's teacher, decide together on a mutually convenient time. Consider all relevant factors: the availability of you and your spouse, scheduling conflicts, and even times of the day you feel particularly grouchy or tired, such as late afternoon.

At the beginning of the school day, teachers need time to get organized, prepare lesson plans, and welcome arriving children, making it difficult to talk to parents. Midday breaks for P.E. and recess are often more convenient times to reach your child's regular teacher by phone.

Stopping by before school starts is tough for the teacher; remember that the school day begins as soon as the first child comes into the classroom.
—Kay Symons, special education and kindergarten to 8th grade teacher for 27 years, South Georgia

Parents coming in to see me in the morning is fine if they keep it brief, but realize that there are many things a teacher has to do to prepare for the day. If it's going to be 15 seconds, that's okay, but if it's going to be a major thing, it has to be planned ahead.
—Lawanna Ford, 5th grade teacher for 25 years, Argonia, Kansas

When it comes to an issue involving their child, parents often think everything's urgent and a serious crisis, and they want to talk to the teacher about it right then and there. This is a judgment call parents really need to monitor. Instead, ask for a meeting outside of class time and briefly let the teacher know what is going on or provide insight about the issue, so the teacher can think about it and be prepared to have a thoughtful discussion.
—Jennifer M., 5th grade teacher for 6 years, Boston, Massachusetts

How Do I Make the Most of Regularly Scheduled Parent-Teacher Conferences?

⊙   Though it can be tempting to dash in with a few questions or issues and let the teacher take charge of the rest of a meeting, being prepared and bringing your own agenda ensures you will discuss the issues foremost in your mind. Organize your thoughts and set goals ahead of time for what you need to communicate and learn during the meeting. You want to go into the meeting with a full understanding of what you wish to gain, so you can have a more effective discussion with the teacher and decide on an appropriate course of action, if needed.

⊙   Consider your child's academic progress, behavior issues, social abilities, and personal dynamics with particular classmates and write down the main issues you want to cover during the meeting. Include outside factors that could be causing his troubles, such as stress at home, health or physical problems, or information about his learning style. Before the conference, ask your child for any in-class work folders he has, so you can be familiar with what he is doing and ready to address issues you notice. Also, look through all pertinent information you have at home—report cards, homework, notes from past teachers, old tests and assignments—to help frame your ideas.

⊙   Set your priorities for the meeting. In the brief time you have to meet with your child's teacher, you probably will not be able to discuss all your concerns and ask all your questions. Note which topics you most need to talk about and address them first. If there are major issues you want to cover during the conference, let the teacher know beforehand so she has a chance to fully prepare for your discussion and make sure the conversation stays on track. If your partner can't attend the conference with you, write down his concerns and questions and bring the list to the meeting.

⊙   Parent-teacher conferences offer a rich opportunity for you to gain insights into your child's progress and deepen your relationship with his teacher. The teacher sees him at work and at play, in large social groups and alone, so approach the meeting as an opportunity to discuss the developmental, academic, and social issues your child faces at school.

⊙   Anxiety over a parent-teacher conference may revolve around uneasiness about how your child is doing. While hopefully you enter conferences with an accurate sense of your child's performance, there is always the fear of unknown problems. It's important that you do not let your anxiety cause an unproductive meeting.

To prepare for a teacher conference, we go over the concerns we have and write them down so we know exactly what to cover. We also give the teachers suggestions. My son is overactive and I suggested his teacher allow him to squish balls with his hands while she talks so he wouldn't run around the room instead. The teacher took that on, and it worked so well that she used it with other classes.
—*Alesha Worra, mom of Brandon, 12, and Travis, 11, Greer, South Carolina*

Let the teacher know what your agenda is before coming in for a meeting, so she can come more prepared to talk about the issue at hand. For instance, make sure to note the specific day, event, or examples of what you are concerned about, just as you want specific examples from the teacher. This way she can be prepared to recall, "Oh yeah, on that day, this is what happened from my point of view."
—*Florence Michel, middle school teacher for 8 years, New York, New York, and Baltimore, Maryland*

Parents can be most effective in conferences by coming in with a list of issues they would like to discuss, really listening to the teacher, asking questions, and most importantly, staying on topic!
—*Alison Gowers, kindergarten teacher for 5 years, West Point, Virginia*

I look at a parent-teacher conference as I would a business appointment. The more prepared you are and the more steps you take in planning, the better it will go. If you are running late and have a bad attitude, then of course it's not going to go well.
—*Suzanne Stoll, mom of Charity, 10, and Jesse, 7, Wampum, Pennsylvania*

My husband and I go together to parent-teacher conferences as often as possible. I find it helps a lot if we both know what's going on with our kids. It shows the teachers that we're on the same team and presenting a united front. In our case, I do most of the talking and my

husband writes everything down. At the end of each meeting, I make it a point to compliment the teacher, telling her my child likes her class or she's doing a good job. Even if it's not the *best* teacher, I can still find positive things coming out of the experience for my child.
—*Rochelle Van Slyke, mom of Chris, 21, Erika, 16, and Amy, 13, Ketchikan, Arkansas*

I absolutely think both parents should go to parent-teacher conferences. I find that often men and women listen and react to things differently. I would read emotional stuff into something a teacher said, while my husband would say, "Well no, what she's saying is our daughter is strong in one area and needs help in another." We would talk about it on the ride home and come away with a better understanding of what had been said. Do whatever it takes to get both of you there.
—*Joanne Brine, mom of Katharine, 9, and Liam, 5, Hopkinton, Massachusetts*

What Can I Do to Help Ensure the Meeting Runs Smoothly?

Be on time for conferences! Better yet, be ten minutes early. Showing up even a few minutes late means less time for discussion, as well as irritation on the part of the teacher or other parents if your conference runs late.

Start the meeting off with a compliment; this sets the teacher at ease, diffuses the tensions in the room, and makes way for a serious discussion. Comment on something your child particularly likes about the class or the teacher, a great recent homework assignment, or just your appreciation for taking the time to talk with you.

Your body language and facial expressions indicate your attitude. Keep constant eye contact, sit without tapping your foot, pen, or fingers, and arrange your upper body in a comfortable, nonconfrontational way.

Stay open to new possibilities, and don't present issues as though you have already made up your mind. To avoid making your statements sound like accusations, discuss how your child feels. You want to open up the lines of communication and work in a collaborative spirit, even when you think the teacher is in the wrong.

@ Be a fair and active listener. It is important to put aside your assumptions and prejudices and keep an open mind during the conversation. Listen to what the teacher actually says instead of interpreting her words to represent what you were expecting her to say, or concentrating on what you want to say next. Do your best to keep yourself from interrupting the teacher when she is speaking to you. If you disagree on an issue and she does not pause to allow you to speak, make a note of it, so when it's your turn to speak you won't forget to bring it up.

@ Remember that the purpose of this meeting is not to hear compliments about your child. Rather, it offers a forum for fostering cooperation and communication between you and the teacher to help your child grow, develop, and learn. Expect to hear about your child's problem areas and be prepared to ask how you can help him. Accept constructive criticism without becoming overly defensive of your child, his behavior, and your parenting skills. On the same note, if you're giving the teacher constructive criticism, do it in a way that is gentle, direct, and specific; malicious words and generalizations will not solve anything.

@ If you're communicating negative information to the teacher, try to speak for a few sentences at a time and then ask for a reaction. If you offer up a long monologue, you are likely to overwhelm the teacher rather than give her time to reflect and respond to each point you bring up.

@ Ask the teacher to elaborate if she uses educational jargon that confuses you, or if you need clarification to gain a more complete understanding of what she is trying to tell you.

@ Avoid lengthy discussion about topics unrelated to the meeting's central purpose, as well as tangential asides. Background information is often helpful, but make sure your real issue does not get overlooked in favor of inconsequential stories or details.

@ Do not waste your time or the teacher's by focusing on what cannot be changed, such as the school's general curriculum. Concentrate instead on the troublesome aspects of your child's school experience within the teacher's control.

Questions you may want to ask the teacher:

✶ To what extent does my child participate in class activities and discussions? Does he raise his hand often? Does he seem shy or disinterested?

✶ How does my child handle taking tests?

✶ What academic progress has my child made?

✶ How well does my child listen and work independently?

✶ Do you think my child is working up to his ability?

✶ How does my child compare to the academic expectations for his grade level?

✶ How are my child's creative thinking and problem-solving skills?

✶ Do you group children by ability in reading or math, and if so, into which group has my child been placed? How often do you reevaluate students and change these groups?

✶ Are there subject areas in which my child struggles, needs extra help, or seems unmotivated? If so, what assistance can the school offer to get him back on track?

✶ Would it be appropriate to test my child for a learning disability?

✶ Do you think my child is being challenged academically?

✶ Does the school have a program for gifted and talented children? Should my child be tested for it?

✶ With whom does my child socialize most in the classroom?

✶ How does my child get along with the other kids in the class?

❂ Take note if the teacher identifies recurrent issues that have come up in previous grades, and check to see if she understands the problems differently than you or his previous teachers.

◉ Ask the teacher about her approach:

✴ What are her classroom goals for the year? On what particular academic or organizational skills is she working? What goals does she have for your child?

✴ What is her grading system for class work, tests, papers, and large projects?

✴ What is her approach to discipline? How does she deal with missed homework assignments, acting out in class, and behavior problems?

◉ Your child's teacher has seen many children and may have advice you can use to deal with homework or behavior problems. She can also tell you the best ways to supplement classroom learning at home.

◉ If you're not sure you're both understanding each other or you just want to conclude the conference by summarizing what has been stated, try backtracking. Repeat back to the teacher what you understand to have been said, recounting the main ideas.

In a meeting with your child's teacher, keep a level head. You don't want to go to the teacher looking like you've already made up your mind on the issue to be discussed. Make sure you're really listening. When you lay out your concerns, do so in a way that is productive, nonconfrontational, and sympathetic.
—Sue Abrams, elementary school principal and former 1st to 5th grade teacher for 22 years, Natick, Massachusetts

First, listen carefully to all the teacher has to share about your child in a conference. Second, ask your most important questions after listening to the teacher's report and observations. Then pick your battles by stating the concerns that you feel cannot be addressed without your involvement.
—Christine R., English, history, and social studies teacher for 32 years, Milton, Massachusetts

My rule is to always try to say something positive first, before I focus on concerns. Don't come in and bombard the teacher. Instead, say something like, "I really like the science project you're working on now, but I'm concerned my son isn't getting it." Then the teacher isn't put on the defensive.
—*Joy Pumphrey, 2nd and 3rd grade teacher for 12 years, Clearwater, Florida*

I use an opening line like, "Help me understand what's causing this problem." Parents and teachers need to have a good attitude: "We're in this together. It's not about us, it's about the child." Openness is great, but not if the parents use this as an opportunity to talk to the teacher in an accusatory way.
—*Claudia Flanders, kindergarten to 8th grade teacher for 34 years, Santa Monica, California*

It's easy for teachers to get defensive, because we always have to defend what we're doing. Parents will come in saying "This is what you should be doing," like one side of the story is written in stone, or they may tell me something happened in my own classroom when I was there. Explain to the teacher what you have heard and tell her you would really like to know what she saw.
—*Mary Chick, kindergarten to 12th grade art teacher for 8 years, Elgin, Minnesota*

I walk in with a prioritized checklist of issues I want to talk about, and I estimate how long each one will take and what I expect as an end result. I also have a goal for myself, some action I want to see happen associated with each issue.
—*Andrea B., mom of three boys ages 15, 9, and 7*

Don't rely on a short conference to fix any serious problems. Focus on the things you can do something about in that period of time. It should not be a complaint session about how your kid thinks the class is so hard. Be more practical about what can be done to help your child, instead of listing the things that are going badly.
—*Ken Pauly, high school social studies teacher for 13 years, St. Louis Park, Minnesota*

Parents' tone when communicating with teachers is very important. Remember, you're a team! Don't get on the offensive; instead, ask what you all can do together to help your child along. Share openly about what your kid is like, and what's helpful or not for your child's interactions and learning. Focus on formulating an effective plan for the year.
—*Ann McCormack, former elementary school teacher in Watertown, Massachusetts*

I always ask toward the end of the conference what my child or I could be doing better. I have found that if there's an issue that the teacher's on the fence about bringing to your attention, this question will likely encourage her to share her concerns.
—*Sibylle Barrasso, mom of Lane, 16, Wellesley, Massachusetts*

How Should I Frame a Specific Problem?

Every teacher has a distinct personal style. By becoming familiar with the particular style of your child's teacher before a problem comes up, you'll be better equipped to figure out which approach will be most effective when addressing the issue.

Learn the rules the system has in place. You won't get anywhere if you come in uninformed, so do your research first. Look through the school handbook and get a copy of the behavior contract or conflict-resolution policies. Knowing about the school's rules and approaches to problem solving will go a long way toward building a solid relationship with the teacher. She'll appreciate that you did your homework first, and you'll be able to understand if she is limited by formal procedure.

Arm yourself with examples. Being too general with your complaints is a bad strategy for trying to mediate a solution. Find out what is being done at the school for students in situations similar to your child's and what strategies have worked best in the past. Similarly, if the teacher calls you in about a problem, ask her to give you specific examples, details, and context.

◉ Keep an open mind as you enter the conference and recognize that strategies that work at home may not work at school, and vice versa. Let the teacher know what steps you have already taken to help address and solve the problem and frame the discussion in terms of working to resolve the problem together. Use "we" language instead of "you" to maintain the feeling of a team effort.

◉ Understand there is probably more than one way to solve the problem your child is having at school. Don't compound the situation by attempting to force one solution. Try to identify as many ways as possible to improve the situation and remember that you may have to compromise with your child's teacher on an approach.

◉ Keep your intense emotions in check as much as possible. Use a steady tone—this sounds easy in the abstract, but can prove incredibly challenging when you start discussing your child. If the conference gets heated and you find yourself becoming upset, take time to cool off. Use a pause in the conversation to check your notes or clarify something the teacher has told you. If you think you need to leave the room to calm your temper, get a drink of water or take a quick trip to the restroom. If you need more time to calm down, gracefully tell the teacher you need to get more information about the problem before you discuss the matter any further, thank her for her time, and tell her you would like to speak again soon.

◉ If you know in advance you won't be able to resolve a dispute with the teacher by yourself, involve a neutral mediator. If you are going to bring an additional person you should politely tell the teacher ahead of time without any indication of hostility or frustration.

◉ Regardless of how you feel at the end of the conference, sincerely thank the teacher for her time. Remember your ultimate aim is ensuring your child's academic progress—not changing the teacher's personality.

If your child is having difficulty with a subject, you need to walk into a conference with the mentality of, "Hey, I'm here so we can work together to figure out what we need to do to make sure that my child's grades improve and he meets with success." Doing so often inspires teachers to give the little extra help needed.
—Martha Ann Chandler, 3rd to 6th grade teacher for 14 years, Florence, South Carolina

If there are problems, come in with an open mind about why or how the situation occurred instead of taking only your child's viewpoint.
—*Anne Marie Fritton, 4th grade teacher for 3 years, Depew, New York*

Realize that your perceptions as a parent are partially attitudinal, and you only know about a problem from your child's perspective.
—*Steve C., 2nd grade to high school teacher for 15 years, Framingham, Massachusetts*

If you have a concern, go to the teacher and say, "Hey, I'm having this concern. What do we need to do to fix things?" Don't be afraid to speak up. Parents and teachers need to work together, as a team. It does take a whole village to raise a child! If you have a question or issue, then call the teacher—but don't scream and yell. Have an open ear and be willing to try different things. Don't say, "It's got to be x and that's it!"
—*Heather Daigle, teacher of all grades, Plymouth, Massachusetts*

What Follow-Up Should Take Place After a Conference?

After leaving a conference, you should have a clear sense of your child's social, academic, and emotional strengths, weaknesses, needs, and development, as well as specific suggestions for what you can do at home to help your child succeed in school. For significant academic or social issues, however, you will probably need to meet with the teacher more than once to fully resolve the problems.

Send a note to the teacher after a parent-teacher conference reaffirming what steps you decided to take, alerting her to anything you may have forgotten, and thanking her. Not only will she appreciate your note and be more willing to meet with you again, but the gesture will also remind her about your agreed-upon plans of action.

☺ Summarize the teacher's suggestions and comments with your child. Discuss with him the strategy for improvement you and the teacher decided upon, and suggest ways he might modify his behavior or daily routine to help remedy the problem. Tell him the teacher's perspective and her observations of his personality and behavior, emphasizing any positive things the teacher had to say about him. Clearly explain any specialists who will be involved in the planned course of action and each individual's role. Ask for your child's feedback and consider whatever thoughts or worries he might have regarding the plan.

☺ Allow some time for any implemented strategies to take hold and produce results before charging back into the teacher's office. No problem can be solved overnight, and some solutions may take a lengthy period of time to prove effective. To see if your plan is working effectively, be consistent with your efforts and follow through. Keep the teacher informed about the changes you agreed upon and the instituted progress.

☺ Schedule a follow-up meeting four to six weeks later, even if the problem seems to have dissipated. Both you and the teacher will get closure, and you both can feel good about helping your child overcome the challenging obstacle. This is particularly crucial if your plan of action does not seem to be affecting the desired results. A subsequent conference allows you and the teacher to talk about what might be hindering the plan's fruition, and what helpful changes can be made to help your child succeed.

Keep in mind that conversations with the teacher about problems are game plans, not promises.
—*Susan Draughn, 7th and 8th grade special education teacher for 24 years, Sunman, Indiana*

When Are Child-Teacher-Parent Conferences Most Effective?

◉ A growing trend in schools is to have the child participate in conferences with his teacher and parents. Schools have found involving the child in these meetings, starting around fourth grade, is an effective way to give the student greater responsibility in the learning process and replace his fears of negative behind-closed-doors discussions with motivation, insight, and open communication.

◉ Not all teachers are comfortable with students attending conferences, so it is important that you bring your child along only if it is the school's policy or you have discussed it with the teacher in advance.

◉ Especially for younger students, have a conference among the adults first and establish an agenda. Don't bring in your child until you've worked together and have a game plan. Your child will feel everyone has a vested interest in him and realize he cannot play you against the teacher. Pulling the child in when developing the plan really depends on the maturity of the child, but could be beneficial in some instances.

◉ During the conference, make sure your child feels you and his teacher are working together on his behalf and on matters related to him.

When dealing with poor behavior at school, discussions among the child, teacher, and parents help to get everyone on the same page. Then the group can discuss concerns and come up with a plan to best help the child succeed.
—Kristen Young, kindergarten to 2nd grade teacher for 8 years, Virginia

Last year, my daughter had difficulty connecting with her geometry teacher, and to address it, my husband, our child, and I went in to meet with the teacher. It really worked. I would do that again if there's a problem with a teacher, because otherwise you hear all this stuff about your kid and then go home and your kid says, "That's not how it works." By having your child at the conference you can address the issue right there, and it saves a lot of back-and-forth parenting.

—*Kim Shepherd, mom of Jessica, 17, Jeremy and Josh, 12, and Jennifer, 10, Indianapolis, Indiana*

Students must feel comfortable approaching their teachers. If there is a personality conflict, you should immediately request a parent-student-teacher conference to discuss any problems that need to be addressed.

—*Jennifer Coleman, 6th to 12th grade teacher for 7 years, Hillsboro, Texas*

Ask your child if he thinks the teacher sees a classroom issue the same way, or if she will have a different answer. If your child has some straightforward answers that make the issue easy to fix, work on that first. Otherwise, contact the teacher via email or phone for suggestions or insights. If this still fails, ask for a meeting to discuss what the team—the parents, teacher, *and the student*—can do to improve the situation. I highly recommend having the student at this meeting.

—*Erika Bare, 6th to 8th grade special education teacher for 3 years, West Linn, Oregon*

Kids need to see the partnership between their parents and teachers, as the school experience really comes together for children when they sense everyone is working together.

—*Cindy Esposito, mom of Jon, Jason, and Chris, 23, Rhiannon, 16, and Justin, 13, Orange County, New York*

When all else fails, a conference including both the child and the teacher can help get to the bottom of a problem.

—*Pam Pottorff, 3rd and 4th grade teacher and 8th grade reading teacher for 5 years, Sioux City, Nebraska*

If an issue arises, the best thing to do is to have a meeting where you all sit down together and figure out what might help. The child gets to be there and you can ask him directly, "What do you think about this? Why do you think we're here? What would help you more?" With everybody in the same room, the kid can't use Mom against Dad, or the teachers against the parents.

—*Laurie Olmstead, 7th and 8th grade math and science teacher for 4 years, Union, Maine*

Managing Child-Teacher Conflict

What Should I Do When My Child and the Teacher Just Don't Seem to Get Along?

◉ If your child and his teacher do not get along, then even with the best curriculum and motivation, the school year is likely to be an academic wash unless you intervene constructively. When a personality conflict exists between your child and his teacher, your challenge is to support your child but not fuel the fire. It's so tempting to do an end run around the teacher—whether complaining to other parents, the PTA, other teachers you are close to, or the principal. But teachers always want the chance to work things out and you need to give them an opportunity to do so, putting aside your skepticism and tackling the issue head-on.

◉ Your first step should be a serious conversation with your child. At one point or

another, everyone encounters a person with whom he does not get along, whether academically, socially, or professionally. Teaching your child to deal with these situations at an early age prepares him for these trials later in life. Explain to him that in life we often have to deal with people we don't like, but cannot react by getting angry, acting out, or refusing to do our work. It's helpful to give him examples from your own life of coworkers, peers, or administrators with whom you have butted heads in the past. Show him how you worked things out constructively. Help him understand that this is an opportunity to show character and rise to a challenge.

◉   It is natural to become concerned if your child returns home from school with stories of how his teacher embarrassed or mistreated him. Nearly all kids go through periods during which they dislike their teachers because they feel they are treated unfairly or receive an undeserved grade. However, before you rush back to the school, have a clear understanding of the story from your child's viewpoint. Ask him for specifics to determine exactly what happened, and find out if it is simply a misunderstanding or if it is a recurring problem. Stay open-minded and consider your first steps an information-gathering mission.

◉   Often, a child's version of what's going on does not match the teacher's. Keep in mind that your child isn't always the most accurate or reliable judge of a teacher's ability. It is critical to hear the teacher's perspective on the issue as well.

◉   Older children, especially middle-school students, are prone to bow to the influence of peer pressure and judge teachers based on other students' opinions. Consider whether your child's gripes are valid or whether he's just repeating what he overheard in the cafeteria.

◉   If your child thinks his teacher is out to get him, make a list of his complaints. Look at the list and judge whether you think the objections are valid, taking your child's personality into account. If he is prone to exaggeration and misinterpretation, proceed more cautiously. Talk to parents of other children in the class and find out if they have received similar complaints from their children or have the same impressions.

◉   Most teachers have their students' best interests at heart. A lot of the problems students wind up having with their teachers are about conflicts of style and personality. Listen carefully to your child's complaints about the teacher. Do they sound like instances of bad teaching or does it sound more like your child is reacting to a new and unfamiliar teaching style or, perhaps, he simply doesn't like the teacher's personality? There is a possibility that some of the things the teacher says to your child or assigns aren't fair, but in the classroom she's in charge.

◉ It is your job to intervene if incidents or comments lead you to believe the teacher or principal dislikes your child. You don't want your child to be labeled a troublemaker for the remaining time spent in that school. Although it is critical that you involve yourself in your child's education, overinvolving yourself may cause even more problems.

It is so hard to hear about an injustice at school, especially if it involves your child. However, it is important to teach your child there are other points of view, and he is part of a larger community in which mistakes are bound to happen. If something does occur that upsets your child, let the teacher know in a note or in person, but remain calm and open to an entirely different point of view.
—*Mary Kavanaugh, kindergarten to 6th grade teacher for 18 years,*
   Williamstown, Massachusetts

I'm a football coach and I can be pretty intimidating in the classroom, even when I'm trying to be my gentlest self. A child interpreting some situations will come home from school with a story that might not be quite accurate, and parents need to assess the situation before they react. Some parents come into my room and kind of embarrass themselves because they haven't really worked through the story their child gave them. Others will turn any situation into a tug-of-war. Instead of trying to resolve a problem, they make it a win-lose instead of a win-win situation. I firmly believe that 99.9% of teachers aren't at home at night plotting and scheming to make a student's life miserable.
—*Edward Sapienza, 9th to 12th grade science, math, and computer teacher for 31 years, North*
   Reading, Massachusetts

If parents think there is an issue between their child and the teacher they should come into the classroom and observe. One parent once went to my principal because she thought I

didn't like her daughter. The principal told her that she should come observe me teach and see her daughter in the classroom setting.
—*Sherri McWhorter, 4th grade teacher for 5 years, Augusta, Georgia*

Don't always believe everything your child tells you. Many times young children will have a very difficult time understanding and taking responsibility for their actions and will blame others. When you completely believe your child's story without hearing from the teacher, you set your child up to be a tattler and to never take responsibility for his own actions.
—*Amy Shaver, kindergarten and 1st grade teacher for 10 years, Bondurant, Iowa*

I tell my parents the first week of school, "If you will believe half of what your children tell you about me, I will believe half of what they tell me about you." Sometimes it's all perspective. Parents, when listening to the child, should try to determine if the teacher's behavior makes sense. If it doesn't, then chances are the story is somewhat exaggerated or incorrect. Parents need to remain calm and not contact the school while they're angry. It's best to express concern in a calm and nonjudgmental way, saying something like, "Susie told me something happened in class yesterday, and I'm concerned about it. Can you tell me what happened?"
—*Kathy Carabine, pre-k and 3rd grade teacher for 16 years, Boston, Massachusetts*

Don't wait until your child is throwing up every morning before talking to the teacher, even if the problem is the teacher. There are ways to figure this out. Document things that happen if the teacher is the problem and take the matter to the principal—that's the worst-case scenario.

What often causes misunderstanding between parents and teachers is parents' readiness to believe anything their child says. I'm not necessarily saying children lie, but a child can have misperceptions. Teachers see your child in an environment with 20 or 30 other students, and you don't have that opportunity. I'm a mom, too! I know firsthand, as a parent, that you think your child walks on water. The teacher sees each child in a different environment.
—*Claudia Flanders, kindergarten to 8th grade teacher for 34 years, Santa Monica, California*

My son's third grade year was tough because he had a teacher he didn't especially like, and who I felt didn't like him. But I tried not to constantly second-guess her decisions—even when my son came home saying, "I got in trouble at school and I didn't do it," I didn't run and call the school ranting and raving. I just said to the teacher, "This is what I heard and I would like to know more about what happened."
—*Jennifer Guss, mom of Fred, 10, Hannah, 4, and Sophie, 2, Montvale, New Jersey*

In middle school, my son and daughter both had the same teacher, one year after the other. My son is smart but disorganized, and we were always told that he was losing things and not turning in papers. We believed the teacher. But when the same thing happened with my daughter, who is a straight-A and very organized student, we realized the teacher was the one who was losing everything!
—*Martha Judiscak, mom of Jimmy, 17, Vicki, 16, and Danny, 11, Knoxville, Tennessee*

Sometimes a teacher does not realize that something she did or said has been offensive or troubling to a student. Give that teacher a call! Explain the situation and let her know you would just like clarification on the matter. It is better to find out the reasons behind your child's complaint in a timely manner. Once the problem has been discussed, future problems can be avoided and a positive relationship can resume.
—*Mary Chick, kindergarten to 12th grade art teacher for 8 years, Elgin, Minnesota*

My oldest daughter has a very strong personality, and she had a teacher who was too laid back for her. It concerned Olivia that he didn't have a firm grip on the classroom, and it made her anxious and uncomfortable that the classroom was really unstructured. My husband and I both took turns going into the classroom and talking to the teacher, but didn't see many results. So we both decided to spend more time helping Olivia. It was a good experience for her to learn about personality clashes and different styles, as well as how to let go.
—*Jennifer O'Gorman, mom of Olivia, 11, Jake, 9, Sam, 7, Annabelle, 4, Luke, 2, and Eleanor, 1, Lebanon, Maine*

My son had a new teacher who wasn't your average, huggable kindergarten teacher—at

times she was abrasive and yelled. We felt we were alone in our feelings about her, and our approach has always been to say to the teacher, "You're the expert at teaching kids in this grade and we're the experts at our kid, so we need to figure out a way to combine our skills—if we need you, we'll call, and if you need us, you'll call." As it turned out, every single parent had the same complaint about the teacher. She was getting used to the school and the school was getting used to her. By the third quarter, everyone got used to one another.
—*Kathleen Spinale, mom of Joey, 9, and Peter, 4, Ipswich, Massachusetts*

Realize that a child's perspective and the teacher's perspective can be two totally different things—even the best of children don't like to put themselves in a bad light.
—*Lawanna Ford, 5th grade teacher for 25 years, Argonia, Kansas*

How Do I Handle Conflicting Perceptions of My Child?

You and your child's teacher may sometimes find yourselves disagreeing about how your child learns best or what is in his best interest. Dealing with a situation in which you disagree with the teacher's approach requires a great deal of respect and discretion.

If you have conflicting views, be sure to fully understand the nature of the disagreement. Find out if there are any areas in which you do agree or common goals you can work toward. Create a plan and follow through both at home and at school, and meet again soon to reevaluate the situation.

If you cannot reach an agreement, bring in a third party for insight and advice.

Listen to and accept, at least in part, the teacher's judgments about your child's social, academic, and emotional development, as she does spend seven hours a day with him in the classroom.

It can be tricky if teachers and parents think differently about a child's ability in academic subjects. If it is a situation where the teacher has your child for more than one year, then I would take action. However, in a normal classroom where a teacher only has the kids for a year, sit down and talk with the teacher and say, "Why have you put my child in the slow reading group? I don't agree." Overall I wouldn't worry about it too much as long as the teacher's not saying anything to your child, like "You're a slow reader," or making your child feel worthless. You can always work on positive ways to work on it at home and to praise your child's achievements. There is no need to go with the teacher's perception of your child being a slow reader or math-struggler.
—*Holly Parker, teacher of deaf students for 10 years, Colorado Springs, Colorado*

Every parent needs to understand what the teacher thinks about her child and his ability level. Misunderstandings build crisis. Parents should know that we are on their side and we make mistakes, too. Really, teachers are user-friendly. We're easy to talk to. We are some of the most understanding people in the world.
—*Lynn M., high school, deaf students, and middle school special education teacher for 21 years, Boston, Massachusetts*

Contact the teacher and find out the other side of the story. Don't speak poorly of the teacher to your child. Show respect and don't undermine the authority of her position. Your child's teacher is a professional and is not going to bad mouth you in front of your child. Doesn't she deserve that same respect?
—*Lawanna Ford, 5th grade teacher for 25 years, Argonia, Kansas*

I had one very problematic parent I just couldn't connect with until I reminded her that it's not about whether we like each other, but rather about what we could do to make her child successful.
—*Claudia Flanders, kindergarten to 8th grade teacher for 34 years, Santa Monica, California*

When Should I Consider Moving My Child to a New Class?

◉ Remember that if the school year is already underway, moving classes could be more damaging to your child's education than the reason for the switch itself. Changing classrooms can cause serious emotional and social upheaval for your child, so the move must be worth the stress involved. For this reason, most schools will not allow a transfer without strong reasons for it.

◉ Taking your child out of his class is rarely the only recourse to a situation. Be open to teamwork and exploring other options.

◉ Most kids will survive one year with a bad teacher. Before deciding to pull your child from a classroom, weigh the emotional versus academic concerns. If your child is shy, has trouble making new friends, or is fragile emotionally, typically you should not make the choice to switch classes.

◉ While most principals try to be accommodating before the beginning of a school year, they often refuse to budge after the school year is underway. If your child and the teacher have a profound disconnect, make an appointment immediately rather than waiting a couple months to see if the issue resolves itself.

There are compromises other than getting the child removed from the class right off the bat. It's not easy to pick a student up from Teacher A and deposit him with Teacher B, even if they're teaching the same class and curriculum. Especially if the student is a problem, now he's the other teacher's problem.
—*Edward Sapienza, 9th to 12th grade science, math, and computer teacher for 31 years, North Reading, Massachusetts*

◉

Moving classrooms is an extreme solution. It may be necessary sometimes, but first you

need to put egos aside, talk, and see what's really going on. When a child and teacher do not get along, it needs to be handled delicately. When teachers get attacked by parents, it's easy to forget the needs of the child, because it becomes personal and emotions get in the way. Then a teacher becomes quick to self-justify. I do my best as a teacher, whenever I make mistakes or people have concerns, to try to welcome criticism because it's ultimately about the child.
—*Niambi Muhammad, 1st and 2nd grade teacher for 4 years, Chicago, Illinois*

My son had one teacher who was horrible. We really tried to make it work because we didn't want him to have an example of bailing out when things go wrong. Sometimes it's just not a good teacher-child combination, though.
—*Claudia Flanders, kindergarten to 8th grade teacher for 34 years, Santa Monica, California*

Thankfully out of five children, there have really been only a few bad teachers. One son had a teacher who was a screamer, which made him overly anxious. She constantly yelled at the kids and forced them to "speak up," and his self-esteem plummeted. I witnessed my kid's entire personality change. Luckily, I recognized that this was happening pretty early on, so I approached the school and was given permission to go into the classroom and observe. We ended up getting him switched to another teacher.
—*Cindy Esposito, mom of Jon, Jason, and Chris, 23, Rhiannon, 16, and Justin, 13, Orange County, New York*

I had a problem with my child's first grade teacher and wanted my daughter out of her class. She would give my child checks for discipline problems, when no other teacher before or since has mentioned any problems. My daughter would come home and say, "I got seven checks for bad behavior today!" I had a conference with the teacher, and we let several weeks go by without seeing any improvement. I then went through the school counselor and had a three-way meeting with the teacher. There was such a political roundabout to get my daughter out of the class that by the time I worked my way up the system, school was out for the year. It affected my daughter's entire school year.
—*Stephanie Lee, substitute elementary school teacher, Lawrenceville, Georgia*

How Do I Know If My Child Just Has a Poor Teacher?

◉ If your child is lucky, he will be blessed with many wonderful teachers. The reality is that he will likely face some average ones, and inevitably a couple lacking the skills, expertise, teaching style, or personality you hoped for.

◉ If you think you are dealing with a bad teacher, understand your options. Except in extreme cases of physical or sexual abuse, most situations will not warrant the school firing or transferring the teacher. Before you do anything else, talk to the teacher about your concerns. It's possible there are reasons for what she is doing that you are not aware of. There are other ways to help the situation:

✦ Talk to parents of children who had the teacher in the past. Ask if any of them had issues with her, spoke to an administrator about her, or resorted to transferring their child out of her class. Be discrete and polite in your inquiries because you don't want to make it known to the teacher or administration that you are considering taking action.

✦ Call the guidance counselor to express your concern that your child has a weak teacher who isn't adequately teaching him the skills he needs to master.

✦ Register a written complaint explaining specifically why you feel your child's teacher is inadequate.

◉ Regardless of what you may have heard about a teacher, give her a chance and assess her skills objectively by the way you see her teaching your child. Even if you respect and trust the people feeding you stories, they may have heard only part of a tale or repeat something that only happened once.

◉ If you have met with the teacher about a problem and tried unsuccessfully to implement a plan, ask to observe your child in class. Being present in the classroom can give you a better feel for what's going on and how to deal with it. If the teacher cites a school rule against parents sitting in on classes, ask the principal for a waiver. When you are in the classroom, watch how she interacts with the students. Observe whom she calls on, what she focuses on, and how she responds to students' questions and answers. Notice how she monitors students' interactions with each other and how she handles discipline issues.

Teachers are like anyone else, and there are some bad ones out there. You can't trust that your child is going to have a good teacher, even if you're in a good school system. If you're really energetic and committed, go to the school at the end of the school year and observe the teachers your child might have next year, and then go to the principal with a request.
—*Kallie Leyba, 1st and 2nd grade teacher for 2 years and mom of Lauren, 11, Lucas, 8, and Samson, 4, Highlands Ranch, Colorado*

I find out if there are problems with the teacher from watching my daughter's reaction when she comes home from school. If something happens one time with your child, just watch the situation. If it happens two or three more times, then it's something to be discussed. It may be more of a misunderstanding, but it could also be something the whole class misunderstood. We had an issue where my daughter thought that she was not allowed to go to the bathroom during reading time, and it ended up being mostly something she misunderstood.
—*Ellen Cameron, mom of Alison, 8, and Hilary, 4, Lexington, Massachusetts*

We had a rough start last year with one of the teachers. My daughter and I were not getting along with her. She was an older teacher who had been around a long time, and we talked several times. She was the kind of person who would give flippant comments that would irritate you right off the bat, but she was one of the best teachers. She ended up spending a lot of time with Nicole after school making sure she got the math and spelling facts straight because she knew it would be a struggle going into upper grades otherwise. We got to know each other and made sure Nicole really got what she needed. She ended up having a successful year.

—*Laura Doctor, mom of Nicole, 10, Cleveland, Ohio*

My daughter had one very negative experience with a teacher who yelled a lot and used negative reinforcement. She constantly kept doubt about herself in my daughter's mind, and my husband and I had to do our own repair damage to build her up a bit. At one point I had to go over her head to the principal to discuss a discipline matter, because my daughter received two poor conduct grades that came out of nowhere. The teacher was furious but changed the grades. I went up to her afterwards and thanked her for doing so, despite her bad attitude. Things calmed down a little bit after that, but my daughter still didn't enjoy going to school, leaving me with no other explanation but, "Honey, we all have people we have to deal with, people we don't necessarily like. It's a life lesson, just something we have to do."

—*Sheila Cross, mom of Emily, 8, Memphis, Tennessee*

If I've heard bad things about the teacher, I don't pass that along to my child. And I try not to believe what other people tell me, because for some reason other parents always want to scare you! I heard rumors that one of my son's teachers was a screamer, and all year I never heard her scream once. Besides, teachers are entitled to bad days. I have bad days with my kids and I only have three of them!

—*Martha Judiscak, mom of Jimmy, 17, Vicki, 16, and Danny, 11, Knoxville, Tennessee*

How Can I Help Defuse a Child-Teacher Meltdown?

Bad relationships can stem from a poor teacher, differences in teaching style and learning style, or simple miscommunication. By strategically getting involved, you can keep a bad teacher-child relationship from deteriorating further.

◎ Tell the teacher the concerns your child expresses, and ask for her insights. Don't be confrontational, listen to her perspective, and come up with potential solutions.

◎ Be aware that the teacher might not remember things perfectly, so unless there was a major incident you are concerned about, focus on fixing issues for the future, not getting the most accurate account of what has already happened.

Listen to your child's and the teacher's concerns before reacting. Then try to help your child and the teacher understand one another.
—*Kristen Young, kindergarten to 2nd grade teacher for 8 years, Virginia*

Speak with the teacher when there is a disconnect, as sometimes the teacher may not be aware of the problem. The success of the child-teacher relationship is mostly on the teacher's shoulders, as she must show your child that she cares about him personally.
—*Sharon Stubbs, 5th and 6th grade teacher for 28 years, Hopkins, Michigan*

Specificity is really important. Telling the teacher your child thinks she's mean doesn't help much. If instead you can specifically say, "On Tuesday my child said this happened," and relate specific incidents instead of generalizing the behavior, it's much more effective. Generalizations just hurt the teacher's feelings and leave the conversation nowhere to go.
—*Claudia Flanders, kindergarten to 8th grade teacher for 34 years, Santa Monica, California*

When your child has a problem with the teacher, approach the situation as a "we," not an "I," and voice specific concerns. Say concrete things like, "My child understands these math concepts and is anxious to move ahead, but I'm not seeing that happen." It's a question of really knowing what is going on in the class and being able to show examples of how needs aren't being met.
—*Sue Abrams, elementary school principal and former 1st to 5th grade teacher for 22 years, Natick, Massachusetts*

Address problems in the child-teacher relationship directly to your child's teacher. Advocate for your child by repeating his concerns in a meeting without him. You can say, "This issue concerns me because I am not sure why my child has this perception. I would like to make you aware of it and hear what you think."
—*Florence Michel, middle school teacher for 8 years, New York, New York, and Baltimore, Maryland*

When Does It Make Strategic Sense to Involve the Principal?

It can be frustrating to find yourself dealing with a bureaucratic system when your child struggles at school. You want what is best for him, but it's often unclear what course of action you should take or whom you should approach with problems, especially when those issues involve his classroom teacher.

Raise issues with the teacher before bringing them to the principal's attention, even if they concern the teacher's style in the classroom or how she handled an incident involving your child. Going above the teacher's head without first addressing the problem with her could lead to resentment that will break down the lines of communication, affect your relationship with her for the rest of the school year, and earn you an unfavorable reputation with the other teachers. Weigh this possibility against the significance of the problem.

After meeting with the classroom teacher, if you are still unsatisfied because she is unresponsive, you were unable to agree on a resolution for the problem, or the agreed upon plan was not successful, then arrange an appointment with the principal and teacher together. This joint meeting assures the teacher that you are taking a course of action to best help your child, instead of going to her boss for retribution.

A principal's job is to balance the needs of the students, the school's faculty and staff, and the community. A good principal takes responsibility for poor teaching in his school and is therefore the best person to approach about a teacher who might otherwise damage your child's education.

© Before you go to the principal with an issue, realize how this move may damage your relationship with the teacher. To decide whether the issue at hand deserves the attention of the principal, ask yourself:

✦ Am I acting impulsively out of frustration or anger?

✦ Am I falling into a pattern of repeatedly bringing my concerns to the principal?

✦ Have I first tried my best to work things out with the teacher?

✦ Is this a matter of school policy?

© For a major dispute that involves a number of parents and affects the entire classroom, ask one or two other parents to accompany you to meet with the principal. There is strength in numbers, and if a principal sees several parents are deeply concerned, she will be more likely to take action.

© Document any retaliation you feel the teacher has levied against your child. Use this when you approach the principal or superintendent about a problem. Assert yourself as you battle to get a fair and effective plan to help your child.

Teachers prefer to be spoken to first before the principal—going above a teacher's head always starts parents off on the wrong foot.
—*Amy Watson, 7th to 12th grade teacher for 5 years, Oyster Bay, New York*

The principal's first question will always be, "Did you talk to the teacher?"
—*Edward Sapienza, 9th to 12th grade science, math, and computer teacher for 31 years, North Reading, Massachusetts*

Parents who go to the principal first up the ante way too fast. It's overkill, like going to a neurosurgeon the first time you have a headache.
—*Claudia Flanders, kindergarten to 8th grade teacher for 34 years, Santa Monica, California*

You always, always, always have to start at the classroom level. Life is not perfect, and there are times when teacher-child relationships need some tweaking or explanation. Sometimes a parent will have an issue with a teacher and won't realize that the real problem is another underlying situation about which the teacher can provide additional information. If the problem is in any way related to a student, my first response will always be, "Have you spoken to the teacher?" Unfortunately, some parents come to me because they spoke to the teacher and they didn't like the answers. For the most part, you go to the principal for issues that are the next level up from the classroom, like class placement or the curriculum.
—*Sue Abrams, elementary school principal and former 1st to 5th grade teacher for 22 years, Natick, Massachusetts*

If there is a classroom incident, you have to go to the teacher first to clarify what happened. If it's coming just from your child, you don't know which direction his comments came from or if his perception is correct. If the teacher had a yelling incident, some parents would want to go to the principal, but it's not fair to go to the top without approaching the teacher first.
—*Ellen Cameron, mom of Alison, 8, and Hilary, 4, Lexington, Massachusetts*

As a teacher, I'm angered and offended if parents go to the principal before talking to me first. It's a big deal. Those are the parents who are going to be talked about in the teacher's lounge all year.
—*Martha Ann Chandler, 3rd to 6th grade teacher for 14 years, Florence, South Carolina*

I work with the child and see him five days a week, so in almost every situation parents should come to me first. Parents should follow the chain of command at the school. Only in extreme cases, such as if a teacher was making fun of a child, should the parent speak with the principal first.

—Barry Mindes, 3rd to 5th grade teacher for 32 years, Norton, Massachusetts

Lean on the principal and her experience. If it's a big problem, then you're probably not going to be the first parent and child who have come in with a complaint about that teacher.

—Kim Shepherd, mom of Jessica, 17, Jeremy and Josh, 12, and Jennifer, 10, Indianapolis, Indiana

There are times when going to the principal is appropriate. For instance, if you have met with the teacher and feel you haven't been heard, the teacher hasn't given you any real solutions or help with your concerns, or the situation hasn't gotten better, then it might be time to talk to the principal. If you feel there is a classroom issue with a new teacher who doesn't have control of the classroom, that's a valid concern and could be a safety issue the principal needs to know about.

—Florence Michel, middle school teacher for 8 years, New York, New York, and Baltimore, Maryland

I have had occasions where I had to get the help of the principal, as a third party witness, to sit in on my meetings with a furious parent. The principal being there is for the support of both parties—the child's parents and me.

—Holly Parker, teacher of deaf students for 10 years, Colorado Springs, Colorado

When Should I Go Over the Principal's Head?

© Some situations arise that remain unsettled despite persistent efforts of the school, child, and parents. If you're engaged in a drawn-out battle with the school's administration, you may find it necessary to go to the next level and address the district school board or superintendent.

© Go into these battles with the knowledge that the superintendent and school board are even more likely to support the principal than she is to support the teacher. Superintendents dislike overruling principals unless they absolutely have to.

© Understand that the superintendent has limited control over the teachers, is unlikely to be able to solve the problems of an individual student, and will not be inclined to override the principal's decision.

Unless it's a really serious incident of child abuse or something equally serious, the superintendent won't be too sympathetic. He can't be because he's too far removed. He is just going to tell the principal to look into it. A good school committee member knows the superintendent is a policy maker, not the purveyor of policy. Trying to put political pressure on him is not the way to go either, because it creates a difficult situation between the child and teacher.
—*Edward Sapienza, 9th to 12th grade science, math, and computer teacher for 31 years, North Reading, Massachusetts*

©

If you have an important issue about your child, you have to go through the right channels: teacher, principal, and then the next in line, like the school trustee. Keep going until you get a satisfactory answer and put it in writing if you need to.
—*Karen Davie, mom of Shea, 9, and Jade, 7, Ontario, Canada*

Academic Issues

What I Should I Do When My Child Struggles in School?

◉ Many kids breeze through early grades, always expecting the new year to pose no more of a challenge than the last. But each new year brings increasing amounts of work, greater complexity, and higher expectations. Sometimes these challenges unexpectedly creep up on a student, which may cause him to feel frustrated and overwhelmed.

◉ As children develop mentally and physically through grade school, their rates of academic success fluctuate dramatically. Even if their ages are relatively close, students will often be in different phases of learning.

◉ Ultimately, you want your child to be able to work through frustration and bounce back when he encounters obstacles or failures. Mistakes and setbacks are an expected and essential part of learning and can be a great stimulus for improvement. Let your child know you are there when he needs you, but don't rush to jump in before he asks.

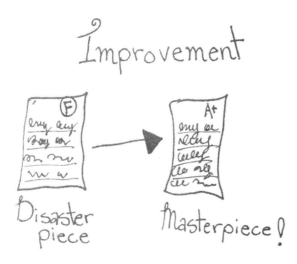

Improvement

Disaster piece → Masterpiece!

© If your child enters a new grade and seems to lag behind his classmates, avoid blaming his teacher from the previous year and criticizing her preparation as inadequate. Instead of focusing on what could have been learned in the past, concentrate on getting your child on track for the future.

© Many children hesitate to admit when they don't understand what is being taught in class because they do not want to appear slow and unintelligent to their teacher and peers. Instead, they go to great lengths to hide their need for help.

© If your child encounters academic difficulties, he may start to feel angry, demoralized, and incompetent. These feelings manifest in a variety of ways, most typically through acting out in frustration and disengaging socially. Take signs of potential academic problems seriously. Meet with his teacher to discuss your observations and brainstorm potential ways to solve the situation.

© When a teacher brings up academic problems with which your child is wrestling, ask to look at concrete examples, like test scores and samples of homework. This helps you get a better sense of where the problem stems from and the best means of intervention. Perhaps he is neglecting a certain subject because he does not understand the material, or conversely, is too comfortable with the subject matter that he neglects to do the extra practice.

© Your child's insights and feedback are vital to tackling any problems in his education. Ask him where his major sources of frustration originate. By encouraging him to express himself and letting him know his opinions are respected and valued, you reassure him that you and his teacher are working with him, not against him.

© There will be times in every student's life when he is disinterested in a subject, or when he is more concerned with his socializing than academics. As long as he has a strong base and a passion for learning, he will eventually bounce back.

First, take a breath. *All* kids struggle at one time or another. Just because a child is having difficulty doesn't mean he's learning-disabled or lazy—it may simply mean it is taking him a little longer to grasp a certain concept. Patience is key. Many parents feel they need to intervene when their children are struggling a bit in school, when in fact it is often better to let them solve their problems independently. Parents *do* need to guide their children, and should be aware of any difficulties they are having in school, but they shouldn't solve the problems for them. Children need to feel school is their thing, not their parents' thing.
—*Kathy Carabine, pre-k and 3rd grade teacher for 16 years, Boston, Massachusetts*

If you suspect there is a problem, there probably is. Take the time to investigate the issue. Watch for mood changes and insist on seeing completed work.
—*Pam Pottorff, 3rd and 4th grade teacher and 8th grade reading teacher for 5 years, Sioux City, Nebraska*

School is a lot more difficult now than when we were growing up, with the academic curriculum compressed ever downward to younger grades, all the way to kindergarten. We're hurrying the children because our educational system is pressured to do this. At certain ages, children's minds develop the ability to perform certain functions, yet we're putting algebra in front of kids before they've reached that level of abstract thinking, which doesn't developmentally occur until age 13 for most kids. So don't get too worried if your fourth grader can't do algebra, as his ability is likely to come later as his brain matures.
—*Martha Ann Chandler, 3rd to 6th grade teacher for 14 years, Florence, South Carolina*

When kids move up a grade, make sure they get the help they need instead of assuming they can do the new work. Some parents assume because their child has done okay in the past, he'll hit the ground running with new stuff, too, but this isn't always the case. They think, "He's been able to do the work all along, why can't he now?" It may be easy to fix, so get help as soon as possible.
—*Deb Brown, kindergarten to 4th grade special education teacher for 26 years, Conyers, Georgia*

Moving from third to fourth grade is a big transition year. Much of the learning in third grade involves memorization, but kids move to higher thinking in fourth grade. Parents are used to children memorizing the stuff and being tested on what they memorize. In fourth grade, kids are tested on their ability to summarize and analyze, which is much harder. Kids are expected to do a whole lot they're not used to doing, and grades often come down as a result.
—*Sherri McWhorter, 4th grade teacher for 5 years, Augusta, Georgia*

Children who have been struggling don't think positively about school anymore and start going on a downward spiral. As a parent, you need to get them to see the positive and fun things about school, like field trips, the playground, gym class, and checking out books at the library.
—*Alison Gowers, kindergarten teacher for 5 years, West Point, Virginia*

How Can I Avoid Report Card Surprises?

If you have been examining your child's work carefully throughout the term, you should have a strong sense of what you will see before his report card is even mailed.

Stay abreast of your child's schoolwork by checking on it every day. Look at his homework, projects, and exams, and pay attention to his teacher's input.

Talk with your child about what he anticipates will be on his report card, both in terms of academics and behavior.

Use midterm grades and progress reports as a way to gauge your child's classroom performance and provide a chance for him to improve his work before report cards arrive.

When the report card comes, it should be an affirmation of what you already know if you've stayed in contact with the teachers. It shouldn't ever be a surprise. The central theme for your involvement should be communication—you don't ever want to be saying, "I just didn't know."
—*Joy Pumphrey, 2nd and 3rd grade teacher for 12 years, Clearwater, Florida*

Ideally, I don't think any report card should be a surprise. By the time it comes home I have a pretty good idea of what will be on it. My son knows that if he's not getting A's, then I need to know why. I make my expectations pretty well known.
—*Jennifer Guss, mom of Fred, 10, Hannah, 4, and Sophie, 2, Montvale, New Jersey*

Ask your child how he thinks he's doing before report cards come out. Ask him what he thinks he's getting for grades and, if he thinks they're going to be good, how he can continue the trend. But if your child is afraid his grades may not be as good as he wants, ask what you can do to help him do better.
—*Kathy Traficanti, 4th to 6th grade teacher for 9 years, Brighton, Massachusetts*

As a working parent, it's hard to know what's going on at school so you're not shocked when the report card comes out. You have to stay up on it all the time, and make sure you are involved if your child is going to be successful. My daughter gets midterm grades halfway through the grading period so we know how she's doing, which is nice because we know when to kick it into gear. When we get the report, we know where she is and where she has to be, but we only have four more weeks to get things turned around. I've contacted the teacher to ask what's going on with some of the grades and if there is something we can do to fix things, like studying at home or extra credit. The teacher will let me know when she's falling too far behind, and if she is, I cut down on TV time and make her spend more time with her homework.
—*Laura Doctor, mom of Nicole, 10, Cleveland, Ohio*

How Should I Approach a Problematic Report Card with My Child?

Ⓟ   Regardless of the grades your child brings home, look for something positive to comment on first. Even a slight improvement deserves a positive comment, and if your child has been having a fair amount of trouble in a specific area, the attention you give to his improvement can encourage him to continue his progress. If your child feels proud of a grade for which he worked hard, compliment him on the success of his efforts. Show compassion and understanding when reacting to a bad report card, even if you feel disappointed. Talk with your child about what went wrong. A grade that comes as a surprise to you can be unexpected and disheartening to your child as well.

Ⓟ   One bad grade or problematic report card does not spell lifelong academic failure. Keep it in perspective; a report card is only one measure of your child's strengths and does not measure his capabilities, but rather the work he produced during a specific time period. A report card is a measure not just of your child's work, but also of his teacher's specific educational values. For example, an exceptional creative writer may do terribly in an English class that stresses the mechanics of writing.

Ⓟ   Report cards don't tell the whole story of your child's semester but they are a good jumping-off point. Don't just look at the grades on the report card; remember to look carefully at the comments as well. Grades should be a measure of academic work and not behavior or attitude, unless there is a designated mark for behavior. A teacher should never punish your child for disruptive behavior by lowering his grades. If you think this is happening, talk to the teacher and set up a more effective way to address the problematic behavior.

Ⓟ   Instead of criticizing his mistakes, guide your child toward finding remedies. By asking him, "How would you grade yourself?" or "What would you have done differently?" you will end up with creative brainstorming, insights, and a way to turn things around.

Ⓟ   Once or twice a year, pull out your child's previous reports cards to look for larger trends in his work. Check to see if your child has been improving, struggling with certain subjects, or staying consistent across the board. Compare the grades your child receives with his expectations and skills. If there's a serious discrepancy, it may be time to sit down and discuss how he can change his approach to work and his study patterns.

☉ Try not to have your child walk away feeling bad about himself because he has not lived up to your expectations. Even constructive feedback can feel disheartening to a child. If your child berates himself over a less-than-perfect mark, reassure him that he doesn't need to be perfect, he just needs to try his best. It is important for children to strive for improvement, learn persistence, and possess the ability to live with occasional disappointing results.

In our society, it's hard not to emphasize the letter grades. So, when the report card comes home, I never make it something that "makes Mommy happy." Rather, I try to turn it back on my daughter so she can feel the pride herself. If there comes a time when she does not do well, I will frame it in terms of "What could you do differently next time?"
—*Patty Potter, mom of Olivia Logan, 6, and Isabel Logan, 3, Ft. Worth, Texas*

Parents need to understand a grade is just a report of how their child is doing. Sometimes the child needs to see the grade he earned and then understand it's his responsibility to bring it up. It's such a great learning experience to ask, "Okay, now what do you need to do to fix this?"
—*Kay Symons, special education and kindergarten to 8th grade teacher for 27 years, South Georgia*

Parents need to concentrate more on whether children are learning. Too often, parents simply present their expectations as, "My kid really needs an A." As a teacher, that's a big turnoff. I try to focus less on the grade and more on the process.
—*Ken Pauly, high school social studies teacher for 13 years, St. Louis Park, Minnesota*

We found our daughter sometimes has confidence issues, and if she has a problem with a report card it isn't always the academics, so we try and take these other factors into account.
—*Natalie Dyess, mom of Michaela, 8, Jacob, 6, and Anna, 2, Lawrenceville, Georgia*

As far as grades are concerned, all you can ask is that your children do their best. Yes, you want them to get into a good college, but if you are overly anxious and overemphasize grades, your kids will start to freak out and think that even a B+ is a disaster.
—*Holly Parker, teacher of deaf students for 10 years, Colorado Springs, Colorado*

What Should My Follow-Up Action Plan Be?

◉ Approach a bad grade as if you were a grade detective. If your child is not performing up to his ability, your challenge is to find out why.

◉ Review files of your child's work after seeing his report card to determine where the bad marks may have come from. Are the report card grades what you would expect based on the semester's work? Has your child had trouble on the tests, quizzes, or homework portions of the grade? Report cards measure grades for several months at a time. While your child may have been working very hard at the end of the grading period and received substantially better grades too late in the semester to make an impact, the first few bad scores of the year may have been hard to bounce back from.

◉ Sometimes teachers make mistakes while entering grades. If the grade on a report card does not seem correct to you or your child, call the teacher to discuss it.

◉ Set up a conference with the teacher to find out what went wrong and what your child can do to bring up his grades for the next round of evaluations, especially if they do not reflect the time and effort he is putting in. Explain to the teacher why you are surprised and concerned about the marks your child obtained. Request to go over samples of your child's work so you can explore together where the problems may be coming from. Ask the teacher what she feels is missing from your child's work and what improvements he can make.

© Look into available school resources, such as a writing center or language lab, and investigate resources outside of school, including commercial learning centers and tutors. Meet with the school's counselor, especially if your child's grade problems stem from behavioral problems or there is a possibility he has a learning disorder.

© Develop a written plan for improvement and outline everyone's role and responsibilities. This plan for your child's success should be as detailed as possible and involve specific things you can do at home to help your child, such as assisting with difficult homework, going over test-taking skills, or working on supplemental material.

© Don't wait until your child's next report card to evaluate the success of your plan. Establish realistic goals for the next grading period, such as having your child hand in every homework assignment completed and on time. Break this down into smaller steps that you and the teacher can monitor and set up a system to keep on top of whether the plan is working, like a weekly update letter or phone call.

If my children's grades are less than what I expect, I just talk to them about it. I ask them what they think happened. If they say, "I don't know," then we go back to look at the work they have done. My son is smart as a whip, but he's so disorganized. When he came home with bad grades we tried to punish him by taking things away and motivating him with money, but that didn't work. You can't buy grades and you can't punish on a long-term basis. I realized these were his grades, not mine. I don't get mad, and I can't stand over my kids all the time. Grades have to come from the child but if there is a problem, it's my responsibility as a parent to get them help.
—*Martha Judiscak, mom of Jimmy, 17, Vicki, 16, and Danny, 11, Knoxville, Tennessee*

Don't attack teachers about the grades they give. Approach it by saying, "I'm just curious what your grading system is like." As a teacher, I would much rather explain a grade than

defend it. I have had parents call me to say, "I don't think you're being fair." I challenge them to come in to the classroom so I can explain my requirements, and lay out their child's portfolio; the grade should be evident.
—*Mary Chick, kindergarten to 12th grade art teacher for 8 years, Elgin, Minnesota*

If a kid is in trouble academically, it is best for parents to call once a week, so they know exactly what we are doing in school and what to look for when it comes to homework. I think most teachers would be open to that weekly conversation. Parents need to be responsible for getting on top of this because teachers are just so busy.
—*Dick Krebs, special education and 7th and 8th grade math teacher for 26 years, Yakima, Washington*

Why Isn't My Child Working Up to His Ability?

Report cards oftentimes reflect a lack of effort more than a lack of skill. Even if your child is a math whiz, he may wind up with poor marks when he doesn't put in the necessary studying hours. When your child receives bad marks, focus on making his schedule more conducive to studying. Set up study times, limit television during the week, and if necessary, cut down on your child's competing engagements to give him more time to concentrate on his schoolwork.

It's helpful to get information from your child's teacher about his work, his grades, and the assignments he has left incomplete. The following are warning signs that your child is not working to the best of his ability:

In elementary school he:

Does well or satisfactorily when he has one-on-one attention from you or a teacher, but becomes restless, slow, or unproductive when he working independently.

✦ Gives up easily.

✦ Withdraws and becomes distracted when someone gives directions.

✦ Always wants to be the center of attention and becomes disruptive when he isn't.

✦ Has difficulty getting along with peers, maintaining friendships, and relating to others.

✦ Throws frequent or inappropriate temper tantrums, and displays rapid mood swings.

✦ Struggles with organization and seems forgetful or preoccupied most of the time.

✦ Makes frequent demands for activities and entertainment, but has trouble staying contented with anything for long.

☉ Later, in middle school he:

✦ Spends more than two hours watching TV or playing video games each night.

✦ Cares more about hanging out with peers than with taking care of schoolwork.

✦ Has friends who are mostly poor students and underachievers.

✦ Puts effort only into a restricted set of subjects or activities that stimulate him, and performs far below his abilities on the rest.

✦ Has difficulty accepting blame for his failures.

✦ Complains constantly about being bored at school and has trouble keeping himself entertained.

☉ Research shows that children's passion for learning steadily decreases from third through ninth grade. Most children enter kindergarten excited about learning, but by the time they reach middle school they see it less as an exciting opportunity and more as a boring burden. Typically, this breakdown of enthusiasm occurs as work becomes more demanding and academic struggles take hold.

☺ Because teachers deal with so many children on a daily basis, it is often the children performing at a satisfactory but below-ability level who get pushed into the background. While gifted children and those with academic, emotional, and psychological problems receive special attention, children who fall in between are often overlooked and not pushed to their full potential.

☺ Motivation may also fizzle when a task is too easy or too hard. Students who feel something is too easy might rush through it, without feeling any satisfaction in their performance. On the other hand, if it is too hard, they may give up quickly, especially if they have learning problems that prevent them from keeping pace with their classmates. Your child may feel it is safer not to try than to risk embarrassment. He may be concerned with how his peers view him and consider it more important to appear cool than competent.

☺ A classroom environment, with too much or too little competition, a teacher he dislikes, or one who conveys low expectations to him may cause your child to stop putting in effort. Lack of interest in school could also be a sign of anxiety or depression.

☺ The most common, and most self-defeating, belief of the underachiever is that he has no control over what happens to him. He fails to take responsibility for his own behavior, believing his actions won't change the outcome, so he assigns the blame for his failures to people or outside conditions. As a result, he hesitates to put effort into things like studying for tests, paying attention in class, and doing homework because he doesn't think such exertion will have any significant impact on his grades. Those who try to help him wind up frustrated by what appears to be his apparent laziness and stubbornness.

If your child seems unmotivated, look at his learning styles. Maybe activities or things planned for the classroom just don't meet your child's needs for the way he learns. Look at what works for you at home, because that might work in the classroom, and share these ideas with the teacher.

—*Nickey Langford, 2nd and 3rd grade teacher for 3 years, Birmingham, Alabama*

The first time I taught 5th graders, I noticed the students came in wanting to learn and do well. They were happy and pleased when they did. But in the 7th, 8th, and 9th grades, out of 100 items on their list of priorities, school is 101. The value of school is just not there. Then, when they get into the 10th and 11th grades and are thinking about graduating, school becomes important again.

—*Dick Krebs, special education and 7th and 8th grade math teacher for 26 years, Yakima, Washington*

What Can I Do to Get My Underachiever Back on Track?

Motivation is the most reliable predictor of success in school. Cultivate qualities in your child that encourage academic success, such as curiosity, creativity, the willpower to achieve and succeed, and the desire to learn. Infuse him with a positive outlook and he will go into tasks with an expectation of success and a sense of control over what he produces.

The first step is changing the expectations of everyone involved. If your child has a history of academic frustration and failure, arrange for him to get work he can complete so he experiences the confidence that comes with success. This prepares him to take on more challenging work. Let him know you don't expect success overnight—you know it will be difficult and there will be setbacks, but you have confidence he can improve with time.

◉ Schoolwork can often be tedious, boring, and repetitive. Teach your child persistence, especially in the face of frustration and confusion when working through a new concept, and encourage him to evaluate his success in terms of what he has gained, not how he stacks up to his friends. Boost his sense of achievement by having him tutor a younger child in an area he knows well.

◉ Underachievers don't handle competition with others well but they compete well with past, less-than-perfect grades because they are able to witness success as they build upon past material that fosters self-confidence.

◉ Academically advanced students may feel frustrated by the slow pace of teaching, and their boredom may manifest itself in the form of inattentiveness, incomplete assignments, and nonparticipation in class discussions. If your child feels bored in class, he may stop working as hard as he used to, drift off, and let his grades fall. If this is the case, find out what enrichment services his school offers to keep him engaged in his assignments.

◉ Success is one of the best motivators. If your child has a taste of how it feels to do well, he will most likely start trying harder to feel that way again. Look for the things your child is especially good at and cultivate them. Give him praise for what he does well.

◉ Be a good role model for your child by showing him you get a sense of satisfaction and accomplishment from the work you do. Always grumbling about your job will set a bad example for your child, while presenting a more balanced view of your hard work will encourage him to do his best. Be honest and realistic—let him know everyone has a hard time with certain parts of their work, and this struggle won't end when school does, so learning to deal with it now will prepare him for the rest of his life.

◉ Teach your child to approach his work with a sense of pride and to take care in checking over his answers and editing his papers. By getting him in the habit of quality control, you raise a thoughtful and self-respecting learner.

◉ Instill the belief that wisdom comes from effort, not innate ability. This encourages your child to persevere instead of giving up quickly because he thinks he'll never be smart enough.

◉ If your child is having trouble with self-confidence, work with the teacher to manufacture small successes to restore his faith in himself. Then gradually raise your expectations to encourage him to continue trying his hardest, even if the results are less than perfect every time.

◎ Help your child look at every challenge as an opportunity and think about success in terms of overcoming obstacles. When something doesn't go according to plan, it's a chance to learn from the mistakes and the experience.

◎ Tell your partner how well your child's doing when you know he is listening. Your child will take pride in what he will consider to be your true opinion.

◎ Praise your child when he deserves it, but don't go overboard. Heaping an abundance of praise on your child will cause him to feel intense pressure to keep succeeding, which will get in the way of his progress and render itself meaningless, if he assumes you praise him for everything. If you react too strongly to his first good grades, he may feel he's now expected to get A's in every class, or that you were shocked he was capable of such high grades. Instead, simply tell him how proud you are he has worked so hard or done so well.

◎ The vocabulary you use when praising your child affects the way he perceives himself. Avoid using words like *brilliant, genius,* and *perfect* to describe your child. Instead, tell him he is *bright, hard working,* and *persevering.*

◎ As children work toward achievement, their grades often rise slowly, and there is rarely a consistent climb upward. Expect to see fluctuations in his performance as he struggles to improve.

I tell my kids, "We're always here, we always love you, and we want you to try your best." When I've seen my oldest slacking off, I've said, "I know you can do better than this and I expect you to try your hardest," but he's a typical 9-year-old. So I say to him, "I love you, and if you don't want to try, you can just continue to be the class clown and have your grades go down. Then, when you're 30 years old, people will remember you as the class clown." We let him see where his strengths and weaknesses are and help him do what he can. We don't accept goofing off—there is a time and place for goofing off and being a kid, and it's probably not during spelling tests.

—*Kathleen Spinale, mom of Joey, 9, and Peter, 4, Ipswich, Massachusetts*

Focus on things your child likes to get him interested in learning. What motivates him? What kind of things does your child like to do when you go out together? Parents can help teachers understand what really gets a kid interested and excited. Look at more creative solutions for helping your child to achieve instead of relying on the school.
—*Niambi Muhammad, 1st and 2nd grade teacher for 4 years, Chicago, Illinois*

Kids are individuals, so what motivates one might not motivate another. Find what works for each child and let their teachers know so they can work with each child's personality.
—*April Tilley, mom of Trent, 7, and Trace, 4, Winston-Salem, North Carolina*

Each of my four children was very different. One was completely self-motivated and never wanted my help. Another needed confidence and praise, and I spent a lot of time encouraging her and standing behind her. Yet another one had all the intelligence but needed to be pinned down with expectations, and I was constantly asking, "Do you think your outside activities are too much? What three things can we do to help you do better?" It's amazing how each child has to be dealt with individually. Some need praise, some need guidelines, and some just need encouragement.
—*Kathy Traficanti, 4th to 6th grade teacher for 9 years, Brighton, Massachusetts*

For kids who are on that line between motivated and not, positive reinforcement is huge. As I walk around my classroom, I tell them things like, "I like what you're doing! It's different than everybody else's." I'll point something out to the kid next to them, who might say, "That's cool, I'm going to try that." I'm lucky because I get to display a lot of their stuff, and a lot of kids who don't get recognized for other things will do something really impressive. Kids walking through the hallway will stop and say, "Wow, that's really cool. I didn't know she could do that." You can try this same type of reinforcement at home—for kids, it's huge.
—*Mary Chick, kindergarten to 12th grade art teacher for 8 years, Elgin, Minnesota*

Goal setting is a good way to make your child more confident. Set small, achievable goals.

You can't start out with something that's completely unrealistic. My daughter was in a reading enrichment class, and they had a contest where, if you read a certain number of books you would get different prizes. My daughter wanted to read 100 books, but that's not realistic. So I went back and helped her to set a more appropriate goal of 5 books a week, and wow, she was really successful in that. It's really deflating if you are trying to reach a goal that's not possible to meet, but when you achieve practical goals, it really builds confidence.
—*Pam Fierro, mom of twins Meredith and Lauren, 8, and parenting multiples guide at www.multiples .about.com, Virginia Beach, Virginia*

Start off by doing away with old family stereotypes of your child like, "You're just lazy," or "You're so unmotivated, what am I going to do with you?" If Mom and Dad focus on negatives, they will be knocking their heads against the wall.
—*Heather Daigle, teacher of all grades, Plymouth, Massachusetts*

Should I Use Rewards to Motivate My Child Academically?

Ideally, all students would be motivated to do their best work simply because they find it satisfying. In reality, some children need extra incentives to get them focused.

An extrinsically motivated student performs to avoid punishment or obtain a reward, such as teacher approval, parental praise, grades, or stickers. Extrinsic motivation often fails to give your child any deep or long-lasting commitment to learning but can help jump-start his desire to achieve.

If you decide to give your child material rewards for improving grades, they should be the smallest, most inex-

pensive rewards that will be effective. Great ways to celebrate as a family are going out together for brunch or an ice cream sundae.

☺ Reward your child, but don't bribe him. Bribing your child to do schoolwork by offering money for each good grade can erode his inherent love of learning by associating learning with rewards instead of an internalized sense of pride. Further, money does not often work to motivate underachievers since they don't think it is ever possible to achieve good grades. When you give your child an award for his hard work, help him understand the full value of his efforts. This way his reason for achieving will be less likely to evaporate when the rewards stop.

☺ A better reward is one that shows your child you know what a great job he's doing. Parental approval is one of the most powerful rewards for children. Ribbons and certificates acknowledge your child's efforts and reinforce motivation for the sake of the task itself.

☺ Don't forget to reward improvement and not just good grades. Improvement deserves recognition, perhaps even more so than another A. Use the element of surprise and give unexpected rewards to celebrate a leap forward.

Rewards for long-term goals can be really useful, but don't give the equivalent of a Mercedes-Benz to a third grader. Offer to have a friend over for ice cream, or give another reward that fits the accomplishment.
—*Claudia Flanders, kindergarten to 8th grade teacher for 34 years, Santa Monica, California*

I expect my daughter to get good grades, but I also hate the idea of paying for them. I'm not going to hold my kids' hands over the fire to get good grades—people are inspired in different ways.
—*Amy Kamm, mom of Ava, 5, and Lily, 2, Burbank, California*

Acknowledgment and affirmation are important. For academic accomplishments, we have done things like have a family celebration at Dairy Queen. In junior high, one of my kids set the curve for the highest test score in the class, so that night I made a cake shaped like a bell curve and we had a "set the curve party," which was just dessert after dinner, but it celebrated the accomplishment.

—*Jennifer Armstrong, mom of Anthony Perkins, 18, Alex Apel, 16, Lucas Perkins, 16, and Anneliese Apel, 14, St. Paul, Minnesota*

We found a way to motivate our kids. We know they can all make A's and B's, so anyone who makes a C gets one hour of labor outside. We tell them, "If you don't want to do this for a living, get going!" It helps motivate them to start working a little harder in class again. My daughter ended up with a C in chemistry, and she was freaking out because she didn't want to do that hour. She went to talk to the teacher because she didn't think she should have a C. The teacher went through her grades and it turns out she had marked her down for not doing a project that she had actually completed, bumping her grade up to a B. One hour of hard labor motivated her to check that out!

—*Kim Shepherd, mom of Jessica, 17, Jeremy and Josh, 12, and Jennifer, 10, Indianapolis, Indiana*

Positive reinforcement is more motivating than any kind of punishment. When kids lose focus it's usually due to boredom or distraction, so having something positive to think about brings the focus back. You could try saying something like, "If you bring home good remarks from your teacher at the end of the week, we will do something special together." Take a trip to the library, get some ice cream, or play a game. It doesn't always have to be a treat. Sometimes all they need is a pat on the back.

—*Pam Fierro, mom of twins Meredith and Lauren, 8, and parenting multiples guide at www.multiples.about.com, Virginia Beach, Virginia*

When my sons were younger, I made the mistake of rewarding both of my younger ones for good report cards. In doing so, I sent the wrong message, with my kids thinking, "Do you love me less because of a bad grade?"

—*Cindy Esposito, mom of Jon, Jason, and Chris, 23, Rhiannon, 16, and Justin, 13, Orange County, New York*

How Can I Engage the Teacher's Help with My Child's Academic Difficulties?

❂ Teachers have little way of knowing how their daily lessons play out at home until it's time to test students on the material. Avoid letting small problems balloon into larger issues by contacting the teacher as soon as you detect something is wrong.

❂ Take context into consideration and find out when and where the problem occurs. Sometimes slipping grades come down to issues as simple as a distracting classmate or post-lunch drowsiness. A little trial and error can go a long way toward finding the ideal working environment for your child. Ask the teacher to try moving your child to a different part of the room, away from loud peers or closer to the teacher.

❂ Figure out whether your child is having difficulty across the board or in an individual subject area, and whether that subject is causing problems for the whole class. Questions to ask the teacher:

✹ Which areas do you think are causing my child's problems in school this year?

✹ Would it be appropriate to test my child for a learning disability?

✹ How can I help my child to improve in school?

✹ What special help can the school offer my child to get him back on track as quickly as possible?

❂ Request that the teacher provide extra attention through after-school tutoring sessions, one-on-one work, or remedial attention.

❂ Come to a consensus with the teacher on what you both expect from your child and what actions you will each take to turn that plan into a reality.

The biggest signal of classroom issues is frustration expressed by your child. Sometimes it's only a ploy to get attention, but usually it signals a problem.
—*Kay Symons, special education and kindergarten to 8th grade teacher for 27 years, South Georgia*

First you have to determine where your child is having a problem. As soon as parents see the beast they're dealing with, they can start working to fix it. The problem may not be an issue the child is having, but rather a teaching style or approach. Some kids come in never having done things that are suddenly expected of them. There's no substitute for going to the teacher and saying, "How do you teach this?"
—*Ken Pauly, high school social studies teacher for 13 years, St. Louis Park, Minnesota*

When Can Engaging an Outside Tutor Help My Child?

◉ If your child expresses concern that everyone in his class is smarter than he is, or feels as though he needs to do more work than everyone else to keep up, he may need tutoring to get the extra attention, practice, and confidence needed for skill development. Also, if you have difficulty helping your child with his work because you are unfamiliar with it or because it creates emotional tension between the two of you, a tutor can be an impartial and knowledgeable helping hand.

◉ If you decide to hire a professional tutor, look for someone who specializes in teaching at your child's level. Ask the teacher to recommend a tutor for him. Often, based on the experiences of students she has taught, the teacher will be able to pair him with a tutor who is a good match for his specific needs. Also, don't overlook older students who did well in the class or school-based tutoring programs. Both are a great deal less expensive and frequently offer the insider's perspective on the teacher and her style.

☺ Before you start hunting for a great tutor, figure out what your goals are. Determine whether he needs help with a specific subject or with honing his learning skills, such as note taking or test mastery.

☺ Consider whether there is a specific approach or technique that works best for your child, and try to describe what he needs in concrete terms. Ask the tutor to describe her teaching methods and training.

☺ Chemistry between your child and his tutor is very important. Some children respond best to a structured, organized approach, while others thrive with a more creative style. While a tutor may have worked wonderfully for a friend or neighbor, she will not necessarily be compatible with your child. Assess your prospective tutor's personality as well as her skills.

☺ Familiarize the prospective tutor with your child's problems, progress, and personality. Show her samples of your child's work and fill her in on his teacher's assessment.

☺ Formulate a written plan detailing areas on which the tutor should focus. Agree upon what the tutor should try to accomplish, how she will approach these goals, and how much time she should budget for each task.

☺ Ask your prospective tutor for references, which should reflect experience with children of similar age and needs. Trust your instincts—even a perfect resume cannot compensate for your wary instincts about a prospective tutor.

☺ For real results, tutoring must occur two to three times a week. Ask the teacher about your child's classroom progress once he begins tutoring. If his confidence in his work seems to be growing, it is a good sign things are working. If your child isn't progressing, talk with the tutor and reevaluate your choice. While no tutor can immediately abolish learning problems, there should be some visible progress within the first eight weeks. Further, your child's tutor should be able to provide progress reports detailing his progress.

☺ Tutoring may address part of your child's problem, but may not necessarily be the solution. If your child continues to struggle despite help from a tutor, you may need to bring in an academic professional to evaluate exactly what is causing your child's difficulty.

◎ The goal of tutoring should be to get your child to the point where he no longer needs the assistance.

If you are having a difficult time getting your child to do work, it makes sense to hire a tutor. You don't want it to be a battleground.
—Susan Draughn, 7th and 8th grade special education teacher for 24 years, Sunman, Indiana

◎

Tutors are never a bad idea if your child is really struggling in a particular subject. He doesn't have to be diagnosed with special needs to work with a tutor. If he is having a hard time learning with the teacher he's working with, call in a tutor to fill in the gaps. He may have just missed a stepping-stone in what the class is working on.
—Erika Bare, 6th to 8th grade special education teacher for 3 years, West Linn, Oregon

◎

Your child may need more help in school than his teacher can give him or simply have trouble working with you, in which case you need to get someone else to look into the problem. Ask a friend who's a teacher or a tutor to work with your child.
—Susan Segaloff, 5th grade, special education, and reading teacher for 12 years,
  Norton, Massachusetts

◎

Homework should never interfere with family life. I always urge parents to step out of the situation when this begins to happen. If a child needs extra help, often a tutor can provide the academic environment and relieve pressure from the parent-child relationship.
—Deborah Berris, 3rd, 5th, and 8th grade teacher for 5 years

◎

Math has been a struggle for my daughter. She feels a lot of pressure dealing with timed tests and memorizing math facts. The teacher and I talked: I was very upset and told her Nicole was just not getting it and I didn't know how to help her. The teacher said if Nicole came to her, they would work through everything, so Nicole started going to talk with the teacher after school a couple times each week. This ended up being a very valuable experience for her.
—*Laura Doctor, mom of Nicole, 10, Cleveland, Ohio*

One of my sons is very overactive, and one teacher told us he would never amount to anything. Our course of action, instead of just yelling and whining, was to prove her wrong. We found a specialist who worked with our son to help him focus, and he brought his grades up by the next year. The teacher did not handle the situation properly, making it our responsibility, as parents, to take action and get our son the help he needed.
—*Alesha Worra, mom of Brandon, 12, and Travis, 11, Greer, South Carolina*

I prefer kids come to me first before getting a tutor to work with them at home. But if your child doesn't want to work with his teacher, or it's affecting his self-esteem, then get a tutor.
—*Amy Watson, 7th to 12th grade teacher for 5 years, Oyster Bay, New York*

If your child has low self-esteem, one-on-one time with a tutor who gives a lot of praise can be a beneficial thing. The key thing to consider is, emotionally, what does your child need most?
—*Julie Kirkpatrick Carroll, 4th grade teacher for 6 years, Benson, Minnesota*

How Should I Evaluate a Learning Center?

Learning centers focus on helping kids keep up with their homework and catch up to their class level by using a diverse range of instructional materials to adapt to each child's learning style.

◎ When looking at this option, check to see if the center is highly recommended by teachers at your child's school or other parents who have used their services. Ask for the names and phone numbers of families you can call to obtain an outside, informed opinion of the center's strengths and weaknesses.

◎ Ask the center how much testing your child will go through at the start of his enrollment, and how often they will retest him to measure improvement.

◎ Look for a center with state-certified instructors with extensive classroom teaching experience. Also find out how the tutors at the center typically interface with classroom teachers. Are they willing to call your child's teacher to keep her updated?

◎ You also can evaluate learning centers by asking the director the following questions:

✦ How are the classrooms set up?

✦ What is the student-to-teacher ratio?

✦ What degrees, experience, and training do teachers have?

✦ What technology do you have to enhance learning?

✦ How do you evaluate students' progress?

✦ What programs do you offer for gifted, average, and remedial children?

✦ What modifications do you make for students with learning disabilities?

✦ How do you adapt to different learning styles?

✦ How much do you charge, and what does this fee include?

✦ Do you provide help with homework?

✦ Do you teach to standardized tests?

✦ How often do you meet with parents?

Parents will call because grades are slipping or the student's attitude has changed. We also get students who are consistently doing poorly, and a few who are not challenged in school and come into the center for further enrichment. Often teachers will recommend a student come in for more help when a red flag goes up, such as low test scores or a telltale report card. We also get a lot of calls when progress reports come out and right after parent-teacher conferences.

—*Kristyn Mulada, educational director of a Sylvan Learning Center for 2 years and former kindergarten teacher, Hanover, Massachusetts*

I had my child tested through a learning center to find out what her strengths and weaknesses were, and then they tailored programs for her. It was kind of pricey to have testing done however; $150 for tests and $600 to $800 or more for her to take summer classes.

—*Stephanie Lee, substitute elementary school teacher, Lawrenceville, Georgia*

When Should I Consider Holding My Child Back a Year?

Retention—holding a child back a year—is an option to redress significant academic or maturity concerns and works best when:

* It's done in your child's earliest elementary years (kindergarten to second grade).

* Your child has fallen so far behind in his developmental or academic skills intervention specialists and individual tutoring do not help.

* Factors other than ability are the cause of academic difficulties.

The first step to considering retention is to have the teacher work closely with your child for the rest of the year to help him catch up to where he needs to be. Hire a tutor to work with him and ask the teacher for anything you can do to support him at home. Also, check out summer programs available to get your child up to speed.

◉ Research indicates that keeping a child back usually hurts more than it helps, so get details from your child's school about how it will affect him. Ask the teacher or principal what your child would be doing if he were held back a year. Going through the same material with the same teacher is not ideal; ask if your child will work with a different teacher or a completely different program. Also check to see if there are remedial programs to assist your child if he were to move on with his class.

◉ Ask the school to provide a written plan of action if your child either stays back a year or moves up and gets extra help. A well-defined strategy should be in place for either option before the next year begins.

◉ Present the decision to hold your child back to him in a positive way. Make sure he understands it is not his fault and he did nothing wrong. Acknowledge your role in the matter by telling him, "We started you in school too early, before you were ready." Make sure he knows that by repeating, he will get a chance to be with new friends and catch up so learning and school will be fun and manageable.

Consider retention when a child is young and very immature, and cannot seem to handle the responsibility of that grade. With older children, it won't do as much good to hold the child back as to get them the extra help they need.
—*Kay Symons, special education and kindergarten to 8th grade teacher for 27 years, South Georgia*

We try not to hold children back because it can become a problem when they're older than their peers. There are many problems that crop up in adolescence with self-esteem, image, and motivation. Usually there is something else wrong when it comes to thinking about holding a child back a year, so you need to investigate what is really going on.
—*Lynn M., high school, deaf students, and middle school special education teacher for 21 years, Boston, Massachusetts*

By the time a student has reached upper elementary grades, holding him back can do more emotional harm than good. Parents often want to retain kids because they're not doing their work, not because they aren't capable of it. When students are younger, they're much more resilient and don't realize the social implications of being kept back.
—*Lawanna Ford, 5th grade teacher for 25 years, Argonia, Kansas*

If children don't have the skills the state requires at the end of kindergarten, or even if they lack social or emotional skills, I definitely feel you should hold them back. As a teacher, that's the hardest thing to tell a parent. But if the child is not ready and is pushed forward, he'll just struggle for another year and see school as a negative place. If he gets another year to build up his confidence and self-esteem, he will start to like school again and come out of the year more on top and not struggling. It keeps the whole experience positive.
—*Alison Gowers, kindergarten teacher for 5 years, West Point, Virginia*

Why Has Cheating Become a Widespread Issue?

℗ Cheating today is much more prevalent in schools than many parents are aware. Research has found that 97% of high school students admitted to questionable academic behaviors and 50% admitted to plagiarism. Cheating has gotten more high tech than the cheat-sheets of old: 15% of students turned in papers from a website or term paper mill and 52% copied straight from websites without citing their sources properly. When surveyed, 33% of students report they cheat because they are lazy or unprepared.

℗ Cheating behaviors are not confined to students known for bad behavior—they cross the entire academic spectrum. Cheating is rampant in the higher ranks where students are competing for top marks. An A student at the top of the class is now just as likely to cheat, perhaps even more so, because he is faced with the pressure of maintaining his good marks.

◉ Because of the widespread nature of cheating, most students don't see it as a problem; acts like copying homework have become commonplace.

◉ Students cheat for all kinds of reasons. Sometimes it's to fulfill their own expectations or those of their parents. Sometimes it's to help a friend. Other times kids cheat because they're lazy and it's often the fastest and easiest way to a good grade.

◉ Students also cheat because they can get away with it. When they see classmates cheating without getting caught, and receiving better grades because of it, they feel pressure to follow suit.

◉ Discuss times you've failed and times you've faced adversity. If your child grows up with a fear of failure, he will eventually face a moment when cheating seems to be the only answer, or at least the most promising one.

◉ Praise your child for his efforts, not his marks. An honestly earned B should be much more rewarding than an A earned by cheating. Reinforce the idea that you're proud of his effort and integrity, or he'll be tempted to cheat just to bring home grades that make you proud.

◉ Character is learned through habit and discipline. Look for ways to nurture the values and integrity you want to see in him. Instill a work ethic and explain that you don't cut corners so your child will be less likely to look for the easy way out.

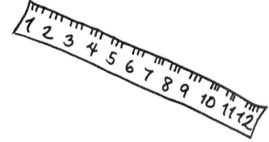

◉ Schools with articulated honor codes and teachers who address cheating have lower incidences of academic dishonesty, so the message must be getting through. If you address the issue with your child as well, you can only increase the positive impact of other discussions.

◉ Look for opportunities to highlight your position on academic honesty and cheating. Whether a book character, movie scene, or news item, media moments provide ways to approach the subject and have an open discussion. Talk about consequences. Articulate how and why cheating robs a person of the opportunity to learn and grow. You also can discuss the consequences you would dole out in such situations.

Unfortunately, cheating is more widespread now than in previous years. There's more and more pressure put on teachers with accountability and testing, which translates to more work and higher standards, so there's increasing pressure put on students. They've got parents threatening them, telling them, "You have to make the grades." I had one child whose parents made him run laps if he didn't get an A. Some students, rather than buckling down and learning, try to cheat. I feel we've brought on some of that ourselves.
—*Lawanna Ford, 5th grade teacher for 25 years, Argonia, Kansas*

Cheating is not as prominent in lower levels. If the teacher displays the information for the full week, by the time the kids have to take the test they usually have the information down. In younger years, it's mostly the children who are really struggling, like those who have learning disabilities, who cheat. With middle schoolers and high schoolers, it's mostly those who aren't being responsible with time or assignments.

When a kid is cheating, parents and teachers need to identify the real problem and attack it from there. Is it that he hasn't studied enough or doesn't understand the information? Does he need to be tutored? Cheating is a reflection of the child's insecurity, because he doesn't know the information and he's afraid of failure. Rather than be on the defensive, go in and find out why.
—*Kay Symons, special education and kindergarten to 8th grade teacher for 27 years,*
South Georgia

It's the little things parents can do as role models that make the biggest difference. When parents do a lot of little cheating on the side, it serves as a powerful role model for their children; even running a stop sign or not paying the late fee on library books can be a big influence if your child is watching. If parents can teach their children virtues, then there won't be a problem with cheating in the classrooms. We have an honor code at our school, and for every assignment, students have to pledge they didn't cheat or lie to complete it. I asked my son once if he wanted me to proofread his paper and he said, "Mom, you can't do that, I have to sign off that I didn't have any help." I was so proud of him.
—*Libby Anne Inabinet, kindergarten, 1st grade, reading, and gifted and talented teacher for*
15 years, Columbia, South Carolina

Parents have a tendency to minimize what cheating really means, which is taking information that doesn't belong to you. I think it's great to show children cheating is not something small, not just a phase kids go through as they try to follow the crowd. Be persistent. Let your child know he is better off getting it wrong than getting it right by cheating.
—Anne Wonson Curry, 5th to 12th grade math and science teacher for 12 years, Rockport, Massachusetts

How Should I React If My Child Is Caught Cheating?

◉ Dealing with cheating is a difficult parenting moment. You may find yourself questioning, "Did I raise him this way?" Tread lightly on the border between discussion and discipline, punishment and lecture. Question your child: "Did you know it was wrong to cheat? What made you cheat?"

◉ Discuss the consequences together and ask him what he thinks an appropriate punishment would be. Make sure the consequences are relevant; taking out the trash for a week isn't a meaningful consequence for copying homework. Remember that often the worst punishment is letting him know how seriously he disappointed you.

◉ Have your child write a letter to the teacher and the school, explaining why what he did was wrong. Fitting consequences are having him tutor a younger student or requiring him to devote more time to work and studying by taking away TV, video games, and computer privileges during the week.

In first grade, my daughter was caught cheating. She wrote some information on her hand before a test. If you don't teach kids right from wrong at this point, they're never going to learn it. I told her I was very disappointed and she had to study to get good grades. She was scared to tell me because she usually does work really hard. She was devastated by my disappointment. At first I wanted to yell and scream, but I knew that wouldn't work, so I sat down and talked to her. I told her, "Whatever we need to do, we will do. You don't have to cheat. If you need my help, I'm here for you. We'll stay up all night if we have to. Homework comes first, above sports and anything else."
—*Mom of a 10-year-old*

We had a massive run of cheating in first grade, which was shocking! My daughter and a friend shared sentences and got a zero on their vocabulary tests. The other mom blew it off, but we did not. It's not like robbing the bank, but she cheated. We made her write the ten sentences again with completely different words and turn them in to the teacher. If she got a grade, great, but if not, she still had to do them. We also made her apologize to the teacher, and the teacher respected that because most parents blow it off.
—*Mom of a 12-year-old*

How Can I Take the Pressure off My Stressed-Out Child?

Children become stressed when they feel too much pressure from their parents, their teachers, or themselves. Stress manifests itself in a number of ways in children, ranging from frequent outbursts and crying to major changes in energy level and a sudden need for constant reassurance.

Young children may revert to more immature behaviors when they feel stressed, including thumb sucking, bed-wetting, trouble sleeping alone, and clinginess. They also may develop a severe school phobia and cry or complain of physical distress when there. Kids often respond physically to stress, exhibiting responses like chewing fingernails, fidgeting, and nervous tics.

⊚ Particularly in gifted children and boys, stress can mimic ADD symptoms such as hyperactivity and difficulty concentrating.

⊚ Stress can create physical symptoms such as stomach pains or headaches. Although it's important to get these checked out by a physician, keep your otherwise-healthy child in school while you resolve the cause of his stress.

⊚ Playing sick is the oldest trick in the book. If your child keeps claiming to be sick, there is a good chance he is trying to avoid someone or something at school. Get to the root of the problem, and rule out a legitimate physical complaint by offering to make a doctor's appointment the same day.

⊚ Children often respond to stress with attention-seeking behaviors and sudden mood swings, especially as they get older. Conversely, some children respond to stress by increasingly isolating themselves, retreating inward and confining themselves to their rooms.

⊚ As children tend to exaggerate the severity of a setback, help your child contextualize the issue and view it as minor. Highlight moments when your child works to the best of his ability and tries his hardest, instead of focusing on final products of perfection.

⊚ If the symptoms persist and the problem doesn't resolve itself on its own, look for outside help:

✴ Look into the school's counseling center. In-school counseling has a number of advantages, such as easy access to your child's teacher and knowledge of the school environment, which can offer a broader perspective on what's going on.

✴ Your child's pediatrician is also a good resource. In addition to ruling out anything physical, your child's primary care physician can recommend a good psychologist covered by your health plan.

⊚ Encourage your child to have high expectations for himself and work toward those goals, but don't push him to perform at a level for which he isn't ready. Children who are pushed too hard and too soon often fall short, and they inevitably feel crushed when they do. Instead of being proud of accomplishments, these children wind up feeling like they're only working to make their parents happy.

Often, school anxieties come from parents putting too much pressure on their kids. As a mom, I'm guilty of that, as I expected my daughter to make all A's because I knew she could. But sometimes, even with her best efforts, she made B's. Parents need to know their children's abilities and be realistic. Observe your children's work habits: If they're trying as hard as they can, then back off. Focus your energy on trying to make a valid assessment of how hard they're trying.
—Martha Ann Chandler, 3rd to 6th grade teacher for 14 years, Florence, South Carolina

I have students saying, "My parents will kill me if I don't get an A on this!" For many parents, good grades serve as a status symbol of good parenting.
—Edward Sapienza, 9th to 12th grade science, math, and computer teacher for 31 years, North Reading, Massachusetts

Some warning signs your child is stressed about school include not sleeping well, not wanting to go to school, not doing homework, and general unhappiness. If you observe any of these, talk to your child and find out what's bothering him so you can deal with the matter appropriately.
—Anne Marie Fritton, 4th grade teacher for 3 years, Depew, New York

How Should I React to My Perfectionist Child Who Stresses Himself Out?

Hidden behind some children's persistent, self-deprecating comments is the belief that if they don't live up to certain expectations, they will be lifelong failures. If you notice your child repeatedly belittling himself, reassure him that you love him no matter what, and encourage him to look at himself in a more positive and realistic way. Don't just attribute comments like "I'm dumb" or "I can't do anything" to momentary frustration. Ask your child to explain why he feels the way he does and encourage him to see the difficulties he faces as challenges rather than reflections of inadequacies.

☺ With performance-based measures now in place to assess schools and individual teacher performance, it is easy for your child to get swept up in apprehension about his scores, leaving him anxious and entirely result-orientated instead of luxuriating in the process of learning itself.

☺ If your child is a perfectionist, he will view even the smallest mistakes as proof of his failures. He will likely opt out of competitive activities or limit his activities to those at which he knows he can excel. He also may tend to leave his work to the last minute and suffer through constant anxiety about getting it done perfectly.

☺ Some children come by perfectionism naturally; worrying so much about making mistakes they keep redoing the same assignment until they feel they have gotten it exactly right. If your child acts this way, try to lessen the pressure he feels to please you, his teachers, or himself.

☺ Tell your perfectionist that success comes through mistakes. Sit down together and have him list things he has avoided or has wanted to do but wouldn't because of his fear, and encourage him to try one of these activities. Explain to your child it's more important to learn new things and enjoy himself than do something perfectly or be the best at every activity.

My son gets upset when he doesn't make all A's on every test or project. We keep reminding him it's okay if he doesn't get a good grade, especially since he pushes himself more than anybody. We make sure he is prepared for tests, while helping him realize that since he is so prepared there's no need to worry. It helps him to know we are there and okay with it if he brings home a bad grade.

—Alesha Worra, mom of Brandon, 12, and Travis, 11, Greer, South Carolina

If my daughter can't do something perfectly the first time, she doesn't want to do it at all. We are trying so hard to make sure she knows no one can do anything perfectly the first time. We also try to take focus off of the grades, which helps too.
—*Sheila Cross, mom of Emily, 8, Memphis, Tennessee*

What Should I Do If I Feel My Smart Child Isn't Being Challenged?

@ Children with advanced skills and intellect may not be able to reach their full potential without special attention and challenges from their teachers. They may not recognize just how far they can go, fear failure, fall prey to boredom, and develop negative attitudes toward class.

@ Standard teaching methods break subjects down into easily-grasped material, making a smart child feel frustrated and bored by learning at such a slow pace.

@ Talk to your child's teacher, explain your concerns, and ask the following questions:

✴ Can you make assignments more challenging for my child?

✴ Does the school have a formal program for gifted and talented children or offer tests to assess giftedness?

✴ What can I do at home to enhance my child's educational experience?

✴ Is there a possibility of my child spending less time with curriculum he has mastered and more time with opportunities?

@ To keep your child's mind stimulated, sign him up at an academic enrichment center, or engage him in intellectual and creative after-school activities such as chess club or art class.

My children are very gifted in reading, so I monitor their homework. If I see it only takes them 12 seconds to do an assignment, they are not being challenged enough. Knowing the teachers helps, because I can have impromptu conferences and take care of the problem really fast.
—*Martha Judiscak, mom of Jimmy, 17, Vicki, 16, and Danny, 11, Knoxville, Tennessee*

How Do I Know If My Child Is Actually Gifted?

◉ In the United States, 5% to 7% of school-age children are gifted; that's three to four million kids. Three decades ago, that number was only 3%, due to the definition of giftedness requiring an IQ over 145. Giftedness is now associated with five separate areas in which a child can be extraordinarily talented: intellectual (those capabilities that are measurable with IQ and achievement tests); academic (those abilities that present themselves most clearly in broad scholastic achievement); leadership; creativity; and the visual or performing arts.

◉ Awareness of the need to challenge children and encourage their educational growth has increased, and the number of gifted programs and children who qualify for them has gone up accordingly.

◉ A gifted child may resemble a slow learner. Sloppy handwriting can point to hands unable to keep up with his thoughts, poor spelling may mean he reads whole words instead of separate letters, and problems with rote memorization may stem from a bent toward creative thinking. Your child might be gifted if he masters new concepts or challenges unusually quickly and easily, excels in specific areas, has a unique strategy for problem solving or an unusual, innovative, and creative way of thinking.

◉ In the classroom, gifted children typically work faster than their peers and may

ask for supplemental assignments. Gifted children also tend to ask questions, make comparisons, and draw conclusions that reveal a deeper level of understanding and insight than is typically found in children their age.

© Gifted children tend to be more inquisitive and challenging to authority, which reflects their voracious appetite for knowledge and understanding rather than intended disrespect. Unfortunately, many teachers misinterpret their behavior as impertinent or pretentious.

© Your child's teacher may recognize that she can't challenge your gifted child and help the rest of the class at the same time. Respect the teacher's honesty, and talk to specialists trained in educating and working with gifted students. Keep the teacher informed of any new information you come across, and work with her and other specialists to gain the best education possible for your child.

A lot of parents come to me thinking their child is gifted. A lot of evaluation needs to be done before most children can be labeled gifted—it can't just be because your child is an early reader. A parent will say, "My child read chapter books at four. Is she gifted now?" The answer is, "No, she just reads earlier than her friends." Time is a really big factor for figur-  ing these things out. Some process things easily, but there's a difference between being truly gifted and having the ability to learn something quickly. If your child really is a prodigy he should be put into a special program, but I wouldn't do it before seventh or eighth grade. —*Kathy Carabine, pre-k and 3rd grade teacher for 16 years, Boston, Massachusetts*

©

Parents will say, "My kid's not being challenged, he's too smart for this," but that's the biggest misconception in the world. Only about 4% of people are truly gifted, and odds are your kid is not gifted or exceptionally talented. If your child is not getting his work done, it's most likely not because he's too smart. However, if your child really is gifted, recognize that gifted students need as much enrichment as they can get outside of reading, writing, and their

school's standard curriculum. Let them dabble in as many different curricula as possible, or in depth in a specialty area. Parents are their children's only advocates. The student himself isn't going to say, "Put me in 4th grade math."
—*Anne Wonson Curry, 5th to 12th grade math and science teacher for 12 years, Rockport, Massachusetts*

You need to be realistic about your child. My older son, who had done school work ahead of many other kids, just wasn't motivated enough to be in the gifted and talented program, so I wasn't going to push for him to do it. It's really about being honest with yourself about where your kids are on the spectrum. Not all of them are going to Harvard.
—*Jennifer O'Gorman, mom of Olivia, 11, Jake, 9, Sam, 7, Annabelle, 4, Luke, 2, and Eleanor, 1, Lebanon, Maine*

When my son was in fourth grade, he'd already mastered the material four years before. The school agreed to have him transported to the middle school every day and allowed him to take his core courses with the eighth grade class. He still took health, art, and gym class with kids his own age, and was with his friends during free time and recess blocks. Because there was no additional cost to the school, they were more accommodating; they also realized he would have ended up becoming a behavioral problem if they didn't intercede.
—*Andrea B., mom of three boys ages 15, 9, and 7*

What Unique Problems May My Gifted Child Face?

Gifted children often have to deal with unrealistic expectations from parents, teachers, and themselves, causing perfectionism that comes out in many forms. Because of the intense, self-imposed pressure your child may put on himself, and the standard of excellence he expects, he may react to difficulty with frustration, anger, or disengagement.

Demanding constant attention and becoming unmotivated and dejected are a few of the many surprising ways gifted children display stress. It can cause a host of psychosomatic problems as well, such as body aches, tiredness, and digestive problems.

To avoid the stress of rejection and the difficulty of finding friends who will understand them, gifted children often become loners. Your child may have difficulty relating to peers his own age because his mind does not work on the same level, and they may see him as conceited or bossy. Alternately, he also may have difficulty developing relationships with older children because his social skills lag behind his academic abilities. When he does find a friend, his demands for intimacy may be so high that he has trouble maintaining the relationship. For this reason, your gifted child may be especially prone to loneliness, which can lead to depression.

Gifted children can come across as smug or obnoxious; the strength of their convictions and the quickness with which they arrive at solutions often leave them impatient with those who lag behind. Some have become so accustomed to adult dialogue they appear arrogant to peers.

Work with your gifted child on his social skills. It's easy to see him as an adult because he talks and thinks on a mature level, but his emotional development will not likely match his intellectual abilities.

I have one son who's 15 and profoundly gifted. He has been accelerated, skipping grades. Academics come easy to him, but his work ethic isn't what it needs to be. He gets the best grades, but he does very little to get them. Socially, it was very challenging. He entered the middle school and was taking classes at the high school. He was treated as a Doogie Howser type, and didn't have a core group of friends. Ultimately, we made the decision to put him in a private school that dealt specifically with gifted children.
—Andrea B., mom of three boys ages 15, 9, and 7

Jackson was reading at 2. Although we were obviously very pleased with his progress, the first two years of his preschool experience were difficult. During this time, he would get frustrated because he was so far ahead of the other children his age. He would look at a map of the United States and see something entirely different than the three-year-old sitting next to him. Because he is our first child, we really didn't have any basis for comparison.
—*Vinca LaFleur, mom of Jackson, 6, and Evan, 4, Washington, D.C.*

What Extra Support Does My Gifted Child Need?

@ Your child needs to feel secure about himself and understand the positive and negative ways in which his giftedness may affect his life. To help your child deal with the unique pressures he faces, give him space to decompress. Let him talk about his concerns without leaping to get involved or solve the problem for him. Overestimating his ability can put enormous amounts of pressure on him to achieve what may be unattainable goals.

@ Encourage your child to cultivate his exceptional abilities. A gifted child tends to have strong ambition to develop his potential, and squelching that ambition may have adverse effects on his emotional well-being. Gifted children often become consumed by activities to the detriment of other aspects of their lives.

@ Help your child set limits for himself. Teach him to manage his time and energy properly and let him know it is okay to take a step back from what he is working on to gain some perspective. He may also start a multitude of tasks at once, then get overwhelmed and frustrated. Teach him to concentrate and finish one thing at a time.

◉ Your gifted child is more likely to question rules and start a power struggle if adults threaten his autonomy, initiative, or creativity. Engaging in an authoritarian parenting style will likely result in friction and stress, but the structure discipline provides is essential to making him feel in control of his life.

◉ Physical activity is a must for gifted children, as exercise helps mitigate stress. Don't let your child become so consumed by academic pursuits that he avoids sports.

◉ While you may have very high expectations for your gifted child, the most valuable goal you can set for his future is that he develops into a well-rounded, well-adjusted adult.

There's a Gifted Program at My Child's School, but My Child Didn't Qualify as I Thought He Would. What Can I Do?

◉ Find out how the school determines eligibility. Most schools rely on a combination of testing, teacher evaluations, input from parents, and rough assessments of a child's creativity. If you think your child performed below his ability on the test his school uses for admittance and all other signs indicate he should be part of the program, ask if he can take the test again.

◉ If your child has a strong academic record, present your case to the school. Try to broker a compromise and ask them to accept your child on a conditional basis.

◉ If your child's inherent ability level is on the cusp of giftedness, consider other factors to determine where he belongs, such as self-motivation, innate intellectual curiosity, his interest in the subject, work ethic, and maturity level when pushing for acceptance into a gifted program. The challenge will either inspire him to push himself or discourage him entirely.

My daughter was involved in a talented and gifted program starting in fourth grade. She had done well academically, and had progressed ahead of most of her peers, as I found out by talking to other parents. She had noticed some kids were leaving the classroom to participate in this program, so I called to ask about it. I didn't want to wait until December, when the next evaluation took place, so I talked to her classroom teacher, who agreed it made sense for her to join the program immediately. I had to ask to get what we wanted.

—Jennifer O'Gorman, mom of Olivia, 11, Jake, 9, Sam, 7, Annabelle, 4, Luke, 2, and Eleanor, 1, Lebanon, Maine

Learning Disabilities

Should I Have My Child Tested for Special Needs?

◉ Every school is responsible for recognizing and diagnosing a student's learning disorders and public schools must provide free evaluations. If your child attends a private school that does not provide comprehensive in-house testing, federal law allows you to request a free assessment from your local school district and have the results reported to you within 50 days.

◉ The Individuals with Disabilities Education Act (IDEA) ensures that federal funding will provide learning-disabled students with the special programs they need. IDEA defines disability to include mental retardation, hearing, speech, and vision impairments, autism, orthopedic impairments, and specific learning disabilities such as dyslexia and ADD/ADHD.

◉ Learning disorders are often difficult to diagnose, as there is no uniform set of indicators and not all teachers have been trained to interpret the subtle signs that distinguish a learning disorder from more common behavioral problems.

◉ Young children may experience developmental delays that dissipate naturally. If you and your child's teacher cannot remedy an issue, however, testing is one way to take action. Ask for a comprehensive psychoeducational evaluation. This involves your child's developmental history, current achievement levels, an IQ test, screening for learning disabilities, and psychological or neurological testing if necessary.

◉ The school must tell you in writing which tests will be administered and how the results will be evaluated. You need to approve any testing before it can take place so before you give your consent, ask for details about the proposed tests, how the results will change the way the school handles your child, and whether the school will use them for anything else, such as tracking decisions. The language and bureaucratic jargon for your child's evaluation can be confusing and overwhelming. If you feel unsure of anything, don't hesitate to ask for clarification.

◉ If testing doesn't diagnose your child with any disorders, it can still point out any areas in which he needs extra help.

◉ There are six main areas in which learning disabilities may reside: oral language ability, reading comprehension, listening comprehension, written language ability, mathematical reasoning, and mathematical calculation.

◉ Do research to gain a better understanding of what your child's evaluation means. Some common learning disabilities include:

✸ *Attention Deficit Disorder* (ADD): difficulty in focusing and maintaining attention for sustained periods of time.

✸ *Attention Deficit Hyperactivity Disorder* (ADHD): very similar to, but even more debilitating than, ADD. The classic symptoms of ADD and ADHD are distractibility, impulsiveness, disorganization, poor memory, short attention span, and poor self-control. Common characteristics of students with ADD and ADHD include grades below ability level, aversion to reading, frequent behavioral difficulties in school, low tolerance for frustration, poor test scores despite sound understanding of material, difficulty finishing tests on time, low self-esteem, poor motor skills, and poor handwriting.

✸ *Discalculia:* difficulty comprehending the symbols and functions of standard math.

✸ *Dysgraphia:* severe trouble writing legibly or quickly.

✤ *Dyslexia:* difficulty processing language, including reading, writing, and spelling.

✤ *Specific Language Disability (SLD):* severe difficulty in another aspect of language skills.

✤ *Sensory Integration Disorder (DSI):* interruption in the brain's ability to integrate information from the body's five basic sensory systems.

✤ *Visual Perception:* difficulty interpreting visual information.

✤ *Auditory Discrimination:* difficulty perceiving the differences between speech sounds.

◉ When consulting a specialist about your child's need for diagnostic testing, share all details you believe to be pertinent to his case. Include observations from people who have worked with him, as well as your own insights about his experiences, behavior, needs, and abilities.

◉ Neither learning disorders nor attention problems correlate with intelligence, so don't hesitate to test your child because you fear that the tests will expose him as low-ability. If he is having difficulties, it is crucial for him to get the help he needs immediately so he can work up to his potential without falling behind his peers.

Really at any point when a child's not succeeding academically, schools should be doing testing.
—*Erika Bare, 6th to 8th grade special education teacher for 3 years, West Linn, Oregon*

Parents should take action as soon as they notice any problems with their child. Even if a child is in preschool and he's not learning his letters, parents need to jump on the ball as soon as they see a problem. This doesn't necessarily mean testing, but they should get him into some kind of program. I've seen too many kids come to kindergarten with obvious problems where the parents have done nothing.
—*Deb Brown, kindergarten to 4th grade special education teacher for 26 years, Conyers, Georgia*

If a child is not retaining information, it can signify a problem, even if he's only in kinder-garten. It's very common for young kids to reverse letters, write them backwards, or start to sound out words backwards. This could indicate dyslexia, but it's really too early for test-ing. It is something to watch. Say to the teacher, "I've noticed this." Every child is different, and it could just take longer for yours to figure things out, but it's better to question every little thing than to ignore the signs completely.

—*Alison Gowers, kindergarten teacher for 5 years, West Point, Virginia*

Every parent needs to understand that what is considered a special need now may not have been 10 years ago. Today, kids can be diagnosed with problems in areas like executive or-ganization skills and memorization. The range of development is huge, and parents shouldn't fear asking the school to test their child. Testing doesn't have the stigma that it used to. It's completely normal: everybody has difficulty somewhere.

—*Anne Wonson Curry, 5th to 12th grade math and science teacher for 12 years,*
    Rockport, Massachusetts

A lot of people don't want their child labeled with a learning disorder diagnosis—parents take it as personal failure—but get over that if your child needs special accommodations in order to get the help he needs. This is especially true in the testing situations, because if a child is learning disabled in some way, he can get special accommodations and not just sit there getting frustrated and doing poorly.

—*Joy Pumphrey, 2nd and 3rd grade teacher for 12 years, Clearwater, Florida*

What we often get from testing is a label—a danger when kids are young. Labels can put your child in a box and he will eventually hear it in some fashion. After hearing it repeatedly, he will start to believe it. When older, however, you may need that label in order to get the individualized help your child needs.

—*Niambi Muhammad, 1st and 2nd grade teacher for 4 years, Chicago, Illinois*

Labels open a legal door. The school cannot serve a child without attaching some name to his problem. That's the way the legal system works, and you have to determine what it is that is getting in a child's way before you can fix it. But any good teacher looks at that as a tiny piece of the child. Half the time, I forget what labels the children I'm working with have. What is more important than the labels is their present level of educational performance, so I talk in ways that adequately describe the child, such as "Joey struggles with sitting in his seat." I give a thorough description of the child, not just, "He has ADHD." Labels are scary for parents, but they are a necessary evil. There's no other way to get in that door to seek help.
—*Erika Bare, 6th to 8th grade special education teacher for 3 years, West Linn, Oregon*

When Should I Opt to Have My Child Privately Tested?

Public schools, overwhelmed by the needs of hundreds of children, will occasionally drag their feet with testing. The biggest complaints about public school testing are that the wait for testing can be long and the quality sometimes questionable. If you feel you cannot wait or need an assessment from a health care or mental health care professional, pursue private testing.

You may also want to have outside testing done if you believe your child's testing results don't accurately portray his abilities, or you think he should be eligible for special education services but the school has determined otherwise. While this option often costs over $1,000, results may lead a school to reconsider its decision. However, bring the results to the school's attention only if you think they are pertinent—for example, if you are trying to get your child admitted into a special program.

Many parents opt to test outside of school because they are concerned about information going into their children's records and affecting future teachers' perceptions. Out-of-school testing lets parents decide what to do with test results.

◉ Good starting sources for private evaluations are pediatricians and psychologists. Talk with your health care provider to go over your options. Health plans can cover certain private tests, such as those for ADHD.

◉ Outside testing can also serve as a periodic reassessment to help the school team monitor your child's progress and determine whether he needs to continue getting special help.

I think you should do outside testing if you disagree with what the school says. Everyone tries to do a great job, but teachers are not with your child as much as you are, and you know more about him. As with any health matter, you can always benefit from a second opinion.
—*Susan Draughn, 7th and 8th grade special education teacher for 24 years, Sunman, Indiana*

Our school has no problem accepting outside testing, but it's usually going to be a repeat of what we would have done. The school is interested in getting information that will help the child, and will do the tests they feel are necessary to understand the problem. We're more than happy to use outside testing results, but they're usually pretty consistent with ours, and you have to spend money to do it privately. The school will do pretty much the same thing for less money.
—*Erika Bare, 6th to 8th grade special education teacher for 3 years, West Linn, Oregon*

You need to have your child tested both in and out of school and come in with outside test results to supplement the testing that the school does. For example, a school will almost never tell parents that their child is dyslexic, because it has to provide remediation for that problem. It's all about money. Parents may miss some of the most important areas where they could get help for their child, because the testing does not reveal a problem. That's how we lose kids through the cracks. Also, the testing the school performs is often inferior. I've seen kids tested for auditory problems in a loud environment. Schools are burdened by costs and laws, and it's the children and their families who end up being the losers.
—*Pat Wyman, former elementary school vice-principal, reading specialist, and founder of www.howtolearn.com, Windsor, California*

Why Should I Test for Vision Problems?

◎ Children with unrecognized vision or perception problems often suffer academically, which can affect behavior as well. Make sure experts aren't overlooking the obvious. Sometimes what appears to be a learning disorder is a sensory problem, such as a vision or hearing impairment. Bring in your child for proper screenings for visual problems on a regular basis.

◎ You can prevent certain kinds of visual problems. Poor lighting for close reading leads to myopia, while excessive television watching and computer use are linked to poor peripheral vision, farsightedness, and visual acuity problems. Other ways to reduce stress on your child's visual system include telling him to hold reading and writing materials at an angle and to take frequent breaks when working at the computer, shifting his focus by looking far away, then up close.

When kids go in to be tested for reading failure, they often simply take a vision exam, which consists of an eye chart test. This has very little to do with a child's ability to read a book. The alternative is comprehensive vision screening, which has been proven to detect and prevent reading problems. Reading problems are easily preventable. Even if schools detect that a child can track words from line to line, he might not be seeing punctuation. Watching too much TV and spending too much time indoors or at the computer arrests the normal development of visual skills. I go to classrooms all over the nation and find that literally 20–30% of the kids have undetected vision problems. That's more than one in four.
—*Pat Wyman, former elementary school vice-principal, reading specialist, and founder of www.howtolearn.com, Windsor, California*

By having twins in the same class, I found out that one needed glasses. The only reason we knew was because they were doing the same work and one was falling behind. In a different situation, it may have been a whole year before we figured that out and he would have already fallen behind.
—*Kim Shepherd, mom of Jessica, 17, Jeremy and Josh, 12, and Jennifer, 10, Indianapolis, Indiana*

What Happens at an Evaluation?

◉ A formal evaluation not only determines whether your child has a disability but also assists you in figuring out what special help he needs.

◉ Those typically involved in the evaluation include:

✳ At least one of your child's regular education teachers,

✳ One of the school's special education teachers or service providers,

✳ A school administrator familiar with special education policies and curriculum, and the resources available at the school,

✳ Other qualified professionals, such as a psychologist, occupational therapist, physical therapist or medical specialist, and

✳ Someone who can go over the evaluation process, answer your questions, and talk about what instruction your child may need.

◉ An evaluation usually consists of multiple components: educational and skill-oriented, medical and physical, psychological, and anecdotal/historical. The educational component assesses your child's current performance, basic academic needs, and sensory capabilities and compares his level of achievement to his ability and IQ. The medical component is an evaluation by a doctor or trained medical personnel, and the psychological component is an assessment by a trained psychologist. The anecdotal/historical aspect involves a series of interviews with you and your child's teachers to find out more about his language abilities and ways of processing information, how he adapts to change, his achievement in school, and his nonacademic interests and abilities.

◉ A proper evauation includes diverse evaluative tools, and will not rely on one single test to be the basis of a child's diagnosis. The people who administer the test must be trained evaluators, should get to know your child before deciding which tests to use, and must administer the tests in a fashion that does not discriminate against your child in any way.

◉ Answer any questions your child may have about the testing and go over what he will have to do. Present the situation as a way for you and the teacher to help him. Visit the place where he will be tested and try to introduce him to the people who will conduct his evaluation; unfamiliarity can impair your child's performance and yield inaccurate perceptions.

What's the Best Way to Interpret the Results?

◉ You have a legal right to see all of your child's records, including the psychologist's notes and test papers from the evaluation. After the testing is complete, call a conference with the people who administered the evaluation and ask them to explain the results. Taping the conversation enables you to listen to it again later in a calmer setting with a clear head. Be sure to inform everyone ahead of time if you plan to tape their remarks.

◉ Request a written report to accompany any oral testing sessions. Make sure beforehand that the examiner is willing to put the results in writing. If not, tape record the oral session and write down any numerical scores. It is important to keep these numbers on record.

◉ The results should highlight not what your child has learned, but how he acquires and manipulates information.

◉ Make sense of the information and results by organizing the documents into those pertaining to your child and those dealing with administrative concerns. Put questions and comments in the margins of the pages, and address them with the appropriate person. Underline and highlight key information or phrases, using simple codes to mark different points like strengths and weaknesses.

◉ If you see problems with the records, like inaccuracies or descriptions that don't match your own observations, ask the principal to remove the materials, request a formal hearing to address your concerns, or write your own note as an addendum to the file.

If your child gets labeled with "x learning disorder," you have the right to know what that means. Ask for clear definitions.
—*Niambi Muhammad, 1st and 2nd grade teacher for 4 years, Chicago, Illinois*

How Can I Further Pursue an Evaluation?

◉   If you have issues with the evaluation that the school conducts, you are entitled to a free second and independent evaluation. If the school disagrees with your assessment and believes their evaluation is sufficient and complete, they must schedule a due process hearing to reach an agreement. This involves an impartial third party—generally a state-appointed lawyer, educator, or special education professional—who listens to both sides and offers a solution.

◉   Examples of conflicts to be addressed in due process hearings:

✤ Disagreements over whether your child's problems stem from an emotional disorder or a learning disability,

✤ Whether your child should receive services like counseling or occupational therapy,

✤ Whether your child should remain in a mainstream classroom or go to a special resource room,

✤ Whether the public school should cover the expense of placing your child in a private school that can better treat his needs, or

✤ Where your child should receive special services—at home, at school, or at another location.

◉   Your legal rights in due process hearings are very similar to your rights in the court system. You can be accompanied by an attorney or another professional to present evidence, cross-examine witnesses, prohibit the introduction of information that was not disclosed to you at least five days before the start of the hearing, obtain a written record of the hearing and of the appeal decisions to which you object, involve your child at the hearing, and receive reasonable compensation for attorneys' fees if you win your case.

When going into a hearing, you must be able to clearly articulate the problem and propose a clear and reasonable solution, and you must have the documentation to back both up. You must also know what the school has in its hand: all of the witnesses they plan to call and information they plan to use. Take a moment to weigh your evidence against the school's and consider what the likely outcome will be. Hearings demand a lot of time, energy, and money from everyone involved. You should be taking this step only if all other recourses and attempts at compromise, such as an administrative review or less formal involvement of third parties, have failed.

What Should I Know about Negotiating an Individual Education Plan (IEP)?

An Individual Education Plan (IEP) serves as a guide to developing an instructional agenda for a special needs student. Because the IEP maps out an academic year in advance, it allows teachers to look ahead as well. Teachers incorporate the IEP into their own lesson plans to help fulfill the student's unique needs. They can organize future lessons and alter the shape of their curriculum to take the student's needs into account.

Most public schools require a student to demonstrate work at least two years behind grade level, or a two-year discrepancy between ability and performance, to qualify for an IEP.

Standards for an IEP differ slightly, but most contain similar features:

* The date of implementation,

* The parent's signature,

✤ The disability or disabilities that make an IEP necessary,

✤ The student's interests and abilities,

✤ Test scores,

✤ Current level of ability in different subjects, ranked by grade level,

✤ Relevant health issues,

✤ Necessary equipment and any equipment loans,

✤ Changes in curriculum,

✤ The amount of assistance that the school will provide, and

✤ Psychologists, reading counselors, and other specialists who will help the student.

© Parents, special education and regular teachers, counselors and doctors, and outside experts can all serve as members of IEP teams, and all affect the success of the IEP. The law ensures that you have the right to actively participate in constructing your child's IEP.

© The function of the school administration at the IEP meetings is to present options to you. You have the right to veto any and all points of the contract. Discuss all options, and ask about the benefits and drawbacks of out-of-school services versus in-school specialists.

© An IEP team starts with information about your child from you, teachers, administrators, and your child himself; discusses his strengths and interests, testing results, and the possible learning disorders they imply; determines a disorder; and then outlines goals for your child along with a plan for achieving them.

© Current performance, classroom placement, and the regular classroom routine are all factors that the team has to take into account when setting goals. What are your child's particular needs? What environment and changes in schedule will best help him learn?

© It's important that the team clearly states how it will help your child achieve each goal, listing changes in classroom routine, flexibility in homework, or special aides, as they become necessary.

◉ Specify any classroom accommodations that the teacher should make, such as giving your child extra time to complete tasks, providing extra tutoring before or after school, seating him nearer to her, or providing him with short breaks in between tasks.

◉ Don't be afraid to ask questions, admit when you don't understand certain jargon, or ask for clarification when something is unclear. You are new to the process, and nobody expects you to know all the technical details. If you hold back, you only do yourself and your child a disservice.

◉ Ask what kind of assistance or supervision you can provide for homework and how you should respond to specific or counterproductive behaviors at home. Share any prior recommendations from previous teachers or educational specialists.

IEPs are very confusing, not just for parents but for special education teachers as well, even though we go through a lot of training. I would rather have an educated parent informed about what's going on. There are Learning Disabilities of America meetings in many towns, as well as extensive literature on individual learning disorders.
—*Heather Daigle, teacher of all grades, Plymouth, Massachusetts*

When parents go into an IEP meeting, often they are overwhelmed, frightened, and confused by all the jargon tossed around in these meetings. Oftentimes they will simply accept the plan the administration offers. The parents can feel like they are alone, when facing a large team comprised of teachers, the principal or an administrator, the specialists, the people who did the testing, and a reading or speech specialist. Here you are, surrounded by specialists who present you with a plan and information on what is wrong with your child and why your child is not performing at his or her potential. Even if the school does identify a problem, you need them to set very specific goals. Be an advocate for your own child, and hold the school accountable for reaching the IEP goals. How will the teacher address those objectives in the classroom?
—*Pat Wyman, former elementary school vice-principal, reading specialist, and founder of www.howtolearn.com, Windsor, California*

IEP plans are often complicated to read and not user-friendly. They involve really long lists of things for the teacher and parents to do, but no ways to measure the growth other than end-of-year results. Make sure that your child's IEP has specific benchmarks along the way.
—*Sherri McWhorter, 4th grade teacher for 5 years, Augusta, Georgia*

Parents should make absolutely sure that they are clear on all of the goals and objectives written in an IEP and how the teacher plans to implement it before they sign it.
—*Holly Parker, teacher of deaf students for 10 years, Colorado Springs, Colorado*

Parents need to feel comfortable enough to ask questions at IEP meetings. Sometimes I start spewing out stuff and I'll think, "Do you have any clue what I'm saying right now?"
—*Deb Brown, kindergarten to 4th grade special education teacher for 26 years, Conyers, Georgia*

Document absolutely everything. If you can't bring another person to meetings to take notes for you, bring a tape recorder. Take extensive notes from the tape, and write back, outlining both your understanding of the issues covered in the meeting and follow-up steps to be taken next. Form excellent relationships with the team of providers working with your child, so they develop empathy for your situation—then your child ceases to be a case, and you become more than just another squeaky wheel parent.
—*Andrea B., mom of three boys ages 15, 9, and 7*

Some parents think an IEP is written to be for an entire year. It is developed for an entire year, but parents and teachers can modify it at any time. Parents would be more relaxed if they realized this. Developing goals for your child is a group effort. The teacher does pretests and figures out the baseline data, but you can and should make goals during the meeting and take them away or add more throughout the year. Some parents rely way too much on what the teacher wants.
—*Pepper Griffith, 1st, 2nd, 5th, and special education teacher for 7 years, Atlanta, Georgia*

How Can I Best Prepare for an IEP Meeting?

◉ To make sure your school-age special needs child receives the best care, become an active advocate for him. The learning curve is steep, so take time early on to find out about special education laws and the variety of resources available to him and your family. Research your child's problem both in books and on the Internet to ensure that the decisions you make are both smart and accurate. Talk at length with similarly situated families to understand the issues and risks involved, what to ask for, and how to craft your requests most effectively.

◉ Create a checklist before you go into an IEP meeting, and don't leave until you have addressed each item. Make notes on the goals and evaluative criteria you want included in your child's IEP, and rank them by importance.

◉ Bring the written results of any diagnostic tests, including write-ups of oral exams or evaluations, to the IEP meeting, and go over them with all the members present. Leave time for discussion and clarification.

◉ Save any email as a record of discussions and plans. Keeping an up-to-date and complete file of correspondence is especially important when there is a significant problem you are trying to resolve or when you are speaking to several different people regarding the same issue.

◉ Organize your observations into categories such as your child's movement, communication, social relationships, thinking skills, self-concept and independence, senses and perception, learning style, and best environment for independent, effective study.

Do as much reading and research as possible about your child's disability, and your rights in the process. *Wright's Law* is what I consider to be the ultimate resource for parents with children in the special education process. Also, the Federation for Children with Special Needs is a great resource.
—*Andrea B., mom of three boys ages 15, 9, and 7*

First of all, treat the IEP team as your ally and understand that everyone has the same goal. You are an equal member of this team, and your voice should be just as loud as that of the learning specialist or the psychologist. The law is very clear about this and any good team will approach it in that way. The team might bring in a draft to the meeting, but this is not your child's IEP. It may be the teachers' ideas, but they need to get your input and make the changes based on what you say. It's not set in stone until after you've had a part in developing it.
—*Erika Bare, 6th to 8th grade special education teacher for 3 years, West Linn, Oregon*

Keep a journal and a folder because if your child is going to be special needs, you can get lost in the amount of paperwork that comes with it. If you have a place where you can jot down things that you think might be significant, it can help support your case. Because you get bombarded with different questions, if you can go into the testing and say, "These are my reasons," it's more valid, and if you have more documentation to back it up, your child will get treated faster.
—*Susan Draughn, 7th and 8th grade special education teacher for 24 years, Sunman, Indiana*

When Should I Hire a Professional Advocate?

◉ Advocating for your special needs child can be a long and difficult process, so you may want to consider hiring a professional advocate to speak knowledgeably for your child's educational needs. A professional advocate can be a psychologist, educational therapist, or even a parent with similar experience battling the school district. You also have the right to request that your own physician, testing consultant, attorney, or counselor be present at the multidisciplinary evaluation team meeting at which an IEP is formed.

◉ The best advocates are articulate, assertive, knowledgeable about special education laws, and able to interpret test results and evaluate programs. Make sure you find someone you trust.

◉ If you have testing done outside of the school system with a specialist, bring that specialist with you to meetings with the school to help you negotiate the services needed for your child. Often, in an attempt to cut costs, schools will be reluctant to provide the types of specialized services that your child needs to catch up developmentally. Having an outside advocate, who has expertise and has evaluated your child and assessed the needed intervention, provides you with a much more powerful bargaining position.

◉ Lastly, understand that hiring a professional advocate has its trade-offs, as it usually slows down the negotiating process and puts the school administration on the defensive.

If you've made a request and the administration says it's not possible or can't happen, don't give up. Talk to someone outside of the school to gauge whether your request is reasonable. If it comes down to it and you're really stuck, I would recommend hiring a child advocate. This is the only time where I would take it to this level. If an advocate comes in, she will be butting heads with the school the whole way. The minute she walks in, the school goes

into legal mode. Most of the time, schools meet or exceed what the law requires, and if they say something is not possible, it probably isn't. There are lots of child advocates you could talk to instead of bringing in a lawyer, who thinks about legalities as opposed to what's best for the child. The advocate should try to work with the school and should be easy to approach about the child's needs.
—*Erika Bare, 6th to 8th grade special education teacher for 3 years, West Linn, Oregon*

Advocates can be a tricky resource. Sometimes they are very good, when they have the child's future in mind. But others don't see beyond the now and whether they can win. I had to deal with an advocate who was pushing an issue that the city wouldn't even look at. So the whole program was stalled, and the child wound up being the loser.
—*Lynn M., high school, deaf students, and middle school special education teacher for 21 years, Boston, Massachusetts*

I would say parents should look into getting an advocate unless they are very educated on IEPs.
—*Heather Daigle, teacher of all grades, Plymouth, Massachusetts*

I've had good and bad experiences with advocates. I had an experience with one advocate who sat with nine teachers for an IEP meeting and said we needed to do this and that, and she hadn't even met the child! She wanted this one little girl, who was very low-functioning and noncommunicative, to be in regular classes, which sickened me. I like inclusion, but different children need different levels. There were nine people staying after school—teachers and specialists who had their own lives—talking to this mother with an advocate who hadn't even met her child. I guess there is a place for advocates, but I've had some bad experiences. Sometimes they think they know it all and they get in there and they don't.
—*Susan Draughn, 7th and 8th grade special education teacher for 24 years, Sunman, Indiana*

It helps to come in with someone who is an expert in these types of proceedings. I've always recommended to parents that they don't walk in there alone. It's hard to sit at a conference table with everyone looking at you. The language tends to be wordy and legalistic, and it's easy to feel intimidated. Plus, these well-intentioned people may be wrong. Parents are not repeat players when it comes to problematic issues at school. They just don't understand how the game is played.

—*Pat Wyman, former elementary school vice-principal, reading specialist, and founder of www.howtolearn.com, Windsor, California*

What Should I Focus on During an IEP Conference?

◉ Ask the IEP team how severe your child's learning disabilities are, what the outcome of the IEP is likely to be, and if they think he will require ongoing assistance throughout his education. Be prepared, though, for some level of uncertainty—teachers and experts cannot always give you definite answers to these kinds of questions. Learning disabilities manifest themselves differently in each child.

◉ Make sure the plan will deal with the underlying learning problem instead of just helping your child to manage his current class work.

◉ Investigate the relationship between the mainstream and special education teacher, and ask each one separately what problems she is facing and how she feels about the others' responsiveness.

◉ If you disagree with the IEP proposal, explain to the evaluation team, politely but firmly, why it does not suit your child's needs. Bring in evaluations and test scores to support your arguments.

◉ Don't give up if the meeting does not go as you planned. Stay calm and encourage the school to keep trying different approaches until you come to an agreement that works for everyone involved. Do your best to work with the team to find something suitable, but remember that it's important to get your child help as soon as possible. You can always ask for more time before accepting the proposed IEP, so don't give your signature until you are sure you completely understand and agree with the plan.

◉   Request a signed copy of the IEP.

Parents need to be a critical part of the conference to develop the IEP—it should not be up to teachers and specialists alone. You need the IEP to specifically lay out what the teacher, the child, and the parent are going to do.
—*Joy Pumphrey, 2nd and 3rd grade teacher for 12 years, Clearwater, Florida*

If I'm uncomfortable, I will stop a meeting. If we've lost communication, I adjourn for the day and pick up later. Parents have done the same for us. You should feel free to say, "Let's stop. Let me think about what you've said. Let me have a copy of the tests and ponder this." Tempers may get heated, and taking a break gives parents time to think about it.
—*Deb Brown, kindergarten to 4th grade special education teacher for 26 years, Conyers, Georgia*

Parents are typically surrounded by experts who either say their child doesn't need help or come up with plans that are tilted in favor of the school. They make the child accountable. When there is supposed to be an ongoing journal log between the parent, child, and the teacher to keep everyone on track, it gets forgotten nine times out of ten because the teacher doesn't have time to fill it in. When the child doesn't make the appointed progress level, the school often puts the blame on the parent and child for failing to fulfill their part of the agreement. When you go into these meetings, do not sign on the dotted line until you have had time to evaluate the plan and talk to the people who are supposed to implement it.
—*Pat Wyman, former elementary school vice-principal, reading specialist, and founder of www.howtolearn.com, Windsor, California*

What If the Plan Moves My Child Out of the Regular Classroom?

◉ By law, your child has the right to the least restrictive environment that can handle his disability effectively. The IDEA states that, to the maximum extent appropriate, special education children should be educated with students who are not disabled. This act attempts to give these students the education they need while integrating them as much as possible into a mainstream classroom.

◉ Your child may end up in his regular classroom, where the teacher will adjust her material and pacing to help him learn. Depending on his needs, he also may see a special education teacher outside of class.

◉ He may spend part or all of his time in a special education classroom, where the teachers and support staff have more training to help with his specific problems. Children with especially severe needs may enter a separate program staffed by specialists.

◉ Consider how much involvement you want your child to have with special services, including the maximum amount of time you think he can be pulled out of mainstream class and how much time for tutoring or with specialists you think he can handle outside of regular school hours.

I know that everybody pushes to get their kids in the regular classrooms, but there are students who need to be pulled out for their own self-esteem. I had one student in sixth grade who couldn't read, and sitting in a language arts class was ridiculous. In some situations, putting kids in regular classrooms is unrealistic because the students get overwhelmed, and parents don't always think in their kids' best interest.
—*Deb Brown, kindergarten to 4th grade special education teacher for 26 years, Conyers, Georgia*

◉

For some kids I think remedial classes are a great necessity; for other kids they are not, and that's when revisions to the IEP are made. Some kids could remain in the classroom with a

special education teacher, for instance, or in a classroom with modifications with a regular teacher who just keeps an eye on them to make sure they're doing okay.
—*Pepper Griffith, 1st, 2nd, 5th, and special education teacher for 7 years, Atlanta, Georgia*

How Do I Ensure My Child's IEP Gets Implemented?

Get contact information for all the people involved in your child's special education program including all principals, teachers, and committee members involved in making decisions for him. They should all be aware of their responsibilities and have a copy of the IEP.

Inform your child's teacher about his behavioral and medication changes.

Keep a record of conversations with officials about your child, including dates, phone numbers, and what you discussed or agreed upon.

If you decide to monitor your child in the classroom setting to see if and how the IEP is being implemented, you should:

Give the teacher prior notice and tell her how long you plan to be there,

Respect the teacher's needs and routines, and keep comments to a minimum until you can speak in private,

Make notes about your visit,

Follow up with a brief conference with the teacher to share your observations, as well as a thank-you note that provides any positive feedback you have.

At the IEP review, find out from the school whether your child is on track with the established plan. Ask what skills he has mastered, what the criteria are for determining mastery, and whether the classroom and special education teacher are applying the same standards. Ask how his work in special resource classes has been translating to his mainstream class work. If he is on track, it may be appropriate to ask whether the goals are sufficiently challenging or whether he can keep up with mainstream classes without out-of-class programs.

☺ Don't expect changes to happen overnight. It can take months before your child noticeably improves, and it's possible that he will need to learn ways to work around his learning disorder.

☺ If a school fails to follow through on its promises and legal obligations, you have the right to a hearing.

With a special needs child, make sure you have a team meeting every few months with the principal, teacher, aide, and special needs coordinator. If you have to set up the meeting yourself, do it—as long as you get to meet with everyone who is involved with your child. Sometimes as a parent, your voice is not heard as loudly as it should be. You have to go in with the point that you know your child better than the school does. Don't let them tell you what you need. You know your child best—go with your gut. You want to be on offense but not *offensive*.
—*Debbie Steeves, mom of Spencer, 8, and Carter, 6, Grande Prairie, Alberta*

My son has dysgraphia, so I negotiated a written agreement that he either be given extra time on written exams or given exams orally via a tape recorder. On the first set of exams given after my son's plan was in place, I asked him how they went and he said fine. I asked, "How much extra time were you given?" "None." "Did you have the option to tell someone your answers instead of writing them down?" "No." I cannot tell you the millions of times that nothing happens if a parent does not stay on top of a plan and how it's administered. You just can't assume that the school will implement the plan. Teachers are human and may just forget. If you don't follow up, your child may not get the additional help he is promised.
—*Pat Wyman, former elementary school vice-principal, reading specialist, and founder of www.howtolearn.com, Windsor, California*

Make sure you keep a journal! On the IEP now, there's a computerized check sheet where you can check things off throughout the year to be sure all the issues are being approached.
—*Susan Draughn, 7th and 8th grade special education teacher for 24 years, Sunman, Indiana*

I've had to file complaints with the Department of Education. According to my son's IEP, he was supposed to have a bus monitor with him on the way to school every day, but they claimed they couldn't find someone to serve on Wednesdays, so the responsibility fell on us. I waited seven months. Finally, I filed a complaint, and sure enough, the next week, I got a bus monitor. It was supposed to start in September, but it started in March. If you see something going on that you disagree with, or you see the school violating their written agreements, speak up immediately.
—*Andrea B., mom of three boys ages 15, 9, and 7*

Make sure your child's teacher is aware of the IEP and has a full understanding of how it applies to the classroom. The IEP has a large focus on accommodations and implementations for classroom use. Make sure that what is supposed to be happening is happening and the teacher is working towards the goals outlined.
—*Erika Bare, 6th to 8th grade special education teacher for 3 years, West Linn, Oregon*

Periodically pull the IEP back out and reread it. This way, if it says that Johnny will know his ABC's, you should then ask how many he knows now. If it's been nine months and he hasn't gotten past D, go to the teacher and say, "You only have three months left to teach twenty-two letters. What can we do to get this done?" The IEP should be something that holds you, as a parent, accountable as well, so that you're working as a team with the teachers and specialists. It gives you something tangible to have and check on periodically to see what your child's doing, because that's what the law says the school should be doing.
—*Holly Parker, teacher of deaf students for 10 years, Colorado Springs, Colorado*

With IEPs, just because you make a choice doesn't mean you have to stick with it forever.

You don't need to wait until the next evaluation comes up if your child is unhappy with the conditions. Parents know their child better than anyone else; they need to be realistic about how their child is doing academically and socially and base their decisions on that.
—*Lawanna Ford, 5th grade teacher for 25 years, Argonia, Kansas*

For our special needs child, we have additional meetings to review her individualized education plan. To show appreciation and to lighten things up, as these meetings tend to get stressful, I always bring cookies and fruit drinks. It's my way of letting everyone know how much I appreciate them, and that I recognize that we all care about this child, are all pulling for her, and want the best for her.
—*Rochelle Van Slyke, mom of Chris, 21, Erika, 16, and Amy, 13, Ketchikan, Arkansas*

How Can I Expect the Teacher to Be Involved in the IEP Implementation Process?

When your child has special learning needs, frequent communication with his teacher is essential. Most teachers have had at least basic training in working with disabled children and know how to manage the classroom while still attending to the needs of the disabled child present. But your child's teacher may not have had much specific training with his individual disorder.

Some teachers find it helpful to explain a student's disability to the class, especially if it is not physically apparent. This helps encourage empathy and understanding in the other children, dissipating any resentment they might have of the special treatment a disabled child will get from the teacher. Other options include you coming to talk to the class or authorizing a specialist to talk to the class and give a disability awareness lesson.

Bad grades can be especially demoralizing for a child with learning disabilities, especially if he is putting in a lot of effort. He can easily lose motivation if he doesn't see any results. Ask the teacher to make some small allowances in grading by, for example, giving extra credit for effort and participation or de-emphasizing certain challenging criteria, like handwriting or spelling, where appropriate. Find out if there are ways for him to earn extra credit through independent projects.

© Homework is also more challenging for children with learning disabilities. To be most effective, homework for special needs children should be short and focused on reinforcement of skills and class lessons. Find out if the teacher is willing to make some small changes to lessen the burden, like shortening assignments or reducing the number of problems she requires your child to complete. Ask her to help your child to break larger projects down into a series of smaller steps or create a calendar of due dates and to look over his work at each stage.

© Make sure you understand the teacher's expectations about your involvement in assignments that come home and know how much or how little you should be helping your child. If your child starts struggling with a particular type or length of assignment, bring this to her attention immediately.

© Remember, a teacher cannot make a multitude of changes at once, so be particular about the requests you make and realize you are asking for modifications that demand more time and energy at the teacher's expense.

Half of the energy goes into administration, paperwork, and record keeping instead of delivery of services. Teachers and student aides are frightened by the prospect of having kids in their classroom who have serious problems they are not sufficiently equipped to handle. The high number of kids in a typical classroom who really need special intervention and a different learning and teaching style are seriously stressing teachers out.
—*Jim Rubens, dad of Matthew, 7, and former state senator, Hanover, New Hampshire*

We have implemented an IEP for my son Nicholas, who is mildly autistic and has ADHD, and actually just had our third yearly IEP review—the IEP started in preschool. So far, the IEP plans have worked very well and we have put together an excellent team of educational and

medical professionals. The teachers have been really cooperative with us in accommodating Nicholas's needs and his IEP, and I became very close with them all. I have also been extremely impressed with the principal at elementary school. He is young and very involved, and even attended the end-of-the-year IEP review meeting, which was a first for us.
—Jennifer D'Oliviera, mom of Nicholas, 6, Irvine, California

Everyone thinks the IEP is the answer, but it's only a game plan of what the child might need. It's not a lesson plan, but people use it like one, and there are so many important things that may not be in the IEP. You need to have a realistic approach to the year. Some things in the IEP may not get done, especially if a teacher wrote it the year before or if people have different ideas about implementing it.
—Susan Draughn, 7th and 8th grade special education teacher for 24 years, Sunman, Indiana

With an IEP, make sure the teacher is following the details of the plan. For instance, if the IEP calls for it, she should be extending time on class tests. A lot of times kids are too embarrassed to ask for it because they don't want to stand out in the class. You should also make the teachers aware of how the IEP came about, any medication your child takes, and so forth. One year I discovered that the time a child was taking his meds wasn't correct and it was interfering with his performance. I have seen a kid go from an F to a B just because of the time he took his medication.
—Amy Watson, 7th to 12th grade teacher for 5 years, Oyster Bay, New York

Problematic Classroom Behavior & Social Issues

Behavioral Issues

Which Student Behaviors Annoy Teachers Most?

☺ Teachers report that the most frustrating behavior they have to deal with is disrespect. This includes being rowdy, interrupting others, shouting answers out of turn, and coming to class unprepared. Disrespectful students cause disruptions in the classroom, forcing teachers to put lesson plans on hold to deal with them. Nearly half of all teachers say they spend more time controlling their classroom than teaching.

Ⓒ Poor listening skills are among the behavioral shortcomings children demonstrate in class. Paying close attention to the teacher helps your child fully understand and absorb information. Teach your child the body language most conducive to learning: sitting up straight, making eye contact with the teacher, taking notes or folding his hands while listening, and not slouching or gazing around the room or out the window.

Ⓒ Set an example for your child by being a good listener yourself. Maintain eye contact as you speak to him, stay interested in what he is saying, and don't interrupt him as he tells you about his day. You can also help him increase his concentration skills by playing games:

✦ Ask him to recite as many colors, states, songs, animals, pop singers, or football players, as he can in 30 seconds.

✦ Have him describe what he smells when you are cooking, what he sees on the way to school, and what instruments he hears in songs on the radio.

✦ Play the take-away game at the dining room table. Everyone closes their eyes except one person, who removes an object from the table. Then the other players open their eyes and guess what he took away.

Ⓒ Practice listening skills by making up a story together in the car. Take turns adding one sentence at a time, and see how long you can make your story.

Ⓒ Work on classroom manners by playing school at home. Play the badly behaved student, waving your hands in the air to be called on and shouting out answers, as a way to comically get the point across.

Children who are constantly moving and talking are a real irritation, but disrespect is the most frustrating and aggravating behavior.
—*Kay Symons, special education and kindergarten to 8th grade teacher for 27 years,*
  South Georgia

The thing I find most disruptive in my classroom is when students are unkind to each other. They understand they shouldn't be disrespectful to adults, but they often don't realize when they are rude to their peers. Parents can help by emphasizing to their children that hurting their friends' or siblings' feelings is just as bad as being rude to any grown-up.
—*Mary Beth Lewison, 2nd and 3rd grade teacher for 15 years in Ludlow, Massachusetts*

As a teacher, rudeness does me in. I will call the student down in front of everyone and say, "That was rude. You need to come apologize." We promote kindness and nice manners.
—*Martha Ann Chandler, 3rd to 6th grade teacher for 14 years, Florence, South Carolina*

There are different levels of disruption in class, and the definition of "appropriate behavior" changes depending on the classroom. If you're in a science lab and you're doing something physically disruptive, there are dangers that don't exist in an English writing course. Parents need to help their children understand that different classroom climates and behavior expectations exist.
—*Anne Wonson Curry, 5th to 12th grade math and science teacher for 12 years,*
  Rockport, Massachusetts

What really begins to grate on you after a while is constant chatter from children who simply do not know when to stay quiet. Dealing with them takes away so much learning time from the rest of the class. That sounds like such a petty thing, but it turns into a constant battle.
—*Lawanna Ford, 5th grade teacher for 25 years, Argonia, Kansas*

How Should I Approach My Child's Behavioral Problems?

℗ Sometimes finding out what your child is like out of the home can be shocking and unsettling, but remember that children often behave differently in school.

℗ Many report cards now have specific sections for marks on your child's in-school behavior. Even if your child excels in school, negative comments on behavior are a serious cause for concern. Many times behavioral comments are pretty vague, such as, "needs improvement." Ask your child what he thinks these remarks refer to.

℗ Ask your child's teacher to be specific about the type of negative behavior she sees him exhibit during school. Look at the context in which the negative behavior patterns seem to pop up: when, where, and under what conditions does the problem recur? Different situational elements may cause or exacerbate the behaviors: time of day, fatigue, certain subjects, personality conflicts, peer influence, or major changes in your child's life. Ask the teacher to clarify her expectations and what your child can do to reach them.

℗ Oftentimes a change in seating assignment will help if another student is distracting your child.

℗ If the behaviors the teacher describes seem confined to or especially aggravated within her classroom, think about how her style of teaching and expectations may be affecting your child's behavior. Let the teacher know what discipline techniques seem to work best at home.

℗ If your child's poor behavior is a constant problem, you need to identify and understand its root. Begin by ruling out physical causes, such as ADD. Problems with hearing or vision, learning disorders, or issues with peers may also cause disruptive or rebellious behavior.

℗ Draw up a game plan, considering short-term solutions for the problem behavior and formulating a plan for the long run. Come up with specific guidelines that you, your child, and the teacher can jointly follow. Make sure you are specific in what you expect, and explain things to your child in clear and simple terms.

◉ Develop a daily or weekly report card to monitor your child's work and behavior. He will no doubt seek to avoid your scrutiny, making this an especially effective scheme.

◉ When discussing your child's behavior problems, focus on his behavior rather than on him.

When it comes to behavior problems, you have to make sure the parents and teachers are together. I expect parents may do something differently at home, but they need to back me up in the classroom. Show your kids you expect them to behave in school and there must be a very good reason for whatever the teacher says there. You don't want to say the teacher is always right, but let them know there's a good reason to follow along.
—*Susan Draughn, 7th and 8th grade special education teacher for 24 years, Sunman, Indiana*

◉

If a child has a behavior issue, often parents feel the teacher is at fault because the problematic behavior is taking place at school rather than home. In one instance, after listening to her son, a parent came to school criticizing and confronting me, which gave her child the impression he could confront me, as well. He felt 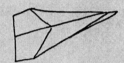 that he didn't have to respect me. I invited her to come in and sit in my office where her son couldn't see her observing the class, and that gave her a clearer perspective on the situation and his behavior. In this instance, it was a home issue the parent didn't want to admit: Marital problems were causing the child to act out in frustration by bullying other kids at school.
—*Joy Pumphrey, 2nd and 3rd grade teacher for 12 years, Clearwater, Florida*

◉

A lot of times kids have behavior problems because they don't understand the classroom work and they figure it's better to act up than show they don't know how to do it.
—*Jody Chambliss, kindergarten, 1st grade, and remedial reading teacher for 15 years, Abilene, Texas*

◉

Accept a teacher's explanation of poor behavior and work with your child to address the behavior and change it. It can be hard to admit your child is not always right—but it can't always be someone else's fault. Too often parents blame others for the actions of their child.
—*Amy Shaver, kindergarten and 1st grade teacher for 10 years, Bondurant, Iowa*

You need to educate your child about what behavior is appropriate, because the greater the concentration put on good behavior, the better your child will learn. And the reverse is also true—the more distracted your child is by disciplinary matters, the less efficient his education will be.
—*Steve C., 2nd grade to high school teacher for 15 years, Framingham, Massachusetts*

When a child is inattentive and off task, he won't be able to learn anything, and this will impact grades and academic success. When I approach a parent about behavioral issues, I say, "These are the specific behaviors your child is exhibiting in the classroom and this is how it's affecting his academic performance." That's what the parent cares about, not that he's running about the room like a little tornado driving his teacher crazy, but that he's not paying attention or completing assignments and will end up with a D in math because of it.
—*Martha Ann Chandler, 3rd to 6th grade teacher for 14 years, Florence, South Carolina*

At times, my sons try to rationalize and excuse their actions, refusing to take responsibility for their own behavior and instead blaming it on a peer or the teacher. I say, "Look at the options you had open to you. You made the wrong choice."
—*Andrea B., mom of three boys ages 15, 9, and 7*

This year my stepson started kindergarten, and I already knew he was a wild boy who often needed his reins pulled in on him. On the second day the teacher told me he was having behavior problems. I said, "You've got to be really firm with him and set boundaries." Then I let her know she had our full support, and gave her some tips on what works for us at home as far as his behavior is concerned, which saved her three weeks of trying to figure it out on her own.
—*Kallie Leyba, 1st and 2nd grade teacher for 2 years and mom of Lauren, 11, Lucas, 8, and Samson, 4, Highlands Ranch, Colorado*

Teacher tricks that parents can use at home to get good behavior include having constantly high expectations and giving kids jobs to do, such as chores.

—Anne Marie Fritton, 4th grade teacher for 3 years, Depew, New York

When it comes to students who have behavioral problems in class, the most beneficial thing is consistency between home and school. It is so helpful when the parents and teacher have the same purpose of trying to help the child, instead of feeling like its an us versus her situation. Emotions can get in the way, and it can feel like you and the teacher are competing for a certain way of doing things, but you need to get past that. Try to be approachable instead of pointing fingers.

—Pepper Griffith, 1st, 2nd, 5th, and special education teacher for 7 years, Atlanta, Georgia

To prevent behavior problems, you need a combination of expectations for excellent behavior coupled with an understanding of a child's individual needs. Some children respond better to behavior contracts. When these are handled sensitively, they can be successful in turning around problem behavior. A daily report home to parents can be another facet of the plan.

—Deborah Berris, 3rd, 5th, and 8th grade teacher for 5 years

In second grade, my son decided he was going to be the class clown. His teacher was great—very energetic and right on top of the problem. She immediately sent a note home, and we sat down with our son and talked about taking responsibility for himself. Right off the bat, we took away privileges, and I had the teacher send me home progress reports every week. As long as he knew those notes were going home, he was fine! And as the saying goes: If you can keep a kid on a behavior for more than 21 days, he's been changed. He's still not a perfect kid, but it toned him down.

—Jennifer O'Gorman, mom of Olivia, 11, Jake, 9, Sam, 7, Annabelle, 4, Luke, 2, and Eleanor, 1, Lebanon, Maine

For really troublesome behaviors, include the teacher and put your child on a behavior modification plan with positive incentives. Be consistent. Use small increments; your child has to be able to feel success. Pick only one or two problem areas, because it takes time to change a behavior. Then when your kid has success in one area, he will be more willing to improve in others.

—*Kay Symons, special education and kindergarten to 8th grade teacher for 27 years, South Georgia*

How Can I Encourage My Shy Child to Participate More in Class?

@ Assess your child's participation by questioning him about his classroom habits: Does he raise his hand often or only when he's sure of the answer? Is he willing to take a chance and guess the answer out loud or does he only answer when called on?

@ Encourage your child to engage, because he will learn much more through active participation than by passively sitting and staring listlessly at the teacher as the conversation swirls about him.

@ If your child has trouble speaking up in class, let him know it's okay to make mistakes while participating. Tell the teacher that your child is shy, and have her call on him in class in a nonthreatening way. Some students just need encouragement to speak in front of others.

If kids are more engaged with the teacher, they're more likely to talk in class. Encourage your child to foster a connection with the teacher through small talk before or after class.

If he can get to know the teacher as a real person, instead of just the adult in the front of the room, he will become more comfortable when he has a question or knows an answer.
—Ken Pauly, high school social studies teacher for 13 years, St. Louis Park, Minnesota

Children who learn to ask for help when they need it in class are much more effective students than those who can't or won't.
—Paul O'Brien, 7th to 12th grade math and science teacher for 27 years, Sheffield, Massachusetts

Class participation depends a lot on the teacher-student relationship. If a teacher gives children permission to be wrong, class participation increases. I have kids who don't want to talk at all, and I try to help them by saying things like, "If you don't know the answer right now, it's okay, I can come back to you," so they feel good about speaking up. Even when I taught older kids, I had shy ones; but I always got them to participate in their own ways, including having them write down their ideas.
—Kathy Carabine, pre-k and 3rd grade teacher for 16 years, Boston, Massachusetts

Should I Worry About What's in My Child's School Record?

☺ Check your child's school records, especially if he has had behavior issues, social difficulties, or a negative relationship with a particular teacher. Getting a copy of his information can go a long way toward easing your fears and answering your questions.

☺ School records should only contain information pertaining to your child's education, and not out-of-school incidents or family information unrelated to schooling. Make sure negative comments, and information potentially harmful to your child's reputation are not in the record to which his future teachers will have access.

@ Certain sections of your child's record are temporary and do not move with him when he transfers or graduates from that particular school. Temporary records include documents about guidance services, parent-teacher conferences, and anecdotal information such as referrals and teacher observations.

@ Some records, however, are permanent, following your child from school to school and remaining on file even after he graduates high school. Permanent records provide quick and easy access to essential information about your child's academic history, including grades, test results, and attendance information, as well as medical records, such as immunization histories.

@ Check through teachers' comments, standardized test results, and any reports from the school counselor, psychologist, or other specialists.

Things generally get purged from your child's school record at the end of each level, such as between elementary school and middle school. However, if your child is brought up for evaluation for a behavior concern, that would remain in there. Unfortunately, this does give teachers an advance feel for that child, which isn't always fair, as what happened in first grade may no longer be a problem by fifth grade.
—Joy Pumphrey, 2nd and 3rd grade teacher for 12 years, Clearwater, Florida

Parents who look through their child's school record might walk out thinking they understand something when they really might not. If you want to find out something about your medical history and go into the doctor's records, how much of what's in there is going to mean something to you? A child could get a 50 on a test, but it could be out of a possible 489 points, which a parent might not know. If you do look through school records, ask to talk to a person who can explain what you need to know.
—Anne Wonson Curry, 5th to 12th grade math and science teacher for 12 years, Rockport, Massachusetts

When I have new students come in, I don't go into their student files. I don't want to set myself up for a predisposed inclination. Sometimes a student just needs to be in a different environment to do his best. If I need to know something, I go to the parent first. I try to stay away from the records because they could be biased, and then I would think something that isn't accurate. I try to give students the benefit of the doubt.
—*Laurie Olmstead, 7th and 8th grade math and science teacher for 4 years, Union, Maine*

Sometimes personality conflicts between a child and teacher affect the records, as they include past teachers' comments.
—*Lawanna Ford, 5th grade teacher for 25 years, Argonia, Kansas*

How Do I Obtain Access to My Child's Records?

☺ If your child's school receives federal funds, the Federal Family Education Rights and Privacy Act (FERPA), an amendment passed in 1974, requires the school to allow you to access your child's records. The school must produce your child's record in its entirety within 45 days of your request. Keep and document a dated copy of your petition with a return receipt for certified mail, or a signed receipt from the school office if you hand deliver it.

☺ Although you are not allowed to remove your child's records from the school, you are allowed to make copies.

☺ You can seek redress if your child's school violates the FERPA law. Try dealing with the school's obstinance locally first, by contacting the principal or superintendent. If you are displeased with the response, you can file a complaint with the Family Policy Compliance Office, U.S. Department of Education, 400 Maryland Avenue, SW, Washington, DC 20202-5901 (www.ed.gov/policy/gen/guid/fpco/index.html).

How Do I Get Something Purged from the Record?

◉ If you find inaccuracies in your child's records, you can request that the school remove the information. Request an amendment and follow through to verify that the school completes the change.

◉ If the school will not let you purge certain information, you still have the right to file a complaint with the aforementioned FERPA Office and add an explanatory note to address the information. By adding comments to your child's record, you have a chance to communicate another side of the story, explain extenuating circumstances, and take back some control over how the records present your child.

◉ You also have the right to a formal hearing if you disagree with the school's decision not to purge the information.

Peers, Bullies, & Cliques

What Role Do Peers Play in My Child's Academic Life?

◉ Your child's social life impacts his entire school experience. Especially in the earlier years, children with solid friendships seem to do better academically and adjust better to yearly changes.

◉ Peer relationships are a crucial guiding element of your child's development because his peers are the individuals with whom he spends the bulk of his day. His relationships are the stimuli for self-discovery and emotional growth. Through them, he learns crucial social skills, like how to interact within groups and manage conflict.

◉ In many ways, your child's social development is just as important as his academic progress because his acquaintances heavily influence his attitude and behavior. If his friends care about academics and schoolwork, your child is more likely to care, too.

◉ As your child starts middle school, he will find peer acceptance and approval increasingly important, and the desire to be liked and accepted will heavily impact his decision-making processes. During the tween years, social circles begin to establish norms for opinions, attitudes toward school, and dress codes, which your child will likely internalize and reinterpret as his own standards.

Peers play a very important role in a child's school life. Get to know the kids your child hangs around with by having them over to your home a lot, and try to get to know their parents as well.

—*Sharon Stubbs, 5th and 6th grade teacher for 28 years, Hopkins, Michigan*

Peer influence is very powerful, especially once kids hit the middle school years. Therefore, you need to make sure your child learns good social skills at a young age. Children should feel like part of a group or a team; they need to learn to share, work together, and cooperate.
—*Beverly Hammond, kindergarten to 4th grade teacher for 31 years, West Point, Virginia*

What Can I Do to Help My Child's Social Development?

© Poor social skills can negatively impact academic work because of the social nature of the school environment. Try to objectively watch your child in social settings, and talk to his teacher to assess how he reacts to the other children in the classroom.

© Teaching good social behavior is especially important for children who have difficulty making or maintaining friendships. Often these children have characteristics that make them difficult to get along with such as short tempers, trouble cooperating with others, or problems responding to social cues.

© Activities at home, such as playing board games, can be useful in teaching your child how to be a good sport—keeping his cool when he gets upset and losing gracefully, while team games like charades can teach him to be a team player, to communicate in groups, and to cooperate with others.

© Encourage your child to take responsibility for his own actions and talk about how he could appropriately handle himself in various situations.

© If your child has difficulty fitting in, he is likely to experience a great deal of pain and may eventually turn to negative or violent behavior. It is your job to worry and intervene if your child has trouble socializing. Ask if he wants you to contact the teacher. Most likely he will answer a resounding "No," but asking opens the door and lets him know you're ready and willing to help.

◉ Remind your child that everyone craves attention. Small acts like flashing a smile or passing an encouraging note can start a friendship. Encourage your child to congratulate his peers on accomplishments, like a well-written poem or a soccer goal. Suggest he save a seat for someone on the bus or volunteer to partner with someone on a project.

At home, parents need to get their loners away from TV and involved in activities. Nothing opens kids up more than being involved in something. They need to know there are adults who value them, take them seriously, and encourage them to flourish. You have to figure out which button to push, and it takes a lot of parental energy.
—*Chris Grimm, 7th grade social studies teacher for 3 years, Ventura, California*

Is There Anything I Can Do to Help My Child Handle Peer Pressure?

◉ Unfortunately, fitting in during early adolescence often means conformity. Most often peer pressure is indirect, so following the crowd can feel like an independent decision even though it may contradict your child's personal standard of conduct.

◉ Your child likely fears being branded or ostracized for speaking up when he disagrees with the group. Let him know his friends will probably wind up valuing his opinion more if he speaks with his own voice and acts from his own values. Often, they are feeling the same way but are too timid to say anything.

◉ Let your child know your values and opinions. Don't be preachy, as lectures will turn his attention off. However, if you see a character on television make a bad decision, such as lighting up a cigarette, it's okay to disagree with the choice and remind your child that "everyone else is doing it" is not a valid reason for doing something.

◉ Encourage your child to think critically before he acts and to consider whether his decisions are truly his own.

◉ Develop your child's self-esteem by supporting his independence. Encourage him to get involved in extracurricular activities that introduce him to different crowds than those he interacts with during the school day.

◉ If you hear about your child's friends or classmates getting in trouble, talk to him about the incident. Ask how he feels about it, whether he thinks his friends did the right thing, and how he thinks you would want him to act in a similar situation.

◉ Tell your child he can always lay the blame on you. Let him know that claiming his parents want him home at a certain time is an effective excuse to get out of a tough situation.

◉ Become friendly with the parents of your child's friends, even if just casually, so you can keep each other informed about concerns that arise.

◉ Keep a constant radar out for issues involving bullying and clique situations. These issues often build in the later elementary school years and become more rampant in middle school.

Middle school is only three years long, but socially they are the most difficult years. Make sure your child knows there's nothing wrong with him, and other students are making choices that have nothing to do with him. Make sure his self-esteem is being affected as little as possible. If he's really struggling, dig into extracurricular activities outside of school, such as a community or church group, so he doesn't feel socially isolated.
—*Erika Bare, 6th to 8th grade special education teacher for 3 years, West Linn, Oregon*

Talk with your child about the friends he hangs around with and about making good choices among peers.
—*Kristi Hartman, 1st grade teacher for 10 years*

In terms of peer influence, be aware of your child's habits and mood. If your child has a solid foundation at home, it will be easier for him to say no to inappropriate or dangerous situations. Personally, I've told my children peer pressure is the one time they *can* lie: make up an excuse, blame it on me, or do whatever they need to get out of a bad situation.
—*Pam Pottorff, 3rd and 4th grade teacher and 8th grade reading teacher for 5 years,*
Sioux City, Nebraska

Peer issues are beginning to surface at younger and younger ages—even as young as preschool. Encourage your child to be his own person, to be a leader, and to come up with his own ideas, and to be creative.
—*Joy Pumphrey, 2nd and 3rd grade teacher for 12 years, Clearwater, Florida*

We use role playing at home to encourage and set the tone for peer interactions—we'll say things like, "Your friends want to do this, how do you feel about that?" From smoking to vandalism to cheating on a test, we make sure when they encounter these things, it won't be foreign. We gear it for their age, like using the example, "What do you do if you break a friend's toy and he wants you to lie about it?" We walk them through it to help them understand how the other person feels. It's important to prepare them for these situations.
—*Natalie Dyess, mom of Michaela, 8, Jacob, 6, and Anna, 2, Lawrenceville, Georgia*

Peer pressure started in preschool for my daughter! I was dressing her for school one morning and put on her colored socks that matched her outfit. She told me she had to wear white socks. When I asked her why she said one little girl wouldn't play with her unless she wore white socks. All I can tell her is to stand up for herself as much as possible.
—*Sheila Cross, mom of Emily, 8, Memphis, Tennessee*

Because peer influence is so powerful, really take the time to get to know your child's friends. Invite them over and talk with them while they're hanging out.
—*Keith Averell, 3rd grade teacher for 27 years, Pleasanton, California*

How Widespread Are Bullying Problems?

@ Bullying is a problem endemic to school systems across the country. The tragic events at Columbine High School in Littleton, Colorado, brought the damaging effects of bullying to national attention.

@ On average, 10% of students are loners. These children are rejected by their peers and lack a solid group of friends, attending school each week with little companionship. The stress of rejection makes it more difficult for a child to concentrate and function during the day, making school an unpleasant place, and leading to academic struggles and behavioral problems and frequent absences.

@ Studies indicate that 75% of children are bullied or harassed at sometime during their school career, 42% of children have personally witnessed bullying, and 56% say they are aware of bullying going on at their school. On any given day, about 25% of students in the United States are victimized by bullies. One child in ten is regularly bullied, and the repeated abuse impacts student attendance records. According to the National Association of School Psychologists, up to 160,000 children stay home from school each day because they fear bullying at school.

@ Most children are bullied in elementary school; in middle school the number of incidents decreases, but the severity increases drastically.

@ More than 60% of victims report that their schools responded poorly—or not at all—when notified of bullying behaviors. This response may be a result of the fact that parents, teachers, and principals alike generally underestimate the extent of bullying in their school communities. Parents obviously do not want their child to be either a bully or a victim, and tend to ignore situations of social conflict.

@ Teachers often are unaware of the extent to which social problems plague their schools because most bullying occurs on the playground or after school, rather than during class time. For this reason, disciplinary measures are more punitive than preventative, and therefore often are ineffectual.

@ Teachers tend to notice the most troublemaking and visible bullies, like those who disrupt class and end up in physical bouts. Other kinds of harassment, done in more covert and targeted ways, generally stay where the bully intends—below adult radar. Bullying between girls escapes the attention of the teacher even more because of its quieter, less disruptive, and nonphysical nature. Many teachers either aren't aware of it or ignore incidents because they don't perceive any immediate danger.

You *hear* about fewer and fewer behavior problems today because principals, and the administration as a whole, are applying pressure on the teachers to keep it that way. A little known secret about the educational system is that teachers get rewarded for keeping things quiet, so they're less willing to rock the boat. Principals receive merit pay, raises, and financial compensation when things are going well; so it turns into a pattern of keeping problems quiet to get more money.
—*Lynn M., high school, deaf students, and middle school special education teacher for 21 years, Boston, Massachusetts*

What Exactly Counts As Bullying?

@ Sometimes it's hard to know if authorities will consider your child's situation bullying, so it is important to understand the different forms of bullying. Direct bullying includes actions such as physical violence, teasing, taunting, and threatening. Indirect bullying happens when bullies intentionally socially isolate others. Bullying falls into three main categories:

✤ *Physical bullying:* The easiest to identify, this category includes blatant physical attacks such as kicking, punching, hair pulling, and pinching, as well as more insidious actions.

❋ *Verbal bullying:* Verbal attacks include name-calling, gossiping, sexist remarks, sexually suggestive comments, racist or ethnic slurs, unwanted phone calls, and threats—anonymous or otherwise.

❋ *Emotional intimidation:* This form of abuse diminishes a person's sense of self through isolation and exclusion. Much more common with girls, this type of bullying includes subtle gestures like facial expressions, body language, note writing, whispering, and snickering. Emotional intimidation goes into full swing during the middle school years as children begin to experience the emotional and physical changes of adolescence.

◉ Bullies use an imbalance of power to dominate a victim. This imbalance can involve differences in age, physical size, strength, or popularity. In some instances, many children may band together to target a single child.

◉ Bullying situations are continuing cycles of physical or psychological intimidation where the aggressor maintains control over the situation.

Who Fits the Bully Profile?

◉ Bullying is a behavioral pattern most often learned at home. Bullies often lack close relationships with their parents; this can inhibit their ability to feel empathy. Also, if a child is physically or emotionally abused, he may internalize the idea that it is appropriate to interact with others using violent behavior.

◉ While there are bullies who suffer from low self-esteem, most tend to be extremely narcissistic, with an egotistical viewpoint that prevents them from seeing situations from other people's perspectives. They desire power, think they have the right to control other people's thoughts, actions, and possessions, are primarily 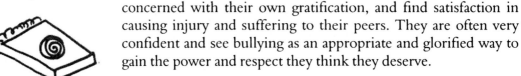 concerned with their own gratification, and find satisfaction in causing injury and suffering to their peers. They are often very confident and see bullying as an appropriate and glorified way to gain the power and respect they think they deserve.

● A bully is intolerant toward people he sees as different, feeling they are unworthy of respect and should be excluded from the group.

● If you observe an incident of bullying or the school calls you in because your child has been involved, recognize the typical defensive reactions of a bully:

✳ He denies he did anything wrong or trivializes the event by claiming his behavior was innocent teasing or fun: "We were just playing" or, "It was just a joke."

✳ He counts on the support of the bystanders to deny the victim's side of the story.

✳ He blames the victim for the problem, effectively escaping responsibility by casting the bullied child as the bully.

Bullies are very domineering children. They are usually outspoken, aggressive, controlling, and think nothing is wrong with their behavior. Usually, they're kids with unsupportive parents, but sometimes they have parents who give them too much attention without censoring their bad behaviors. These parents think their kids are being assertive when they're really being aggressive.
—Kay Symons, special education and kindergarten to 8th grade teacher for 27 years, South Georgia

How Can Bullying Affect My Child?

● The effects of bullying can be devastating and long lasting. Bullying can compromise a child's sense of security and entire well-being, and often isolate him from peers who do not want to lose status or put themselves at risk of being bullied by associating with him.

☺ When your child is bullied he experiences a great deal of mental stress, which can take its toll on his body. He may experience anything from headaches and stomachaches to ulcers. Girls are especially prone to expressing their social anxieties by focusing on their bodies. In extreme cases this can lead to anorexia, bulimia, and obsessive exercising.

☺ Bullying can become an academic issue for your child. A child's grades often suffer when he is bullied because conflicts in school leave him unable to concentrate.

☺ The effects of bullying are not limited to the children directly involved in peer power struggles. Students in schools where bullying occurs often feel less safe. Also, when school officials don't react to bullying, students are likely to respond by becoming more aggressive and intolerant because they interpret such behavior as socially acceptable.

How Do I Recognize When My Child Is Being Bullied?

☺ Victims are often reluctant to seek adult intervention because they believe doing so will only bring about further abuse.

☺ Instead of pressuring your child for information, be patient and remind him he can always tell you if something bothers or hurts him. Keep the lines of communication open by asking about related, but more neutral topics, like classes, friends, and activities.

☺ Even if your child will not admit to being bullied, there are a number of signs that can give you insight into the situation. Look for the following:

  ✴ He shows an abrupt lack of interest in school, experiences a sudden drop in grades, or tries to get out of going to school.

  ✴ He changes his routine to avoid a time period or situation where he is especially vulnerable. For example, he may avoid gym class or the cafeteria or insist you drive him to school. The lunch room and bathroom are the most common

Some kids aren't as vocal about what's going on, so you have to watch for nonverbal cues. Is he happy or miserable? Is he avoiding homework? If your kid loves gym but is suddenly not excited on gym day or isn't sleeping, eating, or smiling, you really need to watch him, especially if he's not a talker. Also, talk to other parents. I knew one mother whose kid was really quiet, and she asked me to let her know if I heard anything from my kids about how he was doing in class or if there were problems. We set up a buddy system so she could keep tabs on her kid.
—*Ellen Cameron, mom of Alison, 8, and Hilary, 4, Lexington, Massachusetts*

sites for bullying, so if he's suddenly starving after school, claiming he lost his lunch money, or always makes a mad dash to the bathroom when he gets home, he may be avoiding these areas.

✹ He comes home with bruises or loses money and other items frequently without plausible explanations.

✹ He becomes preoccupied with some aspect of his appearance such as his weight, hair, or glasses.

✹ He seems fine during the weekends but depressed during the week.

✹ He appears sad, angry, or frightened after receiving a phone call or email.

✹ He shows physical signs of stress and has problems sleeping.

✹ His personality undergoes a major shift. For example, he may regress, acting infantile and overly clingy. He may also suddenly act aggressively toward family members, or develop intense mood swings.

✹ He withdraws from family and social activities he used to enjoy, preferring instead to spend time alone.

✹ He talks about moving, running away, or changing schools, vocalizing a desire to escape his present situation.

◉ A sudden drop in grades may be an appeal to you or his teachers for help, or may be his way of drawing attention away from embarrassing social issues.

◉ Bullies generally pick on shy, quiet, and sensitive types because they are the least likely to defend themselves, retaliate, or report the violence.

How Should I Frame My Discussions with My Bullied Child?

◉ One of the most common misperceptions is that bullying is somehow a normal and necessary part of growing up. If you get a kids-will-be-kids reaction from the administration, point out that all cases of bullying are forms of violence and dismissing the problem only aggravates the situation.

◉ Respond supportively if your child has an experience with bullying and send the message that you are there for him, you believe him, and he is not alone in this struggle. The best thing you can do is make family and home a refuge, where your child feels accepted and loved. Remind him what is going on is not his fault and the blame belongs on the bully, but also talk to him about the impression he makes on others. Help him identify behaviors that trigger or encourage the bully, like acting overly emotional.

◉ Unfortunately, authorities often blame the victim for instigating a bully's abuse. Many teachers and school officials claim the victim is being attacked because he lacks social skills, and will refer him for emotional counseling when the majority of his problems stem directly from the bullying situation.

◉ Avoid barraging your child with questions that may make him feel embarrassed or ashamed. If he sees you angry or upset, he may think he has disappointed you. If you try to minimize, rationalize, or explain away the bully's violence, your child will think he cannot come to you for help.

◉ Tell your child the way to fight back is to inform the school authorities or his teacher about what is taking place. Warn him against engaging in physical retaliation, threats, or other forms of revenge.

◉ Your response is important to teaching your child problem-solving skills. If you impulsively change your child's class or school to avoid the bully without exploring other options, you may teach your child to run away from problems instead of confronting them.

Tell your child, "These are ways some people deal with this kind of situation," or "When I was in school, this is how I dealt with it, what do you think about trying that?" Sometimes you need to take it further. Help him develop a more positive attitude about himself, and let him know this is not something he should put up with, especially if the bully is physically threatening him. There are lots of examples of bullies in literature, like *Bridge to Terabithia.* One of the characters is bullying children in the schoolyard, and the classmates are very concerned. The book shows you need to have more sympathy for the bully as well, because he may have problems at home. Explain different situations to your child and ask how he would handle them. Let him know he shouldn't put up with it, should be ready to encounter it, and that a bully is a person who has problems himself and probably needs help. Tell him to go to the teacher so she can help the bully as well.

—*Kathy Traficanti, 4th to 6th grade teacher for 9 years, Brighton, Massachusetts*

In first grade my daughter was coming home with bruises and broken skin. A girl in her class would come up to her on the playground and bite and pinch her. Her teacher saw a little bit of the problem and would separate them, but eventually I had to take the problem to the principal. The response was, "We'll try to keep an eye on her." Around the same time this was going on, my daughter was standing in line and a boy pushed her. She told the lunchroom monitor and was told to stop whining and sit down. These were not acceptable responses. If there's an issue, there's no sense in waiting—go right down and deal with it. I was told my daughter must have a victim personality. I ended up having to go to the principal. He talked to the teacher first and tried to talk to the administration and agree upon a tactic. The issue was resolved when the girl bullying my daughter was moved to sit up by the teacher.

—*Mom of an 8-year-old*

How Can I Intervene to Help
My Child Deal with a Bully?

◉ Before you step in to confront the problem it's better to see if you can help your child to solve it. Learning how to stand up for one's self is an important skill for dealing with many situations in life. Taking over may also make the bully see your child as a vulnerable target.

◉ Although some bullying requires adult intervention to stop, strike a balance between helping your child and being overprotective. Never hesitate to step in if his efforts to stop the bullying aren't successful. Also, if you fear your child is in any kind of physical danger at school, notify school officials immediately.

◉ Share your plan with your child. Asking what he would like to do about the situation gives your child a sense of control and can help rebuild his damaged self-esteem. If he doesn't agree with your approach but you know it's the best thing, explain to him that even though you value his input, his safety comes first.

◉ Don't let your child focus too much on the problem. Get him involved in new activities and groups to build his confidence and take his mind off the bullying.

◉ It's a good idea to keep your own records. Know the names of those involved and the dates, times, and circumstances of all incidents. This will help you know if the bullying is ongoing. Submit a copy of your report to the school to make sure it also has a written record of the incidents.

◉ Although your child's teacher may not be present when problems arise between students, she may be able to offer insights that help you get a better handle on the situation and serve as an ally to remedy it. She's in the primary position to offer the best help because she's right there with the children every day.

◉ If there are certain times during the day, like recess or lunch, that are especially stressful for your child, ask teachers to provide him with a safe and secure short-term alternative, like going to the library or the gym. Avoid making this a long-term solution, however, because you don't want to give him the idea he can just escape his problems by avoiding them.

◉ If your child's school has antibullying policies and procedures in place, there may be a specific person in the building who is trained to intervene effectively.

Arrange a meeting with that person or your child's classroom teacher and bring your child to make sure he plays a primary role in designing a solution to the problem.

◎ When bullying incidents occur on the bus or the walk to and from school, it is hard for schools to resolve the problem. Adult monitors cannot feasibly be present on the route your child walks or on the bus. If you have time, walk or drive with your child; if you work, have a friend or an older sibling help out.

◎ In almost all cases, it is not a good idea to approach the bully or his parents directly, as they could be defensive, uncooperative, or quick to blame your child. It is more effective to approach the teacher, school principal, coach, or other authority figure first.

It is definitely not your role to approach the other child's parents if the bullying is happening in school. You need to go to the appropriate teachers. Teachers aren't always aware when there's a clique or bully situation. They need to communicate among the special area teachers and the classroom teacher so everyone's aware of it.
—Joy Pumphrey, 2nd and 3rd grade teacher for 12 years, Clearwater, Florida

Starting in the upper elementary grades, issues involving cliques and peer-related situations become much less visible to teachers. Time in the classroom is focused and highly academic, so most peer interactions take place during recess or lunch, when the teacher is not around. I often have to rely on parents sharing with me what has gone on in terms of cliques or peer issues so I can be sensitized and on the lookout for it in the classroom.
—Jennifer M., 5th grade teacher for 6 years, Boston, Massachusetts

Bullying is really isolated to when the teacher is *not* around, which means I'm the last to know. So when parents come to me angry that I haven't done anything to stop this bullying, they don't realize it's the first I've heard of it. Of course I wouldn't purposely let their child be bullied. No way—I would do anything to stop it. However, teachers aren't usually there during recess and lunch.

—*Kallie Leyba, 1st and 2nd grade teacher for 2 years and mom of Lauren, 11, Lucas, 8, and Samson, 4, Highlands Ranch, Colorado*

I don't know if bullying is any worse than it was ten years ago, but I do know we are infinitely more aware of and sensitive to it. We are continually looking for strategies to address it in constructive ways. It's pretty well established that a bully's behavior is usually linked to personal issues of his own. There's a lot of emphasis on general behavior expectations, problem solving, conflict resolution, and empowering kids to stand up to bullies and take power away from them. You have to look at the specific behavior very carefully to distinguish between what's not harmful and what is. It's hard because no one wants to receive a phone call saying their kid is bullying. There's also sometimes a difference in the way parents and teachers handle situations. I've had parents who tell their kids, "If someone hits you, just smack him back." When that's the family message, you're asking children to respond in a way that contradicts what is taught at school.

—*Sue Abrams, elementary school principal and former 1st to 5th grade teacher for 22 years, Natick, Massachusetts*

Make the school aware of bullies as soon as possible, in a way that doesn't embarrass your child or aggravate the situation. You can simply say, "This is what I've been told has been going on."

—*Florence Michel, middle school teacher for 8 years, New York, New York, and Baltimore, Maryland*

Especially with bullying, it is important to speak to guidance counselors to go about fixing the situation or at least making it more tolerable. Last year I had one kid being picked on very badly, and the guidance counselor spoke to all the teachers and isolated the few kids instigating the bullying. That took care of it right away, and the kid hasn't been bullied since then.

—*Amy Watson, 7th to 12th grade teacher for 5 years, Oyster Bay, New York*

If your child is being bullied he needs to go to the teacher, and you need to get administration involved right away. If you feel the problem is not being addressed, don't let teachers or administrators or anyone off the hook. Don't accept "No" or "We don't see any problems here" for an answer. If a child is expressing concerns, there is a problem, and if you don't deal with it, that can cause huge problems later on. Don't push it under the rug. Go as high as you must to get somebody to listen, because it could be your child's safety at stake.

—*Laurie Olmstead, 7th and 8th grade math and science teacher for 4 years, Union, Maine*

Is It Possible to Bully-Proof My Child?

The best way to stay on top of your child's social situation is to keep all the lines of communication open—with your child, his friends, teachers, and administrators. Broach the subject periodically to keep bullying on their radar.

Teach your child a way to approach teachers without sounding like he's tattling. If he is confident and polite and tells the teacher, "I asked him to stop bothering me and he won't listen," then she will know your child tried to stop the problem on his own and will be more likely to pay attention and help him.

Help your child find an ally. Even having one friend to sit with on the bus or check in with during the day can be a great confidence booster for him. If possible, buddy him up with someone older.

Children can resort to extreme options when they feel out of control or desperate about a situation, so teach your child to respond to a bully in an assertive, but nonviolent way. He can firmly tell the bully to leave him alone or even turn and walk away without saying a word. The key is showing the bully that your child will not tolerate being picked on. Make sure he never uses violence.

◎   Role-play specific situations or hypothetical encounters in order to arm your child with comeback strategies.

Bullying is particularly bad in middle school. Some kids seem to be bully magnets, but there are things they can learn to do, and some of them are pretty easy. Like if they are wearing white knee socks and everyone else is wearing black knee socks, buy them some black knee socks. It saves them a lot of anguish.
—*Claudia Flanders, kindergarten to 8th grade teacher for 34 years, Santa Monica, California*

My sons have been picked on at school. We are a little unorthodox because we believe they should defend themselves. We tell them to try to get out of the fight with other skills, but that they may have to hit back in some situations. They may get in trouble, but we don't want them to grow up thinking they can't defend themselves.
—*Alesha Worra, mom of Brandon, 12, and Travis, 11, Greer, South Carolina*

What Should I Do If the School Tells Me My Child Is a Bully?

◉ If you receive word that your child has been bullying others, be honest with yourself. Even though your first reaction will probably be to protect your child, don't blame the other children or the person who brought the bullying incident to your attention. If your child has been acting aggressively or violently, you want to put an end to that behavior as soon as possible so he can learn to control himself and interact positively with other children.

◉ Often, parents of bullies simply consider their child a "leader," and fail to consider the implications of his actions. To look at your child's behavior objectively and recognize whether he is a bully, familiarize yourself with the different ways children manipulate their peers.

◉ Your daughter is more likely to use bullying techniques that involve more subtle forms of intimidation than physical violence, such as smirks, deliberate secret-telling, note passing, and starting rumors.

◉ Begin addressing the issue by working with the school. Strive to be nondefensive and listen openly to their concerns. Find out exactly what happened and ask your child for his version of the events. Be sure to find out what the school has done or is planning to do to deal with the situation.

◉ If the teacher tells you your child got into a fight with another child, you have a long and difficult investigation before you. Ask her how the fight started and whether she witnessed the event or heard about it secondhand. Get a feel for the classroom climate and find out if there is something that seems to spark your child's inappropriate behavior. Talk to the recess teacher to find out whether his behavior is the same in different environments.

◉ Consider why your child has developed aggressive behavior. He may have low self-esteem, academic problems, or problems controlling his emotions, or he may resort to bullying because he doesn't know how else to behave or lacks the social skills to make and maintain healthy friendships. He may benefit from counseling to work out the underlying issues so he can succeed socially.

◉ Let your child know his behavior is unacceptable. Help him come up with new,

more positive ways to handle conflicts. After brainstorming more constructive behavior, use role-play to have him practice the new responses.

@ Nurture empathy in your child and help him develop a vocabulary to talk about
how he feels at home. He may be acting out because he feels powerless or ignored.
Examine his time at home and make sure he is getting enough supervision after
school.

@ Look at your child's peer interaction outside of school and at home. Pay close
attention to the way he acts with siblings. Listen to him talk about his friends and
note whether he belittles or mocks them.

@ Ask your child's teacher about his social life and whether she considers his social circle exclusive and cliquey or friendly.

@ Get to know your child's friends and discourage friendships with kids who behave meanly or aggressively. Bullying can be contagious, and your child may go
along with the negative behavior his friends display even though he is not inclined
to act that way on his own.

@ It is also helpful to talk to other parents, especially those of your child's friends,
and ask them to honestly share with you any concerns they may have.

@ Focus on positive social relationships for your child. Help him find a team or
group in which he can have a structured social experience. He may have difficulty
establishing healthy friendships, so share a few tips with him:

    * He only controls half of a relationship, while his peers control the other
    half.

    * The best way to maintain his friendships is to show his friends kindness
    and respect, stick up for them, and be supportive.

    * He needs to apologize when he's wrong and accept other people's apolo-
    gies.

@ Children often learn good social skills by example, so arrange to have your
child spend time with a responsible older child. If you don't have any family members, friends, or neighbors who can help, try to find a mentor from the Big Brother
or Big Sister programs.

◉ If your child's behavior warrants discipline, think carefully before choosing the punishment. Yelling at him is likely to encourage his aggressive behavior, not squelch it. Try to come up with a constructive punishment, such as canceling play-dates until he can play nicely. Cut down your child's freedom until he shows the behavioral changes you seek.

◉ If your child has hurt or bullied another child, have him write an apology letter. Review it to make sure it expresses true remorse and an understanding of his actions, rather than veiled insults or buried jabs.

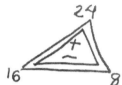

◉ Consider enrolling your child in a conflict resolution, friendship skills, anger management, or self-defense course to help him manage his emotions and reactions.

First and foremost, a parent needs to go into a bully situation with an open mind. Now that I have kids of my own, I understand how you want to defend your child and think he's done the right thing, but don't go into a situation on the defensive. Go in and hear what's going on. Don't assume your child is the same person at home as he is at school. Behavior is dynamic and situational, and this is especially true of adolescents. Most parents would say, "Well, he doesn't do that at home." Unless he has six brothers and sisters, of course he's not going to do it at home because there's no crowd to encourage him.
—*Chris Grimm, 7th grade social studies teacher for 3 years, Ventura, California*

The most important approach to take in bullying situations is one of open communication. A lot of times, a parent appears to be making an accusation rather than engaging in a conversation. If you make accusations, your child will not talk and you're not going to get down to what happened. The first step is sitting down with your child and talking about what's going on in school. If you hear him say, "Johnny's just a wimp," then at least you know where he's coming from. It's important for parents to try to listen. My own first inclination was to ask, "What were you *doing?*" but it's more helpful to approach the situation by asking what he thinks the problem is.
—*Angela McNutt, 6th to 12th grade Spanish teacher for 1 year, Glade Spring, Virginia*

If your child has been accused of being a bully, start by talking to him. Get him to be honest; say, "I'm going to have a conversation with you first, but I will be talking to your teacher as well," so he knows there are going to be consequences. You need to understand where he's coming from and know if it's true. Talk to the school counselor, and explore methods you can work on at home to build empathy.
—Erika Bare, 6th to 8th grade special education teacher for 3 years, West Linn, Oregon

The best thing parents can do when their child is a bully is put forth a team effort with the teachers. Parents should say, "We are stunned. Can we meet with my child and talk this over?" Teachers have taken on too much parenting already, and the parents need to take the responsibility of providing rewards or punishments at home. We all talk about reasonable punishments, and I write the contract up for both the parents and child to sign. Then we make up sheets that include expected behaviors, and the teacher can check off what does and does not happen at school, and the kid can take the form home for his parents to sign. We're talking about creating an intelligent, ethical adult, which doesn't happen without a lot of people helping each child.
—Claudia Flanders, kindergarten to 8th grade teacher for 34 years, Santa Monica, California

Parents of bullies are usually in denial because the bullies take over at home as well. One mother told me her son was bullying her. We tell parents not to engage in power struggles and encourage them to work together with their children to develop effective and healthy communication.
—Lynn M., high school, deaf students, and middle school special education teacher for 21 years, Boston, Massachusetts

I had one student who really needed help with anger management, and from this I realized the first step is acknowledging there is indeed a problem, and not being afraid to tackle it. Start out with guidance counselors—let them spend time with the student—then go from there. The guidance counselors know where to go for outside help.
—Lawanna Ford, 5th grade teacher for 25 years, Argonia, Kansas

I charge my children money if they start trouble. Once my son hit another boy at school for no reason. We charged him $25, which he paid off with chores around the house. That's a lot of money to a young child, and he never did it again.
—*Alesha Worra, mom of Brandon, 12, and Travis, 11, Greer, South Carolina*

My daughter has been following around this one girl, and the two of them together have been known to exclude other girls in their class. We are working on that. When she comes home from school, we get her to walk in someone else's shoes and say, "Well, how do you think that made the other girl feel?" We are constantly reinforcing that sense of empathy. It's a pretty esoteric concept for someone that young to grasp, so you have to turn it around on her to make her understand.
—*Amy Kamm, mom of Ava, 5, and Lily, 2, Burbank, California*

How Can I Teach My Child Not to Be a Bystander?

Most commonly, a child involved in a bullying situation is a bystander, an uncomfortable role to play. The bully makes the environment unfriendly, and if your child doesn't act when he knows he should, he may feel guilty about betraying his values.

Many children do not report bullying because they fear they will be labeled rats if they speak up. Let your child know he needs to tell an adult when he witnesses dangerous or destructive behavior.

Talk to your child about the different kinds of bystanders. Some try to be friends with everybody, but by playing both sides they worsen the situation by giving approval to bullies or deceiving victims, rather than acting as true friends.

Tell your children to find a trusted adult if they ever see any incidents of bullying. They need to find someone they can tell. In this day and age, you can't keep bullying to yourself.
—*Erika Bare, 6th to 8th grade special education teacher for 3 years, West Linn, Oregon*

We had an incident of sexual harassment in the private school my kids were in. The boys in my daughter's class picked a girl each day, and one day was my daughter's day. They made rude noises and made her life miserable for that day. She came home in tears, but also learned a lesson. She watched this happen the first three days and didn't speak up, and when it was her turn, it was horrible and sad. She learned not to sit and watch anymore.

Another incident occurred with my boys, who are twins in a small classroom situation. There are two boys in the class who don't get along and pick on each other, and my boys are friends with both of them. I had to point out to them, "Don't let them pick on each other. Pull them along, use the advantage of there being two of you. If you don't give them support, they won't have any reason to get along." They used that, and it worked out.
—*Kim Shepherd, mom of Jessica, 17, Jeremy and Josh, 12, and Jennifer, 10, Indianapolis, Indiana*

Others spread rumors and, while they are not the source of the abuse, they are key players in perpetuating it.

☺ Prepare your child to react properly when his peers engage in bullying or exclusionary behavior. Instill in him your value system and let him know you expect him to act with integrity.

☺ Offer your child these suggestions for how to get involved and turn the situation around:

✤ He can squelch hurtful gossip or rumors by refusing to pass it along or to combat misinformation with the truth.

✤ He can use humor to diffuse tense situations or to disarm the bully.

✦ He can leave an anonymous note with a teacher or authority figure to explain the situation.

✦ Lastly, if he sees someone being bullied but feels unable to act at the time for his own safety, he can offer consolation later and in private.

◎ Show your child that a bystander plays a major role in bullying and he has the ability to turn a bad situation around. Remind him he is not a neutral player; by not objecting to something he feels is wrong, he is condoning the actions of the bully or clique.

Why Do Cliques Exist Among Girls?

◎ Cliques exist at every school and become increasingly cutthroat as adolescence hits. Walk into any middle school's cafeteria and you will find students arranged into standard groups in the social arena. Cliques become a social mirror. By identifying with a certain group and adopting a set of status and group admission markers, such as dress, hobbies, and attitudes, the child establishes a way to define herself.

◎ In the transition period to young adulthood, your child is taking steps to find her identity and define herself in the social world. This often means separating herself from you. The move from familial attachment to social independence is a natural and healthy one, marking her growth into adulthood.

◎ To gain insight into your adolescent daughter's social world, you need to understand the social structure and roles that operate in cliques.

✦ The *ruler* of the clique usually possesses a number of enviable characteristics, such as designer clothes and good looks, but it is a combination of charisma and manipulation that allows her to reign over her social group while appearing charming to adults. A clique ruler won't take responsibility when she hurts another person's feelings, but believes she has the right to take revenge when she has been wronged. Her most potent weapon is her affection, which she strategically dispenses and withholds. If you think your daughter fits this role, pay attention to how she interacts with her friends, whether she tells them what to do, and how much they follow her.

✴ The *sidekick* is second in command to the group leader. Your child may be a clique sidekick if she has a best friend who seems to have an excessive amount of authority over her.

✴ Another clique member is the *gossip*. She keeps tabs on everyone by pretending to be their friend, and strategically uses the information she gathers for her own benefit. She has power and security in the short term, but the other girls eventually stop trusting her. Your daughter may be the gossip if she acts secretively and always seems to be in the middle of fights.

✴ Occasionally there is the *girl who associates with many cliques* and moves freely from group to group. She has influence in the class, but doesn't use her power in negative ways. Your daughter may play such a role if she doesn't want to exclude people and doesn't seem tied to one group of friends.

✴ The *bystander* is a girl whose allegiance to a clique is a source of conflict and with whom negative peer pressure exerts a great deal of influence. Your daughter may be a bystander if she is always in situations where she has to choose between friends, struggles to accommodate everyone, and has difficulty saying no.

✴ The *fringe member* is on the perimeter of a clique, backs up the leaders and mimics their dress and behavior, has difficulty developing her own personality and figuring out what she wants, and feels insecure in her friendships. She may be willing to do anything to belong to the upper echelons, including participating in risk-taking behavior. Your daughter may be a fringe member if she considers other girls' opinions more important than her own and has difficulty separating what she wants from what the group is doing.

✴ The *scapegoat* is the target of other girls and cliques, most likely because she poses some kind of challenge to the group. Your daughter may be a target for scapegoating if she feels helpless, isolated, and evades difficult situations to avoid being hurt.

© Although clique members live with constant social tension, being part of an exclusive, close-knit group offers the peer validation your child so highly values during middle school years.

© Help your child identify the difference between a clique and a group of friends. Cliques are exclusive and structured around leaders, while friendships are based on a sense of equality and mutual respect. Talk with your child about how kids in friendship groups, as opposed to those in the exclusive cliques, benefit from the security and loyalty of true friends and often have the best self-esteem and confidence.

◉ Just because your child is in a popular crowd doesn't mean her social and emotional worlds are problem-free; such kids often suffer from low-self esteem and know that their friendships are superficial. Your child may become consumed with anxiety as she focuses intensely on her looks and behavior to maintain social status, and she may be facing a tough set of challenges as the popular crowds often engage in risky behavior earlier than their peers and are more likely to get in trouble.

◉ Validate your child's need to be part of a tight-knit social group while reminding her how hurtful exclusion is to other kids, and intervening at the first signs of social power play.

Cliques are absolutely more common with girls. In general, boys can have an argument, huff and puff about it, and then the next day have totally forgotten what they were fighting over. Girls are different. In my experience, at the end of third grade, girls start getting into cliques and forming bonds that create peer pressure. It may be that nothing extreme happens at the beginning, but cliques can begin when the girls are as young as nine years old.
—*Mary Beth Lewison, 2nd and 3rd grade teacher for 15 years in Ludlow, Massachusetts*

I've seen a lot of girls my daughter's age who are already cruel, which I find amazing and disheartening. I've tried to teach my daughter that while she may not like everyone, she can't be mean to anyone. One of the great things about sports and clubs and different activities is she gets to have a different group of friends that she might not have talked to much otherwise.
—*Laura Doctor, mom of Nicole, 10, Cleveland, Ohio*

What Should I Do When My Adolescent Daughter Is Being Bullied?

☙ As you listen to your child talk about a friendship in which you feel she is being victimized, she may make excuses for her abuser. This behavior indicates that this so-called friend has damaged your daughter's self-esteem and conditioned her to believe she can't survive without her friendship, so she is quick to accept apologies and unlikely to demand real proof of friendship.

☙ Help your child examine what went wrong, exploring the dynamics of the friendship together. Working backward through memories of tension and conflict may be useful in determining the root of the problem and the best way to approach the problem or the bullies, themselves.

☙ All bullies use power plays to establish their dominance but girls tend to rely on relational power by threatening friendships and injuring their victim's social status and self-esteem. They can isolate other children by ignoring them or excluding them from an activity, secret, or joke. Because of the insider knowledge necessary for this kind of bullying to work, it often occurs between friends or within close social networks.

☙ Many girls create coalitions to avoid direct confrontation. A popular clique leader will appeal to other girls to join her scheme or fill them in on the juicy details of her fight. She offers them an opportunity to feel like a part of the clique, but maintains the position of power she needs because her popularity dulls her fear that she will become the next victim.

☙ Sometimes the bullying victim isn't who you would assume it to be. A girl who is confident, pretty, smart, affluent, or popular can be targeted if other girls become jealous or think she is conceited. Often, when resentment builds among the other group members, the popular leader of the clique finds herself next in line for group exclusion.

☙ Watch for sudden changes in appearance, hairstyle, posture, or attitude. Your child may react to abuse by trying to disappear—wearing clothes that won't make her stand out or by closing down emotionally.

I had an issue with my daughter because she is very studious and works hard, so girls were teasing her. I told her just to try and get along with everybody and to not take it seriously, which seemed to work.
—*Debbie McCandless, mom of BC, 18, and Sarah, 13, Knob Lick, Kentucky*

© Without sending the message that you think your daughter's being oversensitive, ask her to think about whether the girls are intending to make her feel this way; it may be they don't realize they are being hurtful.

© Don't say things such as, "It's a phase" or "It happens to everybody." Your daughter may feel you are trivializing a painful matter. Avoid disparaging remarks or criticism about her friends, which she could interpret as judgmental or make the situation her fault.

How Can I Help My Daughter Deal with Cliques?

© When cliques start to rule, parents often feel left out of their child's world. Suddenly, you seem to go from arranging playdates and supervising get-togethers to receiving one-word answers about how your child's day went and what her afternoon plans are.

© Cliques can be dangerous because the rules and actions of the group hold a great deal of power over your child. During adolescence, children test the rules and peer pressure can force a child to engage in actions she knows are wrong.

© Clique members often suffer from low self-esteem because their social relationships are often of a precarious nature; they have few true friends in whom they can trust and confide. They may find their status rising and falling in a single day and feel anxious about maintaining their place in the group.

☺ Members of fringe groups suffer the effects of being intentionally left out of the cliques. So-called wannabes often engage in risky, attention-seeking behavior. They desperately want to feel accepted by the A-list crowd, and so fail to develop their own personalities or tend to their own needs. Wanting to belong and finding it difficult to fit in, they often respond to social isolation by acting out in negative or self-destructive ways.

☺ While you can't pick your child's spot on the social ladder, you can get involved by finding out as much as you can and helping her change the way she sees herself in the hierarchy.

☺ Find out about the caste system that controls your child's school. Ask her to diagram the different social groups. You can broach the topic by inquiring about the close friend of hers you haven't heard about, or asking her to identify the different lunch table groups of students in the cafeteria. Ask about the different cliques, and ask her to be specific. What are the standards for admission? What are the dress codes of the different groups? Discuss the advantages and disadvantages of the social groups together. Talk about how the members of the A-list struggle with self-esteem and a constantly shifting social landscape. You'll probably be surprised by her social savvy.

☺ Pay attention to how she talks about the different groups and how she seems to perceive them. Get her to challenge her own preconceptions. Even the most secure children find themselves idealizing the perks of popularity—popular kids seem to have all the fun and are often adored by classmates and teachers alike.

☺ Don't pass judgments on her peers when she shares stories about them. The child with whom she got in a huge fight today may wind up her best friend tomorrow. If she thinks you dislike her friend, she'll be less willing to tell you when they get together and what they do.

☺ Listen and sympathize without always trying to fix your child's problems. Adolescents often want to solve their own problems, but if your child knows she can come to you to vent, she will be much more likely to tell you about her social life.

☺ Remind your child that she isn't alone in her insecurities or her desire to belong. Tell her about an occasion when you felt the same way, or the time a former member of the popular clique confessed how truly insecure she felt at your child's age.

☺ Recognize that the social turmoil you see as petty can be earth-shattering to your child. If she gets the message that you don't care about these difficult experiences, she will be less likely to come to you with problems or share what's happening in her life.

We really need to encourage students to do things together by grouping them together differently, so they get to know different people, instead of allowing them to depend on the same people they depend on all the time. Encourage them to get along with people they haven't had a chance to do things with. Get the quiet kid to play with the louder one, even if he's going to get tired of him, so they can learn to compromise and work together to finish what they have to do. Encourage them to get out of that comfort zone, because it's not always good for progress and growth. It's easy for kids to discredit someone because of something they don't like. Lots of kids do things alike, but because one kid will do one or two things, like be a cheerleader, play chess, or not do as well in school, they separate into these groups when all they have to do is find like interests to appreciate the different things they can do.

—*Angela McNutt, 6th to 12th grade Spanish teacher for 1 year, Glade Spring, Virginia*

Cliques start really early in my school. There are only two sections in every grade here, so you see everybody every day. Parents might get a phone call saying their child seems to be alone a lot, and the sooner they talk to a counselor at school, the better. At the high school, the younger grades are especially cliquey right now. They just started a new thing where they'll pick out kids who get picked on and those who are doing the bullying and set them up in group sessions to work out their problems. I always try to talk about empathy, but junior high kids don't always realize that what they just said made someone feel bad. They don't always make the connection. That's something you need to keep pounding in until they're mature enough to understand it.

—*Mary Chick, kindergarten to 12th grade art teacher for 8 years, Elgin, Minnesota*

First, I don't necessarily think all cliques are bad. I think the essence of any group of friends is that they have common interests. It's fairly natural for kids to find a group to fit in with because everyone is working so hard to fit in anywhere—this can be healthy. It's when these groups become exclusive in a mean way or form rituals and rites where it's impossible or dangerous for kids to be a part of the group, that it becomes unhealthy. There was one group of girls who had decided that to be a part of their group, girls would have to perform certain sexual activities way beyond their age level. To me, harmful clique energy occurs because of a negative focus in the wrong direction, as opposed to playing a sport together or bonding over Pokemon. The energy depends on the bonding force.

—*Chris Grimm, 7th grade social studies teacher for 3 years, Ventura, California*

Cliques generally start around third grade and girls make up the dumbest reasons why you can or cannot join their group. We helped our daughter by inviting friends over a lot, even people on the fringes of these cliques. We told her people are just mean sometimes and they don't think about how they are affecting other people. Also, we made sure she wasn't waiting to be invited places, but instead inviting others to hang out with her. We made it clear that one person who really likes her is better than ten superficial friends. Luckily, it did seem to pass, especially once they hit high school.

—*Martha Judiscak, mom of Jimmy, 17, Vicki, 16, and Danny, 11, Knoxville, Tennessee*

Parent Volunteer

Why Is Volunteering at My Child's School So Important?

● Getting to know your child's teacher by helping out in the school is one of the best things you can do to help your child succeed. Teachers notice active involvement and appreciate it. By volunteering in the classroom, you get to know your child's teacher on a friendly basis, instead of limiting your relationship to parent-teacher conferences. If you build a positive rapport with your child's teacher, she will share her opinions more readily and solicit yours, as well.

● Teachers are likely to raise their expectations for your child if they see you are actively involved in his school experience.

● Another benefit of being involved in the school is it allows you to get to know the teachers in higher grades, so if you are able to request a teacher, you will be better prepared to select the best option for your child.

If you are tired of the monosyllabic responses your child gives whenever you ask him about his day, going into the classroom for a couple hours will allow you to observe firsthand how your child behaves in the school environment, how the teacher manages the classroom, and how the students interact.

Volunteering in the library or on the playground is another great way to get involved because you have the opportunity to see the students out of the classroom.

Get involved. You can't just drop your child off at the door and pick him up when he enters your life again.
—Heather Daigle, teacher of all grades, Plymouth, Massachusetts

Volunteer to help at school. The teachers will be grateful, your child will be proud of you, and you will feel as though you have accomplished something for your community. Plus, you will learn something about what goes on in your child's classroom.
—Kathy Moberg, mom of Eric, 17, Sean, 14, and Kelsey, 12, Saline, Michigan

Being actively involved at the school makes problems easier to handle, because the teacher can just go up to you in the hallway and say, "Your kid is doing xyz," instead of telling you three months later in a conference. Teachers respond better when they see you're involved.
—Kim Shepherd, mom of Jessica, 17, Jeremy and Josh, 12, and Jennifer, 10, Indianapolis, Indiana

The more the teachers see your face, the more attention they will give you. Help out with fundraisers, volunteer to do a special craft, help with the weekly flier, or read with children in the library. If teachers see you are involved, they are likely to spend extra time with your children. They'll also give you more clarification on material because they know you'll take the time to look at it.
—Jennifer O'Gorman, mom of Olivia, 11, Jake, 9, Sam, 7, Annabelle, 4, Luke, 2, and Eleanor, 1, Lebanon, Maine

Even being in the classroom with your child once a month for a couple of hours allows you to see any changes that occur and keeps you up-to-date on everything. Just reading newsletters won't do it—you will be clueless because you won't see what is actually going on.
—*Kendra French, mom of Parker, 2, Fairfax, Virginia*

I didn't do much until after my daughter was in first grade because I didn't see why I should be paying so much to have to do more work! But I've started to be much more involved in the school community. I started taking my daughter to skating parties and going to events at the school. You have to know what's going on; you have to do something yourself so you don't feel like an outsider. It's your responsibility to take the initiative, get involved, and meet people.
—*Laura Doctor, mom of Nicole, 10, Cleveland, Ohio*

What Are the Best Ways to Become Involved in My Child's Classroom?

© Contact your child's teachers at the beginning of the year to offer assistance in the ways you will enjoy the most and can be the most helpful.

© Tell your child's teacher about any skills, hobbies, or interests you may have—including your career—about which the class may enjoy learning. Let her know if you would be willing to share your experience with the class or act as a mentor.

© By volunteering to do tasks such as photocopying or correcting math and spelling worksheets, you give the teacher time to prepare for the next activity of the day.

◉ When you show up to volunteer, get there on time and be prepared to do what you promised. Be willing to bend your own plans to the needs of the school—you are there to help. Remember to have fun, laugh, and keep a sense of humor about your experience.

◉ Ask about any community service opportunities your child's school has in place to expose the children to volunteer work and helping those in need. Get involved in expanding these or in starting a program.

◉ Don't forget to donate. Ask your child's teacher if she could use your empty milk cartons, paper-towel rolls, egg cartons, or other household recyclable material for art projects. Check with his teacher, art instructor, and school librarian to see whether children's or wildlife magazines you have finished reading can be used.

◉ Other ways to volunteer:

✤ Deliver books to the school that teachers order from public libraries.

✤ Volunteer to usher at school productions.

✤ Sew and decorate costumes for class performances.

✤ Make treats for bake sales or for the teachers themselves.

✤ Volunteer to be a guide for visitors during Open House Night.

✤ Film or take pictures of special classroom events for the teacher.

✤ Decorate bulletin boards.

✤ Create a classroom website or student newsletter with writing, poetry, or art.

✤ Plant flower bulbs with your child outside the school or clean up trash from the playground.

✤ Read with a small group of children or to the whole class as a guest reader.

✤ Share your cultural background with your child's class around a holiday with a cooking project or craft.

✦ Help organize events and activities that link parents, teachers, and students, such as a school carnival.

✦ Coordinate a school clothing drive, canned-goods collection, or book swap.

These days, with less money and fewer aides, teachers are much more receptive to parent involvement in the classroom. We especially appreciate volunteers with activities like arts and crafts projects, or at reading time when parents can buddy with a student. In most situations we like to let the children know there will be another person in the classroom. If you show up unannounced it interferes with the teacher's day and children's learning.
—*Kay Symons, special education and kindergarten to 8th grade teacher for 27 years, South Georgia*

Make an offer to your child's teacher to volunteer on days she knows she'll be out of school. It will be so appreciated. Several parents came in and helped when I was substitute teaching, which was fantastic! Often, the parents know the kids in the class better than I do.
—*Stephanie Lee, substitute elementary school teacher, Lawrenceville, Georgia*

Avoid the trap I fell into, where I would be asked to volunteer for something at my children's school, feel like I should be doing something to help, and end up on a project doing the type of work I least enjoy. Now, I give much more consideration before saying yes and make sure the tasks I take responsibility for will be ones I enjoy and will most involve me meeting other parents.
—*Carolyn Stafford Stein, mom of Lena, 10, Audrey, 8, and Natalie, 4, Carlisle, Massachusetts*

The Great Books Foundation (www.greatbooks.org) has a fabulous program to introduce classic works of literature to school-age kids. I volunteer to do this in my children's school. I have a group of ten to twelve kids, and we meet twelve times a year during lunch period. Kindergarteners and first-graders listen to a story, while older kids read a condensed version of a book in an age-appropriate context. I get a teacher's guide with fun questions to spark discussion, like, "Why did Jack climb the beanstalk the third time when he already had a golden goose at home?" We all come together and discuss it. I started doing this with my daughter in 2nd grade, and now she's in 6th grade, so I have met with the same group of kids 48 times. Not only do I know all my daughter's friends, we all feel so vested as a group. I strongly recommend parents look into bringing this program into their children's schools.

—*Shannon McDermott, mom of Catherine, 13, Matthew, 11, and Joshua, 7, Lemont, Illinois*

We send out a letter on orientation day asking parents if and how they would be interested in helping out. Some come in to do special art projects or read to the class, some help organize parties, some cut things out for us, little things like that. It's such a great help to us! It also gets the kids to see their parents involved in the school. It's a plus all around.

—*Alison Gowers, kindergarten teacher for 5 years, West Point, Virginia*

I really appreciate when parents donate bags of candy, boxes of tissues, or juice boxes, or volunteer their time to plant flowers outside our schoolroom. I have one parent who's proficient in Spanish, and she came in to teach short lessons to my fifth graders—she thought this up on her own, too, which was great!

—*Martha Ann Chandler, 3rd to 6th grade teacher for 14 years, Florence, South Carolina*

Get into the classroom as often as you can, even once a week, to work with small groups or volunteer to read a story. I know this is not possible for a lot of people, so take a lunch hour from work to drop in. Make yourself present in the classroom and to the teacher by sending little articles you see about outstanding teachers—anything to support the teacher or school community, so you see the teacher not only when things are going wrong.

—*Claudia Flanders, kindergarten to 8th grade teacher for 34 years, Santa Monica, California*

Why Are Some Teachers Wary of Classroom Volunteers?

◉ Not every teacher will welcome your volunteer attempts—some will get defensive if they feel you are encroaching on their turf.

◉ Some teachers are overburdened, and others are burned out. These teachers may view parental involvement as another task for them to juggle.

◉ When you volunteer in your child's classroom, be supportive and respectful of the teacher's work. Even if you're anxious about the school's approach to your child's education, limit your involvement to that of a temporary assistant and don't take over the classroom.

◉ In a classroom where children with special needs are integrated, volunteers may be privy to certain things. Teachers prefer parents who don't take any confidential information outside of the classroom.

Parent volunteers are helpful, but there are many parents who visit the classroom with hidden agendas. They are there to check up on their child or the teacher rather than help.
—*Barry Mindes, 3rd to 5th grade teacher for 32 years, Norton, Massachusetts*

Some parents are in the classroom every single day, which is really going overboard.
—*Joy Pumphrey, 2nd and 3rd grade teacher for 12 years, Clearwater, Florida*

Often, but not always, teachers rebuff parents who ask to observe a classroom. It's a turf battle between the teachers, administration, and parents. The teachers have the attitude, "We know what we're doing, we're the teachers. You're going to interrupt our work flow if you come into the classroom."
—*Jim Rubens, dad of Matthew, 7, and former state senator, Hanover, New Hampshire*

The important thing when you're volunteering in the classroom is remembering you're there to help the teacher and not sidetrack your child. It helps to talk to your child ahead of time. Say to him, "I'm here to help the teacher with such and such," so that he isn't distracted by your presence.
—Lawanna Ford, 5th grade teacher for 25 years, Argonia, Kansas

As a Working Parent, How Can I Become Involved?

◉ Working full time can put dramatic limitations on the extent to which you can be involved in your children's classes, but there are still many ways to help out. At the beginning of the year, write a letter to the teacher introducing yourself and telling her you want to be involved.

◉ Be honest with the teacher about the amount of time you have to volunteer, but let her know you would love to do what you can. Most teachers will find a way to involve you regardless of your time constraints.

◉ Although it may be difficult for you to visit your child's classroom consistently throughout the year, make an effort to spend at least two hours volunteering in the opening months of the school year. By becoming acquainted with your child's teacher early on, you will find it easier to maintain a positive relationship as the year progresses.

◉ There are many ways to get involved in the classroom, even if you work full time:

🔹 Put together materials for the art class or arrange a class trip from home.

🔹 Take time off from work to chaperone a field trip.

🔹 Help coordinate a school fund-raiser.

🌸 Provide refreshments for an event.

🌸 Give an hour to run a booth at a weekend school event.

🌀 Remember your attendance at your child's special events at school shows him how much you value his education and abilities. Even if you work and have other children, make every effort to be there to cheer him on. If you can't hire a babysitter, bring your younger children along with you. If you absolutely can't make it, find someone important in your child's life who can. Even sending your child's older sibling or grandparent will remind him of his family's love and support.

Whatever your financial or work situation, find a way to be involved, even if that means going an hour late to work once a month. With our school systems, you have to be involved in whatever capacity you can manage so you know how your child is progressing. Have regular conversations with everyone you can—teachers, principals, specialists—and help your children get involved in and be excited about their own education.
—*Jennifer D'Oliviera, mom of Nicholas, 6, Irvine, California*

If you can't come in to volunteer, send a note at the beginning of the year to the teacher saying, "My work schedule doesn't permit me to come in, but I want to help! Please call me for anything you need sent in." You can send in food for a holiday party or stickers for the teacher to use when grading papers. This will let both the teacher and your child know you really care about your child's experience at school. One year, my students wrote poems and we invited parents to a sharing event. The looks on the faces of the children whose parents didn't come were heartbreaking. So if you work, take an early lunch break or try to get a grandparent, babysitter, or friend to be there with your child. Tell your child you can't be there, but ask if he could bring his project home so you can go over it together.
—*Joy Pumphrey, 2nd and 3rd grade teacher for 12 years, Clearwater, Florida*

For a while I was going to college and working, and it seemed as though I was an uninvolved parent. To counter this impression, I made sure the teachers had my cell phone number and

knew there was never a bad time to reach me. I also emailed the teachers a lot and whenever possible I would go over to the school so they knew I really wanted to be involved.
—*Suzanne Stoll, mom of Charity, 10, and Jesse, 7, Wampum, Pennsylvania*

Kids really need to know you're part of the school. It's hard when you work full time and have 101 things to do. I do things I can do from home. This year for Halloween, we used ghost molds to make Rice Krispie treats for all my kids' classrooms, which made my kids feel really good about what we had done together.
—*Kelly Levinson, mom of David, 14, Zachary, 10, Michael, 9, Shaina, 8, and Amanda, 5, Guilford, Connecticut*

For the last two years, the letters coming home from the school and the PTA were full of typos. I write for a living, so I wrote a letter to the principal saying I could edit. I started editing the school newsletter and then writing all the PTA newsletters. Even though I could never come to meetings, I was able to help out and do everything over email.
—*Jennifer Clements, mom of Kaitlin, 8, Ian, 3, and Reilly, 1, Murrieta, California*

Send a note at the beginning of the year, saying, "My work doesn't allow me to go into the classroom, but I'll help you cut, grade, or do menial tasks if they are sent home in my daughter's backpack." This assistance has been a lifesaver for me as a teacher; it takes off an hour of work for me a night. It also lets me know the parents care and want to be involved, and I really feel supported.
—*Kallie Leyba, 1st and 2nd grade teacher for 2 years and mom of Lauren, 11, Lucas, 8, and Samson, 4, Highlands Ranch, Colorado*

How Do I Stay Involved During Middle School?

© Parents of preteens and teens often find themselves in a precarious position. They still want to support their children, but they don't want to squelch the sense of independence that should naturally develop with adolescence. Middle and high school students have to deal with many new social and physical transitions, and sometimes their reaction to these changes is to push away their parents and try to do everything on their own. It comes as no surprise, then, that parent involvement in schools dramatically declines with the onset of adolescence. Yet, research shows that middle and high school students benefit as much from parental involvement as younger children do.

© There are many reasons for the decrease in parental involve-ment as children get older: Schools are bigger and farther away; students take more complex and involved classes; children have more than one teacher; parents are more likely to be employed; and students are starting to become more independent and less focused on the home environment.

© Remaining involved in your child's education as he grows up requires you to engage yourself in significantly different ways than when he was younger. Ways to stay involved include participation in school beautification projects, committees that incorporate parents, and school events such as conferences and concerts.

I hesitate to say parents can help in classrooms in the later years, but there are so many things they can get involved in that affect the classroom. Contact teachers about clubs and activities that are going on. We're trying to set up a trip to Mexico for our older Spanish students, and what would really help me is for parents to say, "I really want this to happen," and put some ideas together to raise funds and support the activity. Also, parents can come in before or after school and say, "I do really well in this area. Could I do some tutoring?" Parents have expertise they think they can't use, but they really can.
—Angela McNutt, 6th to 12th grade Spanish teacher for 1 year, Glade Spring, Virginia

The best thing parents of older students can do is just find a way to prevent their kids from sliding into the teenage years on their own. I hear parents say all the time, "Now that my kids are in middle school, the teachers don't want us there anymore," but a lot of us really do.
—*Laurie Olmstead, 7th and 8th grade math and science teacher for 4 years, Union, Maine*

I used to volunteer a lot, but in middle school I do it much less, and I think that's true of most parents. By then, most kids don't want to see Mom and Dad around school anymore. I think it's good because, by middle school, it's about time for children to take more responsibility.
—*Farida Kathawalla, mom of Tanveer, 13, Westford, Massachusetts*

What If My Child Is Embarrassed to See Me Around School?

Your preadolescent and socially precocious child wants nothing less than a nosy parent constantly checking up on him and frequenting his school. Strike the balance between staying involved and invading your child's space. If your child blushes, runs in the other direction, or sinks down in his seat whenever you're around, find another, less visible way to stay involved.

If your child wants you out of the classroom, you should honor his wishes, but this doesn't mean you need to stop your involvement entirely. Volunteer in a way that crosses onto his turf less frequently, like in the library. This way your child will know you are interested in his life, but will not feel that you are constantly encroaching on his personal space.

Talk to your child before getting involved in activities that will bring you into his sphere on a frequent basis. Check to see if he minds having you in the classroom because, after all, it is his world.

Offers to help at school are nice, but I deal with middle-school students, who will most likely act out if a parent is present. However, helping in the office or with extracurricular activities can get you in the school without threatening your child.
—*Pam Pottorff, 3rd and 4th grade teacher and 8th grade reading teacher for 5 years, Sioux City, Nebraska*

You want to be involved and active in the school, but you also don't want to be overbearing. You want the school to be your child's place. If your child is uncomfortable with the amount of time you are at school, back off. There are many ways to be involved, like baking for parties or planning field trips, where you're not encroaching on your child's sphere and are still doing wonderful things for the school. Talk to the teachers to find out what they need. Send in film and develop it or make photo books at the end of year. Worry more about not intruding on your child than about the teachers. Adults will get over it.
—*Kathy Carabine, pre-k and 3rd grade teacher for 16 years, Boston, Massachusetts*

You don't want to be a classroom distraction for your child. If he is constantly worried, "Mom and Dad are watching" or "Am I going to get in trouble?" he won't benefit from having his parents around.
—*Ruth Anne Manroe, kindergarten to 6th grade teacher for 27 years, Golden, Colorado*

How Can I Best Become an Advocate for School Reform and Improvements?

 Parents have begun to take more active roles in changing old school policies and developing new programs. School systems have responded to this increase in involvement by trying to include the entire school community in the school's operations. Administrators are sharing more of their decision-making responsibilities with teachers and parents than ever before.

◎ Advocating for your child means voicing your opinions, suggestions, and concerns in a respectful and logical way. Understand that your child will learn from your problem-solving approach, so be aware of the example you set.

◎ To prepare yourself to be an effective contributor to the school community, become acquainted with the existing school, district, and state policies that concern your child. Find out why policies exist, when they were first implemented, and if there are any alternative solutions to the problem they seek to fix. If this information cannot be found in the school handbook, call the school to request it or do some simple research online.

◎ If you are unhappy with a teacher's explanation of a policy or arrangement, meet with the school principal to discuss it further. If you are unsatisfied after that meeting, schedule another with a school board member or the superintendent. It's often necessary to work your way up the chain of command to get a full understanding of the issue or to advocate for change.

◎ Being informed on the issues and discussing concerns with other parents is only part of being a successful parent advocate. To be successful in your efforts to affect change in the school system, especially in regard to changing the school budget or procedures, you will need to either work within or in conjunction with the Parent-Teacher Association (PTA).

◎ The PTA offers an established approach to getting involved with a school's policy-making process. This organization serves as a forum in which parents can meet each other and share opinions and interests, keep abreast of what is going on in the school community, and collectively form a group that is more powerful than one parent standing alone.

◎ Look into serving on school advisory councils, committees, or management teams at your child's school. If these positions for parents do not exist, speak to the school about developing a parent involvement program or policy.

◎ If you find you don't have the time to handle a serious position in the school community, you should still be as informed as possible. Attend PTA, school board, and town meetings for the scoop on the latest issues.

◎ Speak up by writing and calling to support or oppose proposed legislation

We can't just put our children in the hands of educators and sit back and watch. We have to advocate and assist their education.
—*Patty Potter, mom of Olivia Logan, 6, and Isabel Logan, 3, Ft. Worth, Texas*

If there's a policy you are concerned about, you can't do the lone ranger routine. Find like-minded people who feel the same way. Talk to a school board member and ask if there are any other parents with the same concern. The lone person on a crusade gets isolated in a hurry.
—*Ken Pauly, high school social studies teacher for 13 years, St. Louis Park, Minnesota*

If teachers and the principal see that you come to PTA meetings and seem concerned about what's going on in the school, they are going to be more receptive to you. They absolutely will pay more attention to your concerns and seriously consider your opinion.
—*Stephanie Lee, substitute elementary school teacher, Lawrenceville, Georgia*

I live in a pretty rural area, and we have at least one school board representative in each town people usually know. You can go to a friend to say, "This is going on in the school and I don't know how to handle it best." If you're really not being heard, you might think about getting someone else from the family involved to say it differently. Sometimes previous teachers can help, especially in those transition years, middle school to high school. Ask them if they saw anything like this when they had your child. If the administration is not aware of the history through those big changes, the issue may simply be pushed aside.
—*Laurie Olmstead, 7th and 8th grade math and science teacher for 4 years, Union, Maine*

It's important to vote for school bodies. Even if you don't send your child to that school, your tax money is going there, so you need to stay informed and involved. When schools have open forums to discuss what the school is doing, it's important for parents be there.
—*Chris Grimm, 7th grade social studies teacher for 3 years, Ventura, California*

affecting your child's education. Find support in the community for your perspective and start a petition drive or letter-writing campaign.

◉ If the school invites parental consideration, get involved in decisions about curriculum and textbook selections. If you have any specific recommendations about how to change the curriculum, participate in school-based evaluations or focus groups.

◉ Be an informed voter during school board elections. The people who are elected hire principals, so by asserting your opinion you are helping secure a spot for the principal you prefer. Know what the candidates stand for:

🔹 How do they feel about issues important to you, such as the school budget and spending for languages, arts, athletics, technology, specialists, and gifted programs?

🔹 Do they harp on any one issue?

🔹 What are their fundamental educational philosophies (traditional versus progressive, core curriculum versus child-centered learning)?

🔹 What are their professional backgrounds?

◉ The most effective way for parents to affect policy change is to slate a new school board. This difficult and time-consuming endeavor can take up to three years, but can be extremely beneficial to the school system. It would be the group's responsibility to find candidates, get them to run, and publicize their campaigns. In your search, look for individuals willing to use the reins of power to examine, not rubber-stamp, school policy.

◉ Understand that it may take you a long time to get a problem solved to your satisfaction. For instance, it took John Ball and the New York PTA fourteen years to outlaw corporal punishment in schools. But, if an issue is really important to you, don't back away from taking it to court, applying more public pressure, or electing more responsive board members.

Part II
On the Home Front

Creating an Academically Nurturing Home Environment

How Can I Create a Supportive Home Environment?

You are your child's first and most important role model. He watches your interactions with other family members, listens to you talk on the phone, and absorbs how you respond to the supermarket cashier. If you value education, your child will as well, and the morals you stress in the home will guide him in the classroom, on the playground, on sports fields, and with his peers.

© Children who have constant love and encouragement from their parents are more likely to enter school with the attitude that they can meet any obstacle head on and defeat it. Nurture your child's curiosity about the world, sending the message that learning is fun, satisfying, and worthwhile. Make home a base from which he feels free to explore, take risks, and approach challenges with a sense of adventure. Foster his abilities, challenge him to improve, and provide support when and where he needs it most.

© Be supportive of your child's problems and questions. You have the opportunity to show him the world on a much broader scale than his teachers can.

© Allow your child to do what comes naturally. Learning is an active process at all ages, and hands-on experience is a child's central route to discovering the world around him. All the academic learning, social skill development, and intellectual and emotional growth your child will experience begins with his poking and prying into his surroundings.

© Studies from the past twenty years show parents who have close relationships with their young children help those children succeed academically in later years. Three kinds of parental involvement at home are consistently associated with higher student achievement: actively organizing and monitoring a child's time, helping with homework, and discussing school matters.

© Talk often with your child about how much your family values learning and education, and bring up examples of the things you continue to learn and ways in which your education has made a profound difference in your life.

© Children who succeed in school:

    ❋ Are curious and inquisitive about ideas, objects, people, and the world,

    ❋ Find pleasure in the process, as well as in the product, of their work,

    ❋ Aren't afraid to take reasonable risks or to fail, and

    ❋ Believe in themselves.

© Just as parents can instill in their children a love for learning, they can also destroy that love. Pushing a child too hard, controlling his academic decisions, or reacting harshly to bad grades will leave him with little desire to learn because of the negative associations he makes with school and learning. Encourage a healthy and positive attitude toward learning by always paying attention to your child's questions, encouraging his interests, and sharing your own.

When you create a nurturing, predictable environment, you give your child a stable base and a sense of security, which will help him deal better with stress and feel confident taking risks.

—*Sue Abrams, elementary school principal and former 1st to 5th grade teacher for 22 years, Natick, Massachusetts*

The biggest factor in a child's success at school is parental involvement at home. The kids whose parents listen to them read will learn to read the fastest. The kids whose parents talk with them regularly have the best vocabularies. And the kids whose parents explore new things with them have the best background knowledge.

—*Amie Parker, 1st and 2nd grade teacher for 7 years, Lynnwood, Washington*

Support at home is number one in determining a child's success at school. Students who know their parents care about their progress and will check up on them perform better than students whose parents don't take an active role. I've had students who were doing poorly until a parent began regular contact with the teachers, and then the students improved greatly.

—*Pam Pottorff, 3rd and 4th grade teacher and 8th grade reading teacher for 5 years, Sioux City, Nebraska*

I think the bottom line is your kids need to feel they are totally adored. I am in love with my kids and they know it. That gives them the ability to go out knowing they are loved and will be okay if they make mistakes.
—*Michelle Turpel, mom of Chris, 19, Haley, 15, Brianna, 8, and Anthony, 4,*
  Thousand Oaks, California

Encourage your children to learn for the sake of learning and to appreciate new learning experiences. Parents should start early with their children's education by providing them with an environment filled with educational sharing opportunities. Examples might include quiet reading time, open-ended problem-solving games, and toys that inspire imagination and role-play.
—*Edward Sapienza, 9th to 12th grade science, math, and computer teacher for 31 years,*
  North Reading, Massachusetts

I think developing self-confidence is important, and it's something kids can't do completely on their own; they need teachers and parents and siblings to help them. Kids also need some independent responsibility. Let them pick out their own clothes. Who cares if they match? Let them set the table. If they break a plate, it's not the end of the world, as long as they are trying. I had one child who was so proud of herself because for the first time she had picked out her coat and zipped it up. Her mother immediately said, "You can't wear that, it's filthy!" It was the first time all year she had gotten her coat herself, and her mother should have been proud of her for that.
—*Alison Gowers, kindergarten teacher for 5 years, West Point, Virginia*

It is crucial to foster the development of healthy, competent children who feel good about who they are. Self-confidence is a critical component in developing a healthy adult. I've seen so many children with low IQs who have succeeded because people have taken the time to make them feel good about themselves.
—*Libby Anne Inabinet, kindergarten, 1st grade, reading, and gifted and talented teacher for 15*
  years, Columbia, South Carolina

Find things to praise your child for. Even a child who is always getting in trouble does something well. Catch him doing something positive. Praise good behavior, good listening, good work habits, and good sportsmanship, so your child knows and sees what kind of behavior is expected of him.
—*Beverly Hammond, kindergarten to 4th grade teacher for 31 years, West Point, Virginia*

Parents have to instill the value, benefit, and love of learning in their child. They have to demonstrate it themselves—for example, after dinner, shut off radios and TVs, and don't even answer the phone for a while. Sit and learn with your child; let him be the center of everything.
—*Steve C., 2nd grade to high school teacher for 15 years, Framingham, Massachusetts*

Especially when kids are young, you want to tap into the things your child really likes and has fun with. While not everything is fun and games, kids need lots of time to relax. Your child is not going to be at a loss because you didn't do something educational today. Don't stress your child out!
—*Niambi Muhammad, 1st and 2nd grade teacher for 4 years, Chicago, Illinois*

How Do I Help My Child Love Learning?

Involve your child in activities that spark his interest and give him new and different ways to learn. Go to museums and concerts to stay culturally fit and check the newspaper for events in your area that may be of interest to your child. Children develop a zest for knowledge when they can connect what they learn to the real world.

◎ Display academic work, as well as artwork, on the fridge and walls so your child sees that you value his academic success just as much as his other talents.

◎ Pay particular attention to the messages you send your child about what you value: Do you give a 100% effort on a test the same enthusiasm as an A+ mark?

◎ Ask your child's teacher to suggest activities that you and your child can do together to expand upon what he is studying in the classroom. Apply knowledge your child finds particularly interesting to real life.

A child's academic success is based on his experiences at home. If your child sees a good work ethic and an interest in his schooling from you, it makes my job easy.
—*Sharon Stubbs, 5th and 6th grade teacher for 28 years, Hopkins, Michigan*

Take your kids to museums or art displays. You don't have to know anything about art for your kids to really appreciate the experience. If kids have seen art outside the classroom, it helps me in class. Sometimes kids will raise their hands when I'm talking about a piece, and they get so excited when it's something they've seen or know something about.
—*Mary Chick, kindergarten to 12th grade art teacher for 8 years, Elgin, Minnesota*

As a Spanish teacher, I encourage my students to eat at Mexican restaurants as often as possible and try to order in the language. I encourage them to talk and make mistakes, because that's how you learn. We also have quite a few concerts kids can go to, just to hear Spanish music and some Spanish speakers, as well. Even if they don't catch every word, it's great for kids to think, "What did he say?" and try to remember the vocabulary from class. Another way to enforce language is to surf the Internet. There are lots of fun language sites, and most primary news sites, like *Time* and even *Discovery*, can be loaded in Spanish. Most DVDs translate into Spanish now, too. Whenever kids are watching a movie, you can just get them to change it into Spanish, even for a few minutes, and it really helps to keep their minds working in that direction.
—*Angela McNutt, 6th to 12th grade Spanish teacher for 1 year, Glade Spring, Virginia*

Go on adventures both outside and on the computer with your kids. Check things out, find out what's out there, and be inventive.
—*Heather Daigle, teacher of all grades, Plymouth, Massachusetts*

Parents need to find out what's going on at school and in the classroom and support that at home. If your child is doing a unit on Italy, go out to an Italian restaurant, watch a movie that takes place in Italy—focus on what your child studies at school and expand on it. It makes it a better experience for your child, and it's a good way to help him get so much more out of some of the things he's working on in school.
—*Holly Parker, teacher of deaf students for 10 years, Colorado Springs, Colorado*

How Can I Foster More Responsibility in My Child?

A child who is independent and responsible at home will apply the same qualities to his education. Picking up after himself before he starts school will prepare your child to keep track of his assignments and school supplies.

Build your child's sense of responsibility by assigning him chores, like doing his laundry, washing the dishes after meals, or feeding the dog. Give him an alarm clock and let him be in charge of when he wakes up and let him pick out what he wears to school. Making these smaller decisions will prepare him to handle important ones as they arise.

Let your child learn from his mistakes instead of immediately interceding when you suspect impending problems. If he chooses to get up fifteen minutes late, then he has to deal with the possibility of missing breakfast and rushing to catch the bus.

Reorchestrating things for your child encourages him to depend on parent intervention to solve problems.

© Giving your child responsibility doesn't mean putting everything on his shoulders. Monitor his efforts, especially when he engages in a time-consuming or difficult activity, and be ready to provide additional support when he asks for help.

Model respectful conduct for your child and don't expect him to act more mature than you!
—*Deborah Berris, 3rd, 5th, and 8th grade teacher for 5 years*

Children mimic what they see. If they see you make time for important things and have a special routine or schedule you follow at home, it helps them develop these important skills quickly. By the time children reach school age, teachers build on these skills already in place.
—*Sharon Webster, 3rd grade teacher and teacher for emotionally disturbed teens for 24 years, Malvern, Pennsylvania*

While molding values and guiding decisions are an important part of parenting, you must have a realistic view of your child's strengths and weaknesses in order to avoid misunderstanding and turmoil. At some point you need to move aside and give your child room to grow on his own.
—*Edward Sapienza, 9th to 12th grade science, math, and computer teacher for 31 years, North Reading, Massachusetts*

Teach responsibility at an early age—every part of a child's success depends on it. A child cannot rely on Mom and Dad to do everything for him, and the earlier he learns this, the better. Your child should be saying, "I need more crayons," or "I need poster board for my project," not "I don't have my project because my Mom didn't get me poster board!"
—*Nickey Langford, 2nd and 3rd grade teacher for 3 years, Birmingham, Alabama*

Our theme this summer is responsibility. We give points for certain chores, and at the end of the summer, if my kids get a certain amount of points, they get a prize. We made it a game for all of their chores, from picking up tennis balls in the yard, to clearing the dishes, to feeding the dog, to setting the table. If I ever say, "I need help with this," I expect them to do it without resistance.
—*Nancy Woods, mom of Jonathan, 10, and Maura, 6, Duxbury, Massachusetts*

A lot of responsibility means a lot of chances to be good at something. My son was the first kid to mow the lawn and walk to school by himself, and he feels great about that sort of thing.
—*Jennifer Guss, mom of Fred, 10, Hannah, 4, and Sophie, 2, Montvale, New Jersey*

My kids are picky eaters, so it's their responsibility to make their own lunches. I freeze sandwiches, and then my kids go into the freezer and grab a sandwich, grab Rice Krispie treats and other snacks I keep in a big tub, and go out the door. Being in charge of their own lunches makes them much more responsible.
—*Kim Shepherd, mom of Jessica, 17, Jeremy and Josh, 12, and Jennifer, 10, Indianapolis, Indiana*

I empathize with Olivia, but at the end of the day her problems are hers. This way she will hopefully learn the importance of making good decisions and taking responsibility for her actions. The minute I start taking on her issues, she'll figure "Well, I don't have to worry about it; Mommy will take care of it."
—*Patty Potter, mom of Olivia Logan, 6, and Isabel Logan, 3, Ft. Worth, Texas*

When Is It Appropriate for My Child to Miss School and How Can I Help Him Catch Up?

◉ Extending scheduled school vacations sends your child the message that you don't value the time he spends in school. Let him know that school is important to you by scheduling appointments and vacations around school hours.

◉ Avoid giving your child rewards for missing school: Keep TV and phone conversations to a minimum and don't let him go to after-school activities. If he really is sick, he will enjoy having the time to rest; and if he isn't, he will learn that staying home isn't fun. If he stays home from school on a Friday, keep him home from friends' houses and activities all weekend to continue resting.

◉ Teachers become irked when you ask them to perform additional tasks like preparing assignments in advance, providing extra tutoring to catch up on missed lessons, or giving makeup quizzes.

◉ Students who miss class work because of trips or extended sickness often feel anxious upon returning to the classroom unless they stay current on assignments during their absence. Although your child will miss out on the instruction only a teacher can provide, keeping up with makeup work will give him a basic understanding of the material covered in class and let him know what questions he should ask the teacher when he returns to school.

◉ A fax machine can be very useful as you try to keep your child on track during sick days. Ask your child's teacher to fax a copy of the weekly lesson plan or any assignments that your child missed. You can also fax your child's homework assignments back to the school so the teacher can correct them.

◉ Get in touch with another parent to arrange a sick-day buddy who can bring work and materials over to your child.

I don't ever think it's appropriate for parents to let their children take a day off from school unless they are sick. There is a direct correlation between attendance and academic achievement. We find some parents do not base family vacations around school vacations and they expect it to be okay with us, but it's not. We have 180 days to teach and each one is important to us.
—*Paul O'Brien, 7th to 12th grade math and science teacher for 27 years,*
  Sheffield, Massachusetts

There's no easy way for a teacher to assign work for kids who have missed class, because it means going back and teaching what the child missed. You can't replace classroom instruction. It doesn't matter where the kids are or for what purpose—when they're out they lose learning time. Every year I had several kids who were out on vacations, and their grades for those terms were lower than for the terms they were in school. And how much time do I have to assign extra work for the following week with 175 kids? It takes a lot of time to prepare work for the whole week a student will be out. Although I've written my own curriculum in advance, honestly, with day-to-day teaching you have to be flexible. If someone's stuck or if a class needs more time on something, you'll spend more time. I won't give the student who's out anything that needs modeling and instruction. Kids need guidance—if they could do it on their own, they wouldn't be in school. I can't say it enough: Keep your kids in school. Take your vacations, but go when everybody else goes. Teachers have to be in the classroom every day of school, too.
—*Susan Segaloff, 5th grade, special education, and reading teacher for 12 years,*
  Norton, Massachusetts

How Can I Get My Disorganized Child on Track?

Some children lag behind their potential because they lack basic self-management and organizational skills and have trouble with concepts like planning ahead, prioritizing responsibilities, and managing time effectively.

Organized students set themselves up for success. Those who consistently use classroom-adopted formats, graphic organizers, editing checklists, and problem-solving strategies realize that taking advantage of the right tools ensures achievement.
—David Lancucki, 3rd to 7th grade teacher for 23 years, King William County, Virginia

There are lots of easy things you can do at home with your child to practice organization skills, like arranging the sock drawer, alphabetizing books, magazines, or CDs, or reorganizing a cabinet. These work because they're hands-on, multisensory activities. To keep schoolwork organized, try color coding everything. In the red reading folder goes anything a child gets which has to do with reading or English; the math folder is green, like money; social studies is blue, like the ocean. Equate the colors with subjects, picking quirky things to make the connection, as it helps kids remember what goes where!
—Lynn M., high school, deaf students, and middle school special education teacher for 21 years, Boston, Massachusetts

Backpacks are trash magnets! Food, money, and papers end up at the bottom. Make a ritual of cleaning your child's backpack out once a week with him and talk about how to keep it better organized. Organization is a lifelong skill children need to learn.
—Chris Grimm, 7th grade social studies teacher for 3 years, Ventura, California

Teachers send home tons of information that can get lost in the depths of backpacks. Establish a routine at home so what you need to send back to school actually gets here. Just as you need to make sure you know what's going on in a job environment, it's the same thing with your kids' school environment. It's part of the home-school connection.
—Sue Abrams, elementary school principal and former 1st to 5th grade teacher for 22 years, Natick, Massachusetts

◉   To help your child improve in these areas, share your best planning strategies, both by example and direct teaching.

◉   An assignment book is a great organizational tool. Get your child into the habit of writing in it every day, even noting when he has no homework. Remind him to look it over before leaving school to make sure he takes home all the materials he will need.

◉   Teachers often give assignments at the end of a period, and your child may be too tired or rushed to write them down accurately or remember details like page numbers. If this happens repeatedly, ask the teacher to initial what your child has written down. That way, she checks it for accuracy and he doesn't spend an hour working on the wrong thing.

◉   Use a color-coded system for different subjects. If your child has a notebook, a folder, and a binder in the same subject, they should all be the same color. This will make it easier for him to grab the proper materials between classes and bring the right ones home.

◉   Another way to help your child organize is to buy him a large monthly desktop calendar on which he can write down his homework assignments, test and quiz dates, and other important deadlines. Mount the calendar in an easily accessible spot in your child's workspace or on your kitchen fridge.

What If My Child Constantly Forgets Things?

◉   Be proactive, especially if you know your child is prone to misplacing or forgetting his things. Put his complete identification, including phone number, on all of his belongings (jacket, textbooks, notebooks, etc.), so if he leaves them in school there is a better chance that someone will return them.

◉   At the beginning of the school year, help your child create a resource list with the names and phone numbers of homework buddies, and note which friends have a home fax machine in case of forgotten homework assignments.

◉ If your child's school doesn't already have one, suggest they start a phone or email system for students to access homework assignments.

◉ Designate a spot by the front door where everything for school goes the night before: gym clothes, books, homework, projects, and permission slips. Organizing completed work into the right spot should be an evening ritual, not a scramble as your child gets ready to walk out the door in the morning. Put sticky notes as reminders in places he's sure to notice them.

◉ If your child has a rotating schedule or special classes like gym and art on specific days of the week, mark this on your calendar so you can remind him to bring in his sneakers or art smock when he needs them.

◉ Consider buying copies of your child's heavier textbooks to keep at home so he doesn't have to lug them around in his backpack every day.

◉ Look into buying a basic fax machine that doubles as a copier so your child can receive missing homework and project instructions from classmates or make an extra copy of his notes to work on.

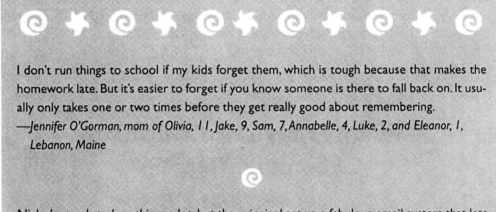

I don't run things to school if my kids forget them, which is tough because that makes the homework late. But it's easier to forget if you know someone is there to fall back on. It usually only takes one or two times before they get really good about remembering.
—Jennifer O'Gorman, mom of Olivia, 11, Jake, 9, Sam, 7, Annabelle, 4, Luke, 2, and Eleanor, 1, Lebanon, Maine

Nicholas tends to lose things a lot, but the principal set up a fabulous email system that lets the parents know what projects and homework teachers have assigned. Every week or so they update it and email it out to all parents. This has been instrumental in helping us keep Nicholas on track.
—Michelle Chartrand, mom of Nicholas, 12, and Olivia, 11, Banier, Ottawa

How Can I Master the Morning Liftoff?

◉ To decrease stress in the mornings, load the car with the items you and your child need for work, school, or daycare the night before. If that's not feasible, place coats, bags, and lunch boxes by the door, so you can grab them easily on the way out.

◉ Designate a shelf, basket, or area in which family members can place items they need to take out the door in the morning. Check the calendar in case your child needs sneakers for gym or a snack for a field trip.

◉ Establish a regular routine: when to wake up, who wakes up whom, and when you leave or your child meets his carpool.

◉ Pack lunches and refrigerate sandwiches—this may be easiest to do while making dinner. Put your car keys with the sandwiches if it helps you remember to add them to lunchboxes in the morning, or put a note on the lunchboxes to remind you.

◉ Have your child pick out the clothes he wants to wear the night before or lay out two outfits for him to choose between in the morning. Choose your own outfit and lay out your clothes the night before to make dressing hassle-free.

◉ Set clocks ahead by ten minutes to help you stay on time in the morning.

◉ Keep breakfast simple, and get your child to commit to a choice the night before. You can make some hot items, like pancakes, French toast, and bacon ahead of time and then reheat them. Save more elaborate breakfast meals for the weekend.

◉ Keep child-sized cups of milk and juice in the fridge so your child can help himself.

◉ If you are a coffee drinker, prepare your coffeemaker and set out a travel mug.

◉ For those desperate mornings when you or your child oversleeps, have breakfast items like muffins, fruit, or granola bars he can eat in the car.

◉ Make getting ready a contest: Can your child beat you at getting dressed or putting on shoes?

◉ Mount an outdoor thermometer where your child can easily see it, and teach him how to read it and dress appropriately.

🌀 Banish television in the morning to avoid wasting the precious time everyone needs to prepare for the day. Instead, play music to energize your kids as they get ready.

🌀 For the last minute, out-the-door rush:

✦ Have toothbrushes, toothpaste, and a towel in the kitchen for quick access if you run late.

✦ Keep barrettes, hair bands, and a brush in a basket near the front door.

✦ Keep a basket of extra socks with shoes by the door.

🌀 Make every effort to keep mornings pleasant, smooth, and positive. Starting off the morning in a negative way has a big impact on your child's day at school.

We do as much as possible the night before, such as packing homework, getting lunch money, signing papers and early-dismissal forms, and putting gym clothes in their backpacks. If anything has to wait until morning—for example, if gym clothes are in the dryer—I write a huge note and tape it to the door where we'll see it in the morning. I put my boys' clothes for the morning in a plastic dishpan in the reverse order that they are put on—shoes on the bottom, underwear on the top. The boys know if it's not in the box, they can't wear it. No negotiations in the morning.
—*Amy Boyle McCarthy, mom of Dylan, 9, and Shawn, 8, Pittsburgh, Pennsylvania*

🌀

I take 15 minutes a night and devote it 100% to organizing for the next day. Get lunch ready, bags for work and daycare by the door or in the car, anything needed for daycare (diapers, wipes, forms) in the car, mail that needs to go out in the mailbox, coffeepot ready, outfits ready for my son and me—right down to the socks and shoes.
—*Nicole Sullo, mom of Antonio, 3, Milford, Massachusetts*

🌀

For each kid we made up bus tickets that had a checklist with all the stuff they needed to get done each morning, and they have to turn them in before leaving to catch the bus. We don't have to ask, "Do you have your homework, permission slips, and lunch?" It keeps them focused and makes organization fun.

—Kim Shepherd, mom of Jessica, 17, Jeremy and Josh, 12, and Jennifer, 10, Indianapolis, Indiana

My boys have used an alarm clock since they were five years old, and instead of telling them what time to get up, I make them use critical thinking. I say, "If we have to leave at 7:30, what time will you have to get up?" Since everyone in our house sits down at 7:20 for breakfast, and they need to factor in brushing their teeth and getting dressed, they will think, "I need to wake up at 7:00." And I'll say, "Well, let's give you five more minutes, just in case something slows you down," and we set the alarm for 6:55. It's a guided process, but they do the thinking.

—Libby Anne Inabinet, kindergarten, 1st grade, reading, and gifted and talented teacher for 15 years, Columbia, South Carolina

Kids need a high-protein breakfast. As a teacher, I can tell which kids ate a bowl of sugary cereal because they're tired by 8:30. Their sugar level is too high in the morning and then drops quickly. Kids need something that will keep them going all day.

—Anne Wonson Curry, 5th to 12th grade math and science teacher for 12 years, Rockport, Massachusetts

I wish parents knew that getting to school on time is really important. We start learning at the beginning of the day, and being on time is a life skill children need to learn as soon as possible.

—Mary Beth Lewison, 2nd and 3rd grade teacher for 15 years in Ludlow, Massachusetts

When my oldest was little, getting out the door felt like a daily fire drill, so I put a timer on and said, "When you hear the timer go off, you have seven minutes until we have to leave." Eventually, it became that they didn't even need it anymore, they would only need a five-minute warning every once in a while. It taught them a lot about time and routine.

—Nancy Woods, mom of Jonathan, 10, and Maura, 6, Duxbury, Massachusetts

How Can I Make Family Dinners Part of the Daily Routine?

◉ The primary moments of family time now happen in the car, instead of at the dinner table, due to the competing demands of activities, sports, and work. According to research by the University of Minnesota, in the past 20 years the number of families who eat dinner together regularly has declined 33%. It has gone so far that we even have an American National Eat Dinner Together Week, from October 1st to 7th, to remind us to gather around the dinner table!

◉ The family dinner hour often devolves into the family half-hour and finally into the fast-food circuit, where you eat on the go between your child's flute lesson and basketball practice. Amid all the scurrying about, it's easy to forget how gathering around a table to eat and talk centers the family, offers a critical time to regroup, and recreates the family culture that binds everyone together.

◉ Studies show that teens who dine with their families five or more times a week are twice as likely to receive A's in school as those who have family dinners two or fewer times a week.

◉ To make family dinners a priority, resolve to eat dinner together at least four times a week even if it's simply take-out pizza. It doesn't have to be gourmet, just relaxed.

◉ Have your child grab a snack to tide him over on nights when you can't sit down to eat dinner until everyone finishes activities or comes home from work. Even if one parent cannot make it home from work in time, it is still valuable to have a family dinner.

◉ Dinnertime should be a time for talking, catching up, sharing tidbits from your day, laughing together, and building intimacy as a family—things you can't do from the sidelines of a game or rushing about in the car. Keep the conversation light and upbeat, as the whole point is to enjoy each other, not to use mealtime to air major grievances or discuss serious issues.

I really try to limit my children's activities, as I don't want a frantic family. The boys do fencing, which meets two times a week in the early evening on the other side of town. On the morning my daughter's not in school she rides horses, and she has dance one late afternoon a week. Even though this isn't a lot, it still leaves us with only two nights a week for dinner at home.

—*Karen Carter, mom of Josh, 7, Dalton, 5, and Alexa, 3*

My general and flexible guidelines to preserve family time and downtime that have worked well are: no activities between 5:30 P.M. and 7:00 P.M. for family dinner. As the whole family supports the person involved in the activity, it must work for all of us.

—*Lisa Kanazawa, mom of Connor, 10, Garrison, 6, and Mitchell, 1, Danville, California*

How Can I Get My Child to Talk About His Day?

Of students aged 10 to 13, 75% say they would like to talk to their parents more about schoolwork. Studies have shown that when parents and children talk about school and school events, children perform better academically.

Ask your child questions about school every day and really listen to what he says. His feelings about school can let you know when he is having a problem with a teacher, work, or a bully. Start this practice early on to establish it as a routine. If you show you are interested in what happens at school on a daily basis, your child will be more likely to come directly to you when there is a real problem, and you will be better equipped to find a solution.

Use active listening with your child to find out more about his day. Instead of jumping in with your own opinions, stay silent for a few seconds to see if he goes on. If he provides you with more information, either respond with neutral comments or repeat what he said to elicit further response.

◉   Talk to your child about how you are feeling, as well. Tell him your goals and the events that take place during your day. These conversations will impart your values to him and also make the conversations more equal.

◉   "Did anyone get in trouble with the teachers today?" This question usually gets conversation flowing, especially with younger children, who will want to tell you the specifics of any atrocities committed in detail, from time-outs during recess to sitting on the red bench by the principal's office. This icebreaker makes it easy to transition to the more mundane and less dramatic details of your child's day, such as what he learned, what games he played, and with whom he spent most of his time.

◉   Try asking silly questions such as, "Did they serve zebra again for snack today?" After your child laughs or rolls his eyes at you, he might just proceed to tell you every detail about snacks that you ever wanted to hear.

◉   Listen to your kids each day after school, whether this means driving slowly, taking a 10-minute walk before household chores in the evening, or sitting and having a snack with them. There might be things your child won't tell you at that time, but because you were listening and opened that window for him, he might tell you later.

◉   Make yourself emotionally available to your child at bedtime, as this is a common time for children to unload their fears and dilemmas. Often, right before he goes to bed your child will tell you about something that has been bothering him all day.

◉   Keep up with the news and share what you are learning with your child. Talking to your child about current events, politics, and history will give him the sense that you consider him intelligent enough to take part in the conversation, as well as give him a better understanding of what is going on in the world around him, which can help him in school.

◉   While young children are usually very excited about discussing the school day with you, middle-school students become virtually mute. The effusive child who used to run home every day to tell you every minute detail of everything that transpired in class suddenly becomes a stone-faced middle schooler who gives up no more than "yes" or "no" responses. To overcome this silence, ask pointed, open-ended questions instead of the usual "How was your day?" Ask about friends, a specific class, or what the coach had them do at practice.

ⓒ Don't be satisfied with one-word answers. Keep asking questions until your child tells you something of substance. Even if he gets annoyed, he will know that you really care.

ⓒ Let your child express opinions, even those contrary to yours, without reprisal or anger. You want him to feel comfortable telling you what he thinks.

Sometimes, when you ask your child what happened in school, he will say, "Oh yeah, well, nothing." When this happens, encourage him to open up and talk about his day. Guiding children is much more effective than direct confrontation. So, instead of rushing him, try asking one leading question over a snack and then a couple more at dinnertime. Always listen carefully and without judgment. In so many instances, if you take the time to listen, your child will talk not only about the basics, but also about more important things, such as a bothersome recess situation.
—*Kathy Traficanti, 4th to 6th grade teacher for 9 years, Brighton, Massachusetts*

I often have to remind myself to stop what I'm doing and really listen to what my kids are saying. It's so easy to say, "Uh-huh," but kids will tell you almost everything you want to know if you pay attention to them.
—*Kymme Simchak, mom of Brandi, 19, Courtney, 13, and Colleen, 10, Seguin, Texas*

If my daughter comes home upset about something, I ask her to tell me the story again to see if it comes out the same the second time. I ask her if it has happened before and if anyone else in class felt the same way. Sometimes I have to let it go because she gets too upset, but I'll have my husband do the same thing when he gets home a couple hours later to see if she's still upset and if this could really be an issue. I avoid bringing it up around bedtime unless I can put a positive spin on it. I'll remind her the next morning to tell me about it if it happens again, and let her know we will get involved should anything happen.
—*Ellen Cameron, mom of Alison, 8, and Hilary, 4, Lexington, Massachusetts*

Keeping our middle school sons talking to us is something we are struggling with right now. Our best approach is to keep the lines of communication open. We try to be as truthful as possible, no matter what the question, hoping this will compel them to keep talking to us. It's scary, and you never really know if they are shutting down or not, but I think it helps that they know we are open and honest with them.
—*Alesha Worra, mom of Brandon, 12, and Travis, 11, Greer, South Carolina*

I used to nag my son, but the more I nagged the less he told me. So I asked him, "What happened? You used to talk to me more." And he told me I was being too nosy. I realized he was growing up and I had to give him his space. I still don't think he tells me everything, but I think it's much better now.
—*Farida Kathawalla, mom of Tanveer, 13, Westford, Massachusetts*

Kids are more likely to tell you what happens on the bus than in the academic classroom. You can have a better discussion with them if you ask the right questions. For example, I ask, "Did anyone get into trouble at school today?" If he says yes, we then talk about why the student acted that way and why it was wrong. Sometimes you have to be sneaky if you want to know what is going on—it doesn't work to just ask, "What happened in school today?"
—*Kerri Charette, elementary school teacher for 10 years, Ledyard, Connecticut*

I don't ask my daughters how school went. Instead, I ask them the best and worst things that happened during their day. It's important to find something positive and end on a good note. I try to ask about specifics—how their friends are doing, who they sat with at lunch, and what subjects they had that day.
—*Karen Davie, mom of Shea, 9, and Jade, 7, Ontario, Canada*

Asking your child questions every day about what goes on in class will allow you to avoid surprise red flags from the teacher.
—*Niambi Muhammad, 1st and 2nd grade teacher for 4 years, Chicago, Illinois*

Television and the Internet: Passivity Central

How Can I Make the Best of the Learning Experiences TV Has to Offer?

◉ Although he may consider it a strictly recreational activity, show your child that watching TV, DVDs, and videos can be an educational experience, too. Teach him to ask critical questions about what he watches, and explain that shows cannot and do not always accurately reflect the real world.

◉ TV has been shown to improve the average child's vocabulary significantly and to give him a more advanced sense of order of events and spatial relationships. Programs such as *Sesame Street* teach shapes, numbers, letters, and other information that helps children as they enter school. Check out PBS, The Learning Channel, and The Discovery Channel for quality programming.

◉ Keeping a dictionary next to the TV will encourage your child to look up words he doesn't understand and will enrich your child's viewing experience.

◉ Make up physical games to play during the commercials, like a jumping-jack contest, and do not put out too many snacks for your child to munch on while he watches.

◉ Offer trade-offs: for every hour of TV, DVD, or video time, your child has to spend an hour running around in the backyard or doing another form of physical activity.

◉ By the time your child turns 18, he will likely have spent more time in front of the television than in the classroom. He will likely have seen 40,000 murders and 200,000 violent acts on television before graduating high school. Parents' concern about the quality of television programs comes with good reason—children have become increasingly desensitized to violence, which has had damaging and long-lasting effects on their social skills, capacity for empathy, and behavior in romantic relationships.

© Studies show that parental monitoring is key to counteracting the negative influence of media violence. By watching TV with your child and having open discussions about the content of shows, you help him put what he sees into perspective.

© The television industry has responded to the public's concern over content by giving consumers more information about programming. Make good use of the violence ratings and viewer warnings by banning or even blocking inappropriate programming.

© Talk to your child when you catch negative stereotypes on television or when you feel concerned that he won't be able to distinguish the fantasy from reality. If you see the hero of a story using violence to solve problems, pose questions like, "What would you have done instead in that situation?"

© Keep the television in a central location so you can easily keep an eye on what your child is watching, and TV viewing becomes a family-centered activity. Don't put a separate television in your child's room, as he will then have the opportunity to watch as much of whatever he wants without your knowledge or approval.

I have to admit our family watches a lot of TV, but we are sure to monitor the quality of shows and my kids have always had bedtimes that preclude them watching too late at night.
—*Martha Judiscak, mom of Jimmy, 17, Vicki, 16, and Danny, 11, Knoxville, Tennessee*

©

As far as TV is concerned, when I do have a situation where my children have seen something bad, such as at a friend's house where the same rules don't apply, I sit down and talk about what's wrong with what they watched. For example, if they have seen something scary, I sit down and we talk about what's real, and make sure they know that things are made more scary for the movies.
—*Suzanne Stoll, mom of Charity, 10, and Jesse, 7, Wampum, Pennsylvania*

What TV Limits Should I Set for My Child?

◉   Studies have shown that your brain is actually more active while you are sleeping than while you're watching TV. This especially harms children, as they spend hours zoning out in front of the screen and their minds are still growing.

◉   Controlling television consumption is one way you can immediately and directly aid your child's success in school. Studies have found that students who watch less TV spend more time on homework, increasing their school success.

◉   Excessive television has recently been linked with long-term behavioral problems in children, such as violent behavior, obesity, shorter attention spans, decreased sociality, poor performance in school, sexual precociousness, and drug use.

◉   Television is perhaps most harmful because it takes time that children could use for creative, constructive activities that would enhance their learning and enrich their personalities. Academic achievement significantly decreases for children who watch more than 10 hours of TV a week, and the average school child watches 27 hours each week!

◉   Many children watch endless hours of TV because their parents do. If you don't care about TV, your kids probably won't either, so turn the set off. During family time and homework hours, catch up on some work or read the newspaper or a good novel.

◉   Limit TV time by allowing your child to go through the TV guide and tape programs for later viewing. This strategy allows you to exercise control over what your child watches while encouraging him to plan ahead and use his time wisely.

◉   Agree on limits that work for your family. Some houses work best with a standard rule of one hour of television per evening, while others do better with a more flexible arrangement.

◉   Discuss the reasons why there are commercials on TV and how advertising tries to get you to buy toys and other items. Teach your child how to be skeptical of the advertising messages, and how to distinguish commercials from other types of television programming. Point out the exaggerations advertisers use.

◉ Some suggestions for family TV limits:

✦ No TV during mealtimes.

✦ No TV on school days, or no TV on school days until everyone has finished all their work and a half hour of leisure reading.

✦ No TV before completing household tasks.

✦ Allot your child a particular number of TV-viewing hours per week, and let him choose how he uses them with your supervision. Unused hours could be cashed in for a small treat.

✦ National TV Turn-off Week is scheduled for every April. Make this a celebratory time, with family game nights and outings. Your child might just learn how easy it is to live without television.

One very basic, but important thing you can do to help your child succeed is to limit your child's TV time. Regulate what your kids watch and turn the TV off, particularly when they have not done homework or to make sure they get to bed on time. Don't let television rule their lives—it shouldn't be the chief source of entertainment.
—*Kathy Traficanti, 4th to 6th grade teacher for 9 years, Brighton, Massachusetts*

Tell your children what you want as far as TV and the Internet goes. I allow my sons two hours of TV per Saturday and one hour from 8:00 P.M.–9:00 P.M. on weekdays. Also, they have to show us what they are playing on the computer. Some people have told me I'm over the top on this, but if my kids know I'm paying attention to everything it will cut down on the bad stuff.
—*Alesha Worra, mom of Brandon, 12, and Travis, 11, Greer, South Carolina*

It's so easy for kids to turn on the TV and veg out. To cut down on the amount of TV my son watched when he was younger, we got an entertainment unit with doors that could be locked. That way when the allotted time for TV was up, it was over without hassling.
—*Sibylle Barrasso, mom of Lane, 16, Wellesley, Massachusetts*

We started a policy in our family beginning in elementary school that there's no TV during the school year from Sunday night to Friday, except for the occasional news segment, educational show, or sports event. Then, during the summer, anything goes.
—*Elise Tofias Phillips, mom of Zeke, 16, Jeremy, 14, and Adam, 12, Newton, Massachusetts*

We have turned on the radio a lot more and play books on tape instead of turning on the TV because a lot of the time we just had the TV on as background noise and I didn't really think about it. Now we'll listen to Dr. Seuss books on tape and my daughter's much calmer—there are no loud commercials to confuse her, and her behavior changes without these interruptions.
—*Kendra French, mom of Parker, 2, Fairfax, Virginia*

My daughter, like her father, is a huge computer person. She would be on the computer way too much if I didn't monitor her. I tell her she can play one or two games and set a time limit. I monitor TV the same way. A lot of times I say to her, "It's beautiful outside! Do you even know what you are watching?" Sometimes it just becomes second nature to turn the TV on.
—*Sheila Cross, mom of Emily, 8, Memphis, Tennessee*

I have a friend who does the No TV from Monday through Friday rule and all those kids want to do over the weekends is watch TV—it becomes this forbidden fruit. I like to enforce a healthy balance.
—*Nancy Woods, mom of Jonathan, 10, and Maura, 6, Duxbury, Massachusetts*

How Can I Ensure My Child Uses the Internet Safely and Productively?

The Internet has become an important part of how we learn and interact in the modern world. Children have to become computer and Internet savvy at increasingly younger ages, as technology enters the classroom and the computer becomes the site of social intercourse in earlier grades. Help your child take advantage of this invaluable resource and teach him how to use it properly and effectively.

If you are not computer literate, learn to use the computer alongside your child. Take advantage of local programs at libraries and community colleges that teach beginners how to use the computer and Internet, or ask a librarian to show you some basic steps.

Many kids are computer experts, so let your child teach you. Ask him to show you what he's learned, and find out his favorite websites.

Take advantage of the wide variety of educational software available to help your child become comfortable with the computer and enhance his learning opportunities. Ask your child's teacher to recommend fun and informative software your child may enjoy.

While the Internet provides a wealth of opportunities for your child, it does pose a number of valid safety concerns, including running into inappropriate material on the Web, sharing personal information with a stranger, and being harassed through email, instant messaging, or postings.

The best way to help your child navigate the Internet is to spend time using it with him. Watch him as he surfs around and chats with friends. Instruct him not to give out personal information such as his full name, address, phone number, passwords, school name, after-school activities, and picture. Let him know that his conversations with strangers could be potentially dangerous, as people he interacts with online may not be as honest or benevolent as they seem.

Keep your family computer in a public place so you can better supervise its use and monitor how much time your child spends on it.

There are a number of games children can download off the Internet, many of which contain excessive violence and sexual content. To stay on top of your child's activities, check out resources like GetNetWise (www.getnetwise.org), a free service from public interest groups and Internet corporations, or FamiliesConnect (www.ala.org/iconn/familiesconnect.html), an American Library Association service. These sites provide information to help you make informed decisions about the Internet.

ⓔ Invest in filtering devices. Like the television's V-chip, many Internet browsers offer parents the option of filters that block out inappropriate websites.

Lately, my kids have been consumed by instant messaging, and will walk into our house and go straight to the computer. We have been somewhat successful in limiting them on the computer to thirty minutes a day.
—*Elise Tofias Phillips, mom of Zeke, 16, Jeremy, 14, and Adam, 12, Newton, Massachusetts*

Jack is very interested in the computer and we let him use more than I thought we would. But, he really likes educational programs so it actually works to his advantage. For a lot of these things, it's better not to set very rigid rules because in doing so you inadvertently make the activity more desirable. If one of our children has a natural interest in something, we by all means encourage them to explore it. In our house it's more about establishing a routine than enforcing rigid rules.
—*Vinca LaFleur, mom of Jackson, 6, and Evan, 4, Washington, D.C.*

I have a parental block on our computer so I can see all the websites my son visits.
—*Jennifer Guss, mom of Fred, 10, Hannah, 4, and Sophie, 2, Montvale, New Jersey*

The computer is in a room adjacent to the family room so I make it a point to walk through the room often, very quietly without a big announcement.
—*Martha Judiscak, mom of Jimmy, 17, Vicki, 16, and Danny, 11, Knoxville, Tennessee*

Reading

How Important Is Reading?

◉ The skills a child acquires from reading form the building blocks of the learning process and are crucial for academic success. Not only is reading involved in almost 90% of all schoolwork, it raises IQ and standardized test scores as it teaches abstract thought and increases vocabulary.

◉ Reading to younger children greatly improves their early reading and writing skills. The fact that only half of all parents with children ages 3 to 5 read to them on a daily basis helps explain why 40% of students enter kindergarten behind where they should be.

◉ In addition to exposing students to new ideas and writing styles, reading also teaches them how to concentrate intently, see subtleties in literature and in life more acutely, and gain more enjoyment from class discussions. As much as 75% of what students learn comes from what they read.

How Can I Make the Most of Reading with My Child?

Reading aloud to your child increases his vocabulary, expands his knowledge, improves his listening skills, stimulates his imagination, sharpens his observation skills, promotes self-confidence, and builds problem-solving skills. It also allows him to enjoy and appreciate literature that is too challenging for him to read himself.

Find a regular time and place for reading every day. Choose a time when you and your child are relaxed, such as before bedtime, and read for as long as he is interested. Before you begin, make sure he is settled and ready to focus.

Vary your tone and pace, and make reading enjoyable by using different voices and expressing the emotions in the text. Create suspense and anticipation, while giving your child time to absorb the content and pore over the illustrations by reading at a slow speed.

Children often look like they are distracted when they really are paying attention. Fidgeting and squirming doesn't necessarily mean your child isn't listening. If you have trouble getting a very young child to sit still through a book, try reading to him in the tub.

Ask questions to make sure he stays interested and engaged. Check to see if he remembers the order of events. Get him to tell you, in his own words, what he thinks the book is about. Ask what he thinks will happen to the main characters at various points in the story.

Encourage your child to follow the text on the page as you read to him. Pointing to the words as you read helps him learn how to pronounce difficult ones.

Help your child discover the meanings of words he hasn't seen before, and make sure he feels comfortable asking questions about the story. Encourage interruptions and respond to his insights with comments like, "Good thinking!"

Ask your child more "why" than "what" questions, such as, "Why do you think the character made that choice? Why do you think the story ended that way?" Analytical questions help your child become a better thinker.

⊚ Encourage your child to tell you his own stories, and challenge him to come up with alternative endings to the stories you read together.

⊚ At several key points throughout the story, ask your child to predict what will happen next and discuss whether the events in the story could really happen.

⊚ Discuss any moral of the story, as this gives you a chance to subtly impart your values and ethics.

⊚ Reread your child's favorites again and again. Relate incidents in the book to occurrences in your child's life.

⊚ Never take away reading time as a punishment for your child. Instead, offer extra story time as a treat he can earn.

⊚ Don't stop reading aloud together once your child begins school. Research shows that children whose parents continue reading to them and listening to them read become more competent readers.

⊚ Some intriguing questions to ask your older child when reading aloud:

✳ Do you find the characters interesting and believable? Do you relate to any one in particular?

✳ Where does this story take place? Is the book set in the past, present, or future? What season is it?

✳ What distinguishes the characters from one another? Which characters are the main ones and which are supporting?

✳ Teach your child to identify the basic story line as well as the characters, their relationships, the roles they play, what they should or need to do, their personalities, unique identifying traits, personal obstacles to overcome, what is at stake, how a character changes, what he learns, how we learn about the characters' major conflicts, points of view, and what we know as readers that the characters don't.

⊚ Also point out how information is conveyed in a book including description, narration, symbols, metaphors, irony, allegory, parable, sentence structure, vocabulary, contrasts, and parallels.

It's never too early to start reading to your children. Once they reach school age, taking time out of every afternoon and evening to work on the reading skills they are learning in school is a good way to be involved.
—Debbie McCandless, mom of BC, 18, and Sarah, 13, Knob Lick, Kentucky

How Can I Expand My Child's Vocabulary?

⊙ Keep a list of new words you and your child encounter as you read. Ask him to share any new words he has learned, give him age-appropriate crossword puzzles, and read newspaper articles together to find new words. Keep poetry magnets on the refrigerator.

⊙ The best readers are often the best spellers. Review spelling and vocabulary lists with your child and use the words in your everyday conversations to reemphasize them.

⊙ Help your child analyze words by showing him how to break them down into syllables, and teach him the meanings of common roots, prefixes, and suffixes.

⊙ Teach your child about context clues that will enable him to guess the meaning of a word by looking at the words around it. If he gets stuck on a word, tell him to skip it, move on, and then reread the sentence.

⊙ When your child asks you what a word means or how to spell it, find it together in the dictionary.

Whether or not your child's teacher assigns it, require 30 minutes of reading a night, because it greatly increases vocabulary and world knowledge.
—*Julie Kirkpatrick Carroll, 4th grade teacher for 6 years, Benson, Minnesota*

Teach your children how to use a dictionary when they're young and make sure they continue to use it when they're older. Kids don't like to use dictionaries because a lot of the time they're using collegiate dictionaries, and the meaning isn't there for them. They should have an appropriate dictionary with pictures and few words to start out with, and then move up to intermediate dictionaries up through grade 8.
—*Susan Segaloff, 5th grade, special education, and reading teacher for 12 years,*
   Norton, Massachusetts

⊙ Many libraries offer books with audiotapes, which your child can use to track the words on the page as he hears them.

⊙ Play the Dictionary Game: One family member opens the dictionary and points to a word. Each of the others writes down what he thinks is the definition, and then everyone reads his guess aloud. The person with the closest definition wins. A variation on this game can teach your child spelling skills.

How Do I Instill a Love of Reading in My Child?

⊙ Good readers only become so by hours spent reading. From comic books to Thoreau, it doesn't really matter what your child is reading, as long as he sticks with it.

⊙ Instill a passion for reading by making library trips a weekly event about which your child can get excited. To make the most out of these visits, get your child his own library card. Also, ask the librarian to recommend an age-appropriate book series. Kids often fall in love with a series' style and characters, content to read book after book in the series.

@ Consider giving your child a monthly book allowance to encourage him to buy new books. Your willingness to spend money on books shows him how much you value reading. Subscribe your child to a children's magazine that will foster his interest in reading.

@ Always include a few gift-wrapped books as part of birthday and holiday presents to your child.

@ Keep a plethora of reading materials available in your home in easy-to-reach places: the bathroom, the family room, and especially by the TV. They do not have to be expensive—peruse yard sales or secondhand bookstores to find good books for your child.

@ Keep a bag of books in the car for an easy and educational way to keep your child entertained. Take the books along on errands to places where you might have to wait, like the doctor's office or bank.

@ Help your child create a special reading space where he feels comfortable. Something as simple as a few pillows and a poster can personalize an area of the house and make reading feel like a special activity.

@ One night of the weekend, bedtime rules are off! Tell your child he can stay up as long as he wants to enjoy a good book in the comfort of his bed.

@ Encourage your child to swap books with friends.

@ Be sure your child sees you reading frequently, as this reinforces the message that reading is important and enjoyable, and not something he simply has to do for school. Children who see their parents choose reading over television or other leisure activities are more likely to do so themselves.

@ It's impossible to enjoy reading if someone makes you do it, so don't push your child to read more than he wants to, even if you would like to see him reading more. When he does read for pleasure, give him positive feedback.

@ Ask your child about what he is reading. Treat him like an expert in the field—

everyone enjoys being admired. Ask what he likes and dislikes about a book, and take his opinions seriously.

◉   Help your child carve time out from his extracurricular activities for free time to enjoy a book for pleasure. If he doesn't have the time to read what he enjoys and only reads what he is forced to for school, his love of reading will invariably diminish.

I started reading to Maggie when she was in my womb, and when she was about 6 months old I took her to the library. I think exposing her to books by reading to her every day, joining two book clubs for children, and really limiting TV turned her into an avid reader.
—*Abby Gilhooley, mom of Maggie, 2, Chatham, Massachusetts*

Treat books as treasured articles and then your kids will, too. Bring books to special places, like a picnic or to grandparents' houses.
—*Mary McNamara, mom of Catherine, 7, and Patrick, 3, Wellesley, Massachusetts*

Read to your children as soon as they have more than a 2-minute attention span. When Sam was an infant, I would read *Us Weekly* or the newspaper to him—something I wanted to read on my own. I would just use a singsong voice and he would love it—he had no idea what I was reading about and he didn't care, it just taught him about words.
—*Danielle Cohen, mom of Sam, 3, Westford, Massachusetts*

We go to a kid-friendly bookstore where my daughter can explore and pull books off the shelf. We make games out of it: How many green books can you find? How many books can you find about elephants? We make it fun so she looks forward to going to the bookstore every time, especially now that she is developing interests we can explore. As great as the library is, you have to be quiet there, so kids can't be themselves. We found a place that lets her run around and be herself and she has so much more fun—she asks to go the bookstore almost every day now.
—*Kendra French, mom of Parker, 2, Fairfax, Virginia*

My son feels that his world is too busy to stop and read a book. So, during the summer we make library trips and take out books once a week. We also have "Mom's quiet time," where we'll sit on the couch and I'll read a little bit of what I'm reading to him. If he gets bored he can get up and run around but I always encourage him to sit as long as he can.
—*Suzanne Stoll, mom of Charity, 10, and Jesse, 7, Wampum, Pennsylvania*

If your child's favorite activity is skateboarding, read a magazine about that with him. Reading is reading. If he is reading comic books or books about rollerblading, that's great!
—*Dick Krebs, special education and 7th and 8th grade math teacher for 26 years, Yakima, Washington*

I was not a reader; I hated reading when I was a kid and not until later did I enjoy reading for pleasure, so I tried to do it differently with Olivia. Mostly, we model reading and expose her to it as much as possible. We read with her every night and she sees her father and me read a lot around the house, from books to the newspaper. We go to the library and check out books and really encourage her to make choices about the books she reads. We never forced reading upon her; instead, we made it just a fun thing to do.
—*Patty Potter, mom of Olivia Logan, 6, and Isabel Logan, 3, Ft. Worth, Texas*

Start a family book club, and set a time frame for when everyone has to have the book read by—either reading together or separately. Then discuss what you have read and share opinions.
—*Julie Kirkpatrick Carroll, 4th grade teacher for 6 years, Benson, Minnesota*

How Do I Choose the Best Books for My Child?

◉ When choosing books to read aloud to your child, give your reading selections balance and range. Exposing your child to all forms of literature, from science fiction to fairy tales, newspaper articles to riddles, will encourage him to be a well-rounded reader and improve his analytical skills.

◉ Consider your child's abilities when picking out books for him and match book length and difficulty to his listening skills and attention span. If you bring home books he thinks are too childish, he may become disenchanted with reading, but if you push him into reading material he finds too difficult, he may give up on reading for pleasure entirely.

◉ Allow for more independence with reading material as your child gets older. Children often turn to mature subject matter you may find yourself questioning. While it is okay to exert some limited influence, keep in mind that your child is reading out of curiosity, and restricting his choices will only make him less willing to share his reading experiences with you.

◉ Pick out books written by Newbery Medal–winning authors. Books win this award based on their excellence as American literature for children, and you can identify them by the gold or silver emblems on their front covers.

◉ Pick stories with clear messages and social contexts to help your child learn basic values and develop decision-making skills. These stories can also help your child understand difficult or trying times.

◉ Although many books for younger readers have pictures, get some without them so your child can visualize what happens in the story or illustrate it himself.

◉ For excellent suggestions on newly released children's titles, The American Library Association (ALA) compiles a list of notable children's books selected by librarians throughout the United States. Visit the association's website at http://www.ala.org.

It's very important to read books, but it doesn't matter what they are. If your child doesn't like to read novels, find out what he enjoys and supply it. My son is passionate about sports, but he's not into Harry Potter books, so I'm not going to make him read those. He likes to read the sports page of the newspaper. He runs out to the mailbox and will sometimes even leave the rest of the newspaper there and just bring in the sports page because he's so excited. Since that's what he enjoys, we subscribed to *Sports Illustrated for Kids.*
—*Libby Anne Inabinet, kindergarten, 1st grade, reading, and gifted and talented teacher for 15 years, Columbia, South Carolina*

Think about what books your child would be interested in. If you have a child who is interested in fire trucks, you're not going to get him to read about gardening. I've found that getting them interested in a certain author works also. Then you can say to them, "This is by that author that you like," which gets them into the book faster. Young kids like books with a lot of repetition because they feel as if they can read themselves even though they're reciting from memory. Saying the words while looking at them helps them think, "Maybe that says cat." Older kids like books with characters the same age as they are that they can identify with. If your child is struggling with an issue, find a book about it. For example, my younger child has ADHD, and so we got a lot of books about it. It got him interested in books and showed him that other kids had ADHD, too, so it was no big deal.
—*Kathy Carabine, pre-k and 3rd grade teacher for 16 years, Boston Massachusetts*

I allow my son a broad range of reading material—not all kids' books! He's really into building tree houses, so we went to the library and got a bunch of books on that.
—*Jennifer Guss, mom of Fred, 10, Hannah, 4, and Sophie, 2, Montvale, New Jersey*

Use librarians. They know books and what types your child might be interested in. They also make it easier to locate what you're looking for. You can ask the teacher what your child's reading level is or use this trick: Have him turn to any page in the middle of a book and read it aloud. Any time he hits a word he doesn't know or can't say, put up a finger. If you put up

one to two fingers the book is going to be easy for him, three to four fingers will be a challenge, and four or five will be too difficult. At a four or a five you should be doing some shared reading and have discussions about what's going on.
—*Susan Segaloff, 5th grade, special education, and reading teacher for 12 years, Norton, Massachusetts*

How Can I Encourage My Reluctant Reader?

© Studies show that as students move through the grades, voluntary reading decreases and negative attitudes toward reading increase. Often students' interest in reading begins to taper off around the time they enter middle school. Although your child may have loved reading when he was younger, extracurricular activities and friends often become more appealing than books. Also, as the amount of assigned work increases, he has less time to read for pleasure.

© Although your child may have built a strong reading foundation in his earlier years, a hiatus from reading can often prove detrimental to his reading skills and overall academic development.

© All kids will go through stages during which they read a lot and others in which they barely touch a book. This happens especially at periods of high stress or change, such as the transition to high school. Let your child move through these phases naturally and without forcing him to read, but allow him to read whatever he wants, including comics and books you think have little redeeming value. The most important thing is that he keeps reading.

© Try tying in reading choices to TV and movies. Check to see if there are any new movies or shows based on children's books, like *Holes, Harry Potter,* or *Stuart Little,* and consider reading the books yourself so you can discuss them with your child. For your older child, see the movie after he has finished reading the book. This experience can bring the book to life.

© Going to the theater can bring drama alive for your child and may encourage him to read the play later. Classics, like Shakespeare, have new dimension when witnessed live.

🌀   If you spend a lot of time in the car with your child, pick out a book-on-tape to listen to together as you drive. When read aloud, good literature can be a visceral experience.

🌀   While busy kids may not have the time to read a lengthy novel, a brief magazine article may be a more appealing length. Anthologies of short stories and poetry also offer quick reads.

🌀   Children who are just starting to take an interest in books tend to leaf through them without stopping at many pages or reading many words. Provide them with magazines to facilitate this first step. These kids will slowly spend more time on each page and actually start reading what's there.

If a child is averse to reading, it's often because he has a reading problem.
—*Kay Symons, special education and kindergarten to 8th grade teacher for 27 years,*
   South Georgia

🌀

Lots of students who don't like to read just don't know how to choose books. At our school, we have a reading program where students are supposed to read a certain number of books, and the librarian at my school says some will come in and pull a book off of the shelf without even looking to see what it is! Talk to your child about what interests him and what he would like to read about before you assume that he just doesn't like to read.
—*Jody Chambliss, kindergarten, 1st grade, and remedial reading teacher for 15 years,*
   Abilene, Texas

🌀

If your child is not assigned any particular kind of reading, encourage him to read various genres and explore. Get books on tape and have your child read as the tape plays. There's always an author and a genre for a child, but it's nice to explore several areas, not just mys-

teries or realistic fiction. Explore historical fiction, too, and explain that fictional characters have real backgrounds. Ask your child questions to lead him to books he will be interested in. Take him places then get books that follow his curiosity. For instance, if you go to the science museum and your child is interested in magnets, find books at his level about them.
—*Susan Segaloff, 5th grade, special education, and reading teacher for 12 years, Norton, Massachusetts*

Giving a child difficult reading materials when he isn't ready can cause him to lose interest and motivation. Easy reading actually helps comprehension more, and gives young readers a motivating sense of accomplishment.
—*Betty Edens, 2nd and 3rd grade reading teacher for 18 years, Hillsboro, Texas*

Although my husband and I are avid readers, my three older sons had a tough time getting excited about reading. They would see us read all the time, and were surrounded by reading materials, but they simply could not sit still for stories—they had no interest in them. I finally attended a workshop to pick up more tips because getting those three to love reading was not getting any easier. I learned a few different tactics, including having magazines and books lying around the house and allowing them to use comic books as reading material if nothing else worked. Eventually they started to improve.
—*Cindy Esposito, mom of Jon, Jason, and Chris, 23, Rhiannon, 16, and Justin, 13, Orange County, New York*

One of the things I've really had to talk to my students about is how long it takes to read. We time them so they see how long it actually takes to read a chapter, and many of them realize it doesn't take as long as they thought it did. Then it's easier for them to break it down so it doesn't seem so long, like reading just one chapter a night.
—*Jody Chambliss, kindergarten, 1st grade, and remedial reading teacher for 15 years, Abilene, Texas*

How Can I Help My Struggling Reader?

◉ If reading is a problem for your child, seek help—reading problems rarely resolve themselves without extra attention to specific skills.

◉ If your elementary school child's teacher tells you your child is struggling with reading, or if she gives your child an unexpectedly low grade on reading, work with the teacher to pinpoint your child's difficulties and find out where the problem lies. Is it his pronunciation, speed, or comprehension?

◉ The end of first grade is a good checkpoint to assess your child's reading capabilities. If your child has difficulty with reading and is lagging behind his peers, talk to the teacher to see if he should go to a reading specialist for help and testing.

◉ Around third and fourth grade, reading becomes crucial for success in most academic subjects because the emphasis shifts from learning to read to reading to

With a student who is reading below grade level, start at a level that he can understand. Make sure the vocabulary is within his range and look for main ideas together. Show your child how to use clues to find the main idea. Explain signal words that denote things like cause and effect or similes and other conventions.
—*Kristyn Mulada, educational director of a Sylvan Learning Center for 2 years and former kindergarten teacher, Hanover, Massachusetts*

My oldest child has had some difficulty with reading, so she has been leaving the classroom a few times a week for special reading instruction. Although she has benefited from this, she has expressed some anxieties about making up the normal classroom work she misses. We have worked together with the teacher to make sure it all gets done.
—*Linda Henell, mom of MaKena, 8, Sean, 5, and Cameryn, 3, Marco Island, Florida*

learn. So, if your child has difficulty reading or has low reading comprehension skills, his overall academic achievement will decline.

☉ Most important, find something your child is interested in reading about and that will help spark his passion for the world of books.

Homework

After 8 Hours at School, Why Does My Child Have So Much Homework?

Schools today give more homework than ever before—students face three times as much homework now as they did in 1980. Global competition and the fear that American students are falling behind the rest of the world academically have prompted this craze.

Homework builds your child's comfort with material by going over it again. It increases your child's academic learning time, improves his recollection and overall understanding of classroom material, encourages him to practice more comprehensive and inquisitive thinking about classroom topics, and can pique his interest in learning more about a subject.

More broadly, homework provides your child with the opportunity to become an independent learner. It also builds important personal skills, such as organization and time management, and helps children realize learning extends beyond the classroom. The long-term benefits of slogging through hours of tedious homework include the development of self-discipline, self-reliance, and independent problem solving.

While some parents believe homework creates additional academic stress, it can

Homework ideally gives my students more practice and repetition to ensure the things being learned go into long-term memory.
—*Sherri McWhorter, 4th grade teacher for 5 years, Augusta, Georgia*

Homework is important, but should be used for enrichment, not just to generate more work.
—*Nickey Langford, 2nd and 3rd grade teacher for 3 years, Birmingham, Alabama*

A lot of teachers give so-called busy work, but often it's only the parents who see it as merely something to keep their child busy.
—*Niambi Muhammad, 1st and 2nd grade teacher for 4 years, Chicago, Illinois*

I really wish homework didn't have "work" in the title.
—*Patty Potter, mom of Olivia Logan, 6, and Isabel Logan, 3, Ft. Worth, Texas*

The most successful students do their homework completely, on time, neatly, and thoughtfully. They get help when they don't understand something by asking questions in class, clarifying with peers, and staying for help after school. They also begin to study for tests ahead of time, a little each day, and not just the day before.
—*Claudia Fox Tree, 7th grade special education teacher for 15 years, Lincoln, Massachusetts*

actually decrease anxiety. Students who regularly complete their homework assignments typically receive higher scores on classroom tests than those who do not. This performance gap increases as children progress in school. So, while your child may be able to achieve satisfactory marks in early elementary school even if he fails to complete homework assignments thoroughly, it is much less likely he will be able to maintain this pattern through middle school.

@ Research shows that if students with low scores on achievement tests devote themselves to completing their homework regularly, they will gradually catch up to their peers and ultimately receive grades comparable to those of higher-ability students who spend less time on homework assignments.

@ Science and social studies homework assignments have been shown to influence academic achievement more than any other subjects. Reading and writing follow, and math homework has the lowest overall impact.

@ The best homework assignments are clear, manageable, consistent with your child's achievement level, and directly related to his classwork. Above all, they should encourage deep thinking and problem solving, teach your child to think critically about the topic he is studying, and allow him to process the information more permanently.

How Much Time Should Homework Take?

@ At the beginning of the year, find out whether your child will receive homework each night, how much time the teacher thinks is appropriate for the average assignment, and the rough schedule for big projects.

@ If your child spends countless hours on homework, observe his work habits. Is he wasting time, dawdling, daydreaming, taking frequent breaks, or being overly perfectionistic? You may find the underlying problem isn't the amount of homework given.

@ Tell your child to keep track of how long he spends on homework in each subject so you can determine the most time-consuming areas. This will also help him recognize how much time he needs each day for homework and how much time he needs to study for tests, which makes scheduling much easier.

Every child will take different amounts of time with homework, but if it's a constant source of stress to get homework completed, contact the teacher immediately.
—*Libby Anne Inabinet, kindergarten, 1st grade, reading, and gifted and talented teacher for 15 years, Columbia, South Carolina*

With homework, one rule of thumb frequently mentioned is 10 minutes per grade level, so 40 minutes would be the typical amount of homework for a fourth grader. This is just a guide, and I always tell my students' parents, "If your child is spending more than one hour every night, then let me know."
—*Julie Kirkpatrick Carroll, 4th grade teacher for 6 years, Benson, Minnesota*

Elementary school homework should never take over an hour. If it does, then there's something wrong—either the teacher has given too much work or the child doesn't understand it.
—*Sherri McWhorter, 4th grade teacher for 5 years, Augusta, Georgia*

Let the teacher know if you feel the workload or the level of difficulty of the homework presents frustration rather than positive reinforcement.
—*David Lancucki, 3rd to 7th grade teacher for 23 years, King William County, Virginia*

If you have a concern, present it as, "I'm concerned about the amount of homework. My child is really struggling." Next, ask, "What are your suggestions?" Focus on solutions to better help your child. This approach keeps teachers from feeling they have to defend themselves from a parent saying they're in the wrong.
—*Florence Michel, middle school teacher for 8 years, New York, New York, and Baltimore, Maryland*

@ Some kids have a tough time getting their homework done or projects completed in a timely manner because they obsess about getting things right. In this case, it is your job to help your child understand the difference between having high standards for his work and obsessing over details.

@ In general, the amount of time your child spends on homework should gradually increase as he moves through the school system. Prepare for this change as he enters each new grade.

@ If your child consistently spends much longer on homework than the teacher says he should, send her a note asking how he should proceed. Should he leave the remainder of the assignment blank? Is she willing to adjust the amount of homework she gives? Can she offer advice to reduce the amount of time he spends doing work?

@ Talk with other parents in your child's class to determine whether their children are also dealing with copious amounts of work. If the problem is widespread, consider holding a group discussion with the teacher to address the issue.

@ If homework proves an ongoing struggle and your child's grades do not reflect the time and effort he puts in, ask to meet with the teacher to resolve the problem.

How Should I Be Involved in Daily Homework?

@ Teachers rely on homework to strengthen and review classroom work, often counting on parents to help clarify misunderstandings and confusion. In essence, you become an adjunct of the classroom, providing the tutoring, editing, or advice your child needs to grasp the material.

@ Homework allows you to take an active role in your child's education and serves as a bridge between your world and your child's classroom. By reviewing the content and checking his work, you become involved in your child's academic progress.

◉ Find out what your child's teacher expects in terms of homework. What does she want your child to learn from the assignments: time management or responsibility? Review material or learn new material? The directions should be clear and your child should know, without guesswork, what the teacher expects of him.

◉ Time management is a critical skill which your child needs your help to master. You can help him by deciding together how much time an assignment will take, marking a time for him to start his work, and checking in when the work is finished. This will help your child learn how to manage his time and pace himself.

◉ Figure out how your child works best. Does he do better with the pressure of deadlines, or is he good at doing work gradually? If he meets deadlines but always seems to be cramming everything in at the last minute, help him create a calendar of mini-deadlines to follow.

◉ Offer to clarify instructions or steps that initially seem daunting or confusing, quiz your child on memorization assignments, such as vocabulary words or multiplication tables, and proofread homework for mistakes. Drop hints when he gets stuck on a homework problem and brainstorm strategies when he can't think of a solution.

◉ Make homework time family time. Have all family members do their own homework at the same time in the same place to enforce the importance of education as a family. If you don't have any work, do a crossword puzzle or read, as long as you are doing something productive and quiet.

◉ Ask your child to explain his work and teach it to you. This helps him understand the assignments better, gets you involved, and bolsters his self-esteem because you show interest in skills he can teach you.

◉ Ask to see homework after the teacher returns it. Go over the assignments and discuss the teacher's comments and problems that have arisen.

◉ Reward your child's progress with plenty of praise, and display his best work on your fridge.

As much as possible, be available during homework time. Children enjoy showing you what they are learning. They are also less likely to get discouraged if they can ask for help easily.
—*Erika Bare, 6th to 8th grade special education teacher for 3 years, West Linn, Oregon*

When you ask your child if he has any homework, do not accept the answer, "I have none," or, "I did it at school." Ask him to let you see his work and tell him you enjoy seeing what he is doing in class. Even straight-A students can go through periods where they slack off. Continue to check your child's work every week.
—*Laurie Olmstead, 7th and 8th grade math and science teacher for 4 years, Union, Maine*

Sit down with your child while he is doing schoolwork. You can read the paper or a book, balance the checkbook—anything—just be there for your child.
—*Pam Pottorff, 3rd and 4th grade teacher and 8th grade reading teacher for 5 years, Sioux City, Nebraska*

When it comes to parents' involvement with their children's homework, it truly depends on the child. I give different advice to different parents, although I emphasize to all of them that a child's effort is the most important thing. Especially around fifth grade, the goal of homework is to get children to be increasingly independent in their work. Backing off and being patient is often hard for parents to do, as they hate to watch their child struggle to figure out how to solve a problem or answer a question. The way I approach this in the classroom is by  telling the kids, "You may think I'm being mean by not telling you the answer, but I'm actually helping you in the long run. I want you all to work through it and figure it out for yourselves." This being said, if a child struggles every night with homework, then parents have to become engaged.
—*Jennifer M., 5th grade teacher for 6 years, Boston, Massachusetts*

Parents can help by modeling problems. With math, for example, work through one problem together with the child. Then ask questions to guide him through the rest of the assignment. It's important to give encouragement and praise and not use a harsh attitude.
—*Betty Edens, 2nd and 3rd grade reading teacher for 18 years, Hillsboro, Texas*

How Can I Avoid Overdoing It?

© Doing homework independently builds confidence and fosters good study habits and responsibility. If you get over involved with the process and start doing the assignment instead of encouraging your child's work, you will interfere with this crucial learning process.

© Be available for assistance, advice, and review, but don't let your child's homework become your responsibility. Think of yourself as a homework consultant, not a participant. If your child works in his room, stop by periodically with words of encouragement, drop off a snack, and offer praise. Constantly pushing your child to get his homework done on time can condition him to depend on your forceful voice to finish his work. It's best to allow him to realize he can take the initiative.

© Even if your child does not complete his assignments on time or does a poor job, resist the temptation to jump in and do the work as this will keep him from getting the help he needs.

© Dependent children often coerce their parents into giving them an inordinate amount of help with their work. Teachers may inadvertently encourage this behavior by asking parents to get involved with the work of underachievers.

© Children need to experience the consequences of their decisions. If your child doesn't start his book report until the night before it is due, let him suffer the consequences of handing in an essay below the caliber of his normal work, instead of staying up all night with him and writing something spectacular. He will be much more likely to start his paper in advance the next time around.

◉ There's nothing wrong with lending your expertise and problem-solving skills to help your child struggle through a particularly challenging or difficult homework problem, but make this an exception to the norm.

◉ Encourage your child to use resources to find tough homework answers (such as the Internet, encyclopedias, and atlases).

◉ Ultimately, by allowing him the space to complete the tough stuff on his own, you will give your child a sense of accomplishment and foster a healthy independence and confidence in his own problem-solving abilities, especially as his successes start adding up.

◉ If you are unsure of how much assistance to give your child, clarify with his teacher your role in helping to correct his work.

Instead of pointing to an error and saying, "This one's wrong," say, "I see one that's wrong in this row. See if you can figure out which one it is." Or if a word is misspelled, let your child figure out which one it is. Spelling the words for him instead of asking, "How do you think it's spelled?" prevents your child from developing homework autonomy.
—*Joy Pumphrey, 2nd and 3rd grade teacher for 12 years, Clearwater, Florida*

◉

Not giving your child a chance to be on his own, make mistakes, and learn from those mistakes really hurts him. Parents often try to micromanage their child's school life.
—*Sue Abrams, elementary school principal and former 1st to 5th grade teacher for 22 years, Natick, Massachusetts*

◉

I let my daughter work on her homework by herself. When she comes to me with questions and says she doesn't understand, first I make her reread the instructions. She would like me to tell her exactly how to do it, but I won't. I want her to be able to do it on her own because I know she can. I do check her homework once she's done, however, and point out mistakes so she can fix them.

—*Sheila Cross, mom of Emily, 8, Memphis, Tennessee*

If parents help at home too much, the student's daily work looks good, and there's no way for a teacher to know if it was a struggle unless the parent or child communicate with her. Parents arrive at a conference, and I say, "He seems to be finding this difficult in class." And they tell me, "Yeah, we've been working on that two hours every night." I wonder, "Why didn't you call me and let me know?"

—*Lawanna Ford, 5th grade teacher for 25 years, Argonia, Kansas*

If the parent's idea of helping with homework is to do large portions of it, it will teach the child he can rely on others to do his work.

—*Laurie Olmstead, 7th and 8th grade math and science teacher for 4 years, Union, Maine*

If parents correct homework, the teacher doesn't have a good grasp of what the kid knows. If it comes back into school perfect, then she thinks he understands everything.

—*Jennifer Guss, mom of Fred, 10, Hannah, 4, and Sophie, 2, Montvale, New Jersey*

The single biggest mistake I see is parents doing their children's homework. The teacher assigned the work for a reason, and I can guarantee it was not to see if parents can still do the work they did when *they* were in school.

—*Erika Bare, 6th to 8th grade special education teacher for 3 years, West Linn, Oregon*

When Zach has trouble with his homework, I tell him to do what he can and then ask me for help afterwards if he still needs it, so I'm not helping on every question. You have to balance your involvement.

—*Joy Ortega, mom of Zachary, 11, and Elijah, 3, Reading, Pennsylvania*

I don't view homework as my responsibility. It's my children's responsibility, just like making lunch and brushing teeth, and if their grades are slipping, they don't get to do other things, like play with friends. My daughter would try to engage me to do her homework for her, so I had to leave her in her room to do the work on her own, and if it didn't get done, it didn't get done. If you're pouring so much effort into homework that you're almost doing it for them, the teacher doesn't know what they know, and neither do you, and then everyone is surprised when they don't do well at test time.
—Jennifer O'Gorman, mom of Olivia, 11, Jake, 9, Sam, 7, Annabelle, 4, Luke, 2, and Eleanor, 1, Lebanon, Maine

Which Homework Routines Are Most Successful?

◉ The most important part of homework time is consistency, so help your child develop a regular habit and routine of doing work. Base this on what time of day your child concentrates best, which activities take place after school, and when an adult can help out. For example, your child may feel exhausted immediately after school and need to relax and reenergize before tackling homework. Solicit your child's thoughts about when and where he prefers to do homework, and make a mutually agreed upon plan.

◉ Encourage your child to get the hardest homework out of the way first: he'll be focused for the difficult assignments and will have easy exercises left when his energy starts to fade. Also, urge him to work first on the assignment with the closest deadline, then tackle larger, long-term projects.

◉ Set the kitchen timer as a reminder to start homework so your child can develop independence and personal responsibility in his homework routine. It can also be an objective way to announce when it's time for total focus and time to run off for a break.

Set a homework deadline at least half an hour before your child's bedtime, or else he will not learn one of the most important values of homework: time management.

You may find it helpful to organize a homework playgroup, giving classmates time to play together once or twice a week before joining forces on homework. With his peers around, your child might be more enthusiastic about doing his homework.

Don't allow TV or phone calls during homework time. Even when children don't have homework, make this a time in which they read or do extra studying. Involve even the youngest children in the house so they get used to the routine.

Use homework time to do parent homework alongside your child. Let him see you engrossed in some kind of work: reading, balancing your checkbook, doing a crossword puzzle, or writing a letter. This way, you make homework a shared ritual instead of a private ordeal.

If your child doesn't have homework on a particular night, have him read for at least 30 minutes.

Have a consistent homework routine. Find a time that works best for your child, and an appropriate length of time. Then, every school night have him spend the designated time on something school-related. If he has no homework one night, it can be a great time to read or practice basic math facts. Knowing he has to spend that time no matter what discourages procrastination and sets up great work habits.
—*Erika Bare, 6th to 8th grade special education teacher for 3 years, West Linn, Oregon*

Have a specific time for homework to get done each night. It's a mistake, however, to schedule this time right after school. Kids need downtime before they do their homework, so that's when they should go outside and play, have a snack, or do something else that's not school-related.
—*Mary Beth Lewison, 2nd and 3rd grade teacher for 15 years in Ludlow, Massachusetts*

When doing homework, students need to set aside a certain amount of time, before or after school, to have all the supplies together they may need, because it speeds things up considerably and allows for minimal distractions.
—*Lawanna Ford, 5th grade teacher for 25 years, Argonia, Kansas*

Try giving your child some sort of a booklet, or post something on the fridge that lists the homework for the night. Then make it his responsibility to figure out, "If I give this much time for this and that, will I still have time to do what I want to do?" Even for tasks not related to homework, get your child to figure out if he can get several things done in a certain amount of time and talk with him about it. If he didn't get something done in two hours, is it because it simply took too long, or because he started daydreaming?
—*Angela McNutt, 6th to 12th grade Spanish teacher for 1 year, Glade Spring, Virginia*

We try to do homework right after school. The boys fight it the most, but if they want to do something else they aren't allowed to until all the homework is done. Not giving in is the key. It's so easy to say the heck with it, but if you don't make homework a priority, it won't ever become one.
—*Kim Shepherd, mom of Jessica, 17, Jeremy and Josh, 12, and Jennifer, 10, Indianapolis, Indiana*

Does My Child Need to Cut Down on Extracurriculars to Make Time for Homework?

Many extracurricular activities, especially those involving leadership, can boost academic achievement and personal confidence. School-sponsored or team activities that occur after school hours help bond your student to his peers. However, extracurricular activities should never interfere with your child's education. Even academically oriented activities such as Odyssey of the Mind or French club must take a backseat to homework, reading, and studying.

My 16-year-old son got involved in too many things and his grades started to reflect this. We told him he had to cut back on his activities, but gave him the option of deciding, among all the things he did, which ones he would give up.
—*Diana, mom of 6 children, Oklahoma*

Keep homework excuse notes at a minimum. If the excuse really is valid then that's one matter, but if it's something like "The family was running late," "We didn't grab it," or "Sam had soccer practice and didn't get to it," then maybe priorities need to be rearranged for homework.
—*Nickey Langford, 2nd and 3rd grade teacher for 3 years, Birmingham, Alabama*

Factor in homework as a significant component of your child's weekdays. Set clear boundaries on the number of extracurriculars in which he is allowed to participate so neither homework nor family time suffer. Make it clear to your child that family and school take priority over anything else in which he might be involved.

If you find your child is too busy or tired to finish his homework on certain days or if his teacher tells you he is sluggish, tired, or unfocused in school, cut back on after-school activities. Any schedule that routinely keeps your child up late at night doing homework needs to be restructured. Your child will be hard-pressed to explain uncompleted homework when the cause is a baseball game or soccer tournament.

In organized sports, a large number of volunteer coaches are working parents who hold weekday practices late in the afternoon or in the early evening hours. Suddenly, homework has to get done either right after school, when your child wants to shut down his brain after seven long hours in class, or after an evening practice, when your child becomes cranky and easily discouraged. The minute homework starts feeling rushed, your child's frustration level will likely escalate.

ⓒ Consult your child before deciding he has to end an activity and ask him for input about which activities to cut. After all, this decision is not a punishment, but rather a constructive change. He'll be less resentful if he has some say in the matter.

ⓒ Keep in mind that recreation and activities can be as important as schoolwork. Don't cut everything but school out of his life, or he might lose his academic drive entirely.

How Can I Keep My Child Focused and Energized During Homework?

ⓒ Some kids need regular breaks to get up, stretch, or just jump around on the couch before focusing again on homework. Observe what seems to be the extent of your child's attention span, usually between twenty and thirty minutes, and create five- to ten-minute breaks.

ⓒ Your child's attention span should influence the timing and duration of study breaks but homework should train him to stay focused for increasingly extended periods of time.

ⓒ Suggest a break when you sense your child is frustrated with his work. Taking time away from the material for a few minutes often makes a problem easier to tackle when he returns.

ⓒ On subjects your young child dislikes, give him short, fun breaks to make it feel less like a chore. For example, he can pretend homework is a marathon race, and do stretches between subjects.

ⓒ Have a snack available at break time. Kids get tired when doing work for extended periods, so offer refreshments that give your child a boost of energy. Also, take this time to talk about how his homework is going.

ⓒ Help your child break large homework assignments into smaller, more manageable tasks. While some kids depend on delving deep into one assignment and seeing it to completion, others thrive on the variety of switching things around, which keeps them more interested and focused. A variation on this is to mix up the time spent on different types of assignments, such as spending ten-minute intervals on spelling, then math, then grammar, and circling back.

☺ As children get older, they can concentrate for longer periods of time and require fewer breaks. To encourage this, talk about concentrating in terms of maturity by saying things like, "You're getting so old, you only need breaks every 35 minutes!" Also, as your child gets older, build in breaks around when an assignment is completed instead of when a certain time period is up.

☺ Declaring homework time for all of your children can eliminate the distractions siblings provide. You can even make up simple homework assignments for a younger sibling, such as coloring, art projects, or letter tracing.

If your child is in a very structured classroom where there's not a lot of moving around, it may be tough for him to sit down and concentrate on homework in the evenings.
—Julie Kirkpatrick Carroll, 4th grade teacher for 6 years, Benson, Minnesota

How Can I Create an Ideal Homework Space for My Child?

☺ Help your child feel comfortable and ready to concentrate by creating a homework area.

☺ Before setting up this space, figure out whether your child works best in his room, in a home office, or in a more public setting where he can ask questions freely, such as at the kitchen table.

☺ Determine how much background noise your child prefers when doing homework. Some kids need complete silence, while others do better with the comfort of soft music or the sounds of laundry being done. Having company or comforting sounds, like dinner being prepared or dishes being washed, may make your child feel less isolated. However, television should always be off during homework, studying, and reading time, as it is overly distracting.

 Experiment to see what type of setup works best for your child's homework habits. This could be sitting in a stiff chair at a desk, lounging in a comfy chair, sitting at the kitchen table or on a stool at the kitchen counter, or sitting on the sofa and working with papers spread out over a coffee table.

Make sure your child's study area is free of distracting clutter. A neat workplace sets the tone for serious studying and allows your child to spread out his work.

I bought my daughter a desk we keep in my home office. When she has homework, we go to the office together to work, with me on my computer and available to check in or help when she needs me. She loves working up there with Mommy.
—*Laura Doctor, mom of Nicole, 10, Cleveland, Ohio*

My kids like to do their homework in the kitchen, where I'm available to them for questions but not interfering.
—*Sarah Essick, mom of Lauren, 12, and Parker, 7, Johnson City, Tennessee*

It really depends on the child. Daydreamers can't work in their rooms because they get distracted really easily. They need to work in a place where you can keep an eye on them and help them stay on task. However, some kids work better in their rooms, especially if they live in busy homes.
—*Anne Marie Fritton, 4th grade teacher for 3 years, Depew, New York*

I find it works best if I sit by my son's side, available for questions. I also call any work I bring

home from the office my homework, which my kids see me do as I tell them I'm going to try to do my best.
—*Bryann Bromley, mom of Ben, 11, Emma, 8, and Spencer, 4, Chestnut Hill, Massachusetts*

My son gets easily distracted and will say it's too easy or he's bored, but I just tell him it's required and he has to do it. I send him into a different room, like the dining room, away from the other kids, and make sure he's at it until he's done.
—*Jennifer O'Gorman, mom of Olivia, 11, Jake, 9, Sam, 7, Annabelle, 4, Luke, 2, and Eleanor, 1, Lebanon, Maine*

What Should I Do If My Child Constantly Struggles with Homework?

© Often children get home and realize they don't know how to begin their homework. To cut down on confusion, advise your child to look over the homework directions before leaving school and clarify any questions with the teacher at the end of class.

© Keep a handy list of homework contact numbers. If your child is unsure about homework directions or expectations, encourage him to call a classmate.

© If your child experiences confusion, ask him to pinpoint where the work became difficult. Is the assignment too hard, is he having difficulty organizing, or is he simply unclear on a concept?

© While it's sometimes necessary for you to step in, encourage your child to talk about his problems one-on-one with his teacher. This will give him a sense of responsibility and self-confidence.

© In many cases, the homework's difficulty level is the reason for the problem. Help your child comprehend the instructions, and if that doesn't work, talk to the teacher about modifications. She may be willing to scale down assignments, extend a deadline, or allow for an alternative assignment that better matches your child's learning style and skills. She could also send home individualized homework or practice for the areas in which your child lacks specific skills, as kids who fail to master basic skills early lag behind in later years and experience chronic difficulties. Focus on strategies to help your child master the material instead of berating the teacher.

If a child comes home crying about homework, it's often news to the teacher. If you rush into school yelling, "I can't believe this homework!" the teacher won't understand where you're coming from. Some kids in the classroom may be finding it too easy, while others think it's impossible. Parents are often reluctant to come to the teacher because they fear it's a problem just their kid is facing. So when parents come to me saying, "The homework is taking my child an hour," I can then say, "These are six-year-olds. Do 20 minutes and stop."
—*Kallie Leyba, 1st and 2nd grade teacher for 2 years and mom of Lauren, 11, Lucas, 8, and Samson, 4, Highlands Ranch, Colorado*

Homework should be a review, not something your child doesn't know how to do. It also shouldn't take hours and hours. So if you get into a deadlock with your child over getting it done, or if you think there's too much homework—such as a page of 50 math problems of which your child can't do more than five right—immediately talk with the teacher. Let her know your child doesn't understand the assignment. Ask, "Has the material already been covered in class? If so, my child seems to need help because he is not getting it. How can I help?"
—*Joy Pumphrey, 2nd and 3rd grade teacher for 12 years, Clearwater, Florida*

Homework is supposed to be an extension of the school day. Students need to make the first attempts to figure things out. When your child is frustrated and comes to you for help on a problem, first sit down and make sure he understands the instructions. After that you can ask him, "What are you having a problem with?" and intercede. Contact the teacher when your child seems overwhelmed.
—*Kay Symons, special education and kindergarten to 8th grade teacher for 27 years, South Georgia*

Check with the teacher to see what homework is fundamental and absolutely needs to be done and what is supplemental. Have your child concentrate on the most important homework first.
—*Keith Averell, 3rd grade teacher for 27 years, Pleasanton, California*

If your child is having trouble with homework, have him phone a friend who usually does well in the class. Studies have shown that students who teach or help teach their peers are effective because they use the same language and are at the same stage developmentally; they are really able to understand each other.
—*Laurie Olmstead, 7th and 8th grade math and science teacher for 4 years, Union, Maine*

How Can I Help My Child Struggling with Math?

Although you may have your own problems with math, it's important to pass on a healthy approach to this difficult topic to your child.

If your child seems increasingly frustrated with math, teach him to break complex math problems down into smaller components, examining each piece separately before integrating them together into a final solution. Give him easier examples to work through to boost his confidence before tackling more difficult problems.

Teach your child to read word problems slowly and carefully to make sure he understands what type of math function will solve the problem. He should underline any facts the problem gives him, draw a diagram to describe it, and ask himself, "What does the problem want from me?"

Keywords in the phrasing of word problems are clues to the math function a solution requires. For instance, *is* means equals, *less* means subtraction, and *into* means division.

🌀 Use real-life situations to help clarify new math concepts your child finds particularly confusing:

✴ Physical objects, like apples or bananas, can help your child visualize and solve math problems.

✴ Use cooking to reinforce math. Teach your child how many teaspoons are in a tablespoon, how many tablespoons are in a cup, how many cups are in a quart, and so on. Help him figure out how to double and halve recipes.

✴ Board games like Monopoly, Life, and Yahtzee, and card games like Go Fish! and Gin Rummy are fun, easy ways to teach your child counting and problem solving.

✴ Giving your child a weekly allowance can teach him how to manage, budget, and save money and think about monetary values.

✴ Use time in the car to practice memory and math skills. Turn errands into fun activities by having your child figure out gas and mileage word problems.

✴ Work on estimation and prediction skills around the home. Cookies piled on a plate, pages in a book, M&M's in a bag: Ask your child to guess how many there are in total.

🌀 Show your child how to check his work using estimation. The estimation method for checking response accuracy only requires that he round each number in the problem to the nearest multiple of five or ten and recalculate the answer using these new value approximations. Another easy method for checking work involves recomputing the solution using the inverse operation—for example, checking addition using subtraction.

🌀 Neatness counts! Teach your child to write his numbers neatly, as sloppy number writing causes 25% of all errors.

✴ Some parents and teachers instruct children to make European sevens (with a horizontal line through the rising line of the seven) to cut down on confusion between sevens and ones.

✴ Your child can use graph paper to keep the numbers neatly aligned.

So many kids have math phobia. I spend the entire seventh grade year trying to get kids to understand there's not just one right way to do a problem anymore. One thing that makes a huge difference in test scores is parent attitude. Parents who say, "I was never good at this," have children who think they can't do it either and can't rise to a higher level. If a parent says, "That was hard for me too, but I know you can do it," the attitude difference you see is incredible.

—*Laurie Olmstead, 7th and 8th grade math and science teacher for 4 years, Union, Maine*

It's so important for children to know basic facts by heart. All higher math comes from knowing the basics. The easier it is for a child to recognize what 6 X 8 is, the less he will struggle in higher grades with adding and subtracting fractions.

—*Kerri Charette, elementary school teacher for 10 years, Ledyard, Connecticut*

So many people think they were never very good at math, yet we are constantly doing math without even realizing it. Even in the sentences we speak, there are mathematical patterns to the words we use. Everything around you is mathematical. Many kids just lack the confidence to do well or just don't understand what's going on in math class.

—*Edward Sapienza, 9th to 12th grade science, math, and computer teacher for 31 years, North Reading, Massachusetts*

Memorizing basic math tables is as important as memorizing the alphabet. So many kids have trouble in algebra because they don't know math facts, and they reach a level of anxiety that will make them blow a whole test. Kids figure they can just use a calculator on tests, but when they can't, it's not as simple. They need those building blocks to be able to go back to the basics of a problem and reduce anxiety in a testing situation.

—*Anne Wonson Curry, 5th to 12th grade math and science teacher for 12 years, Rockport, Massachusetts*

How Can I Avoid Homework Battles?

◎ Homework frustration can mount when your child doesn't understand your explanation, or when you show him a way to solve a problem that differs from the way his teacher has presented it in class. Tell your child, "When you get upset it becomes impossible for me to help you and impossible for you to learn. Can you tell me how your teacher showed this in class? Do you have any handouts or notes so I can see what she did and learn her approach?" Often this process of explaining things out loud will help him come to the answer on his own.

◎ Avoid heated emotional exchanges over homework. If your child lashes out at you, disengage without anger, saying, "I'm not the person who should be helping you with this. We're both too frustrated. Let's figure out a different solution so it isn't this hard on either of us." Tell your child to go as far as he can with the assignment and then write down questions to ask the teacher the following day, or to call a classmate for help.

◎ Avoid criticizing how your child does his homework, as long as he does it well and on time. Let his temperament set a pace that works best for him.

◎ If homework battles become a constant part of your life, seek outside help. You don't need to hire an expensive tutor if your child continually expresses anger and frustration at your suggestions: a high school or college student can play a neutral role while helping him complete his work.

◎ Try using homework incentives and tools such as a spinner. Fill in each section with a privilege your child would like, such as "stay up 30 minutes after bedtime" or "choose one favorite dinner item." Your child can earn a spin each time he completes his homework according to your agreed-upon rules.

Homework doesn't need to become a battleground if you help your child develop good study habits and skills. Beginning in kindergarten, you need to provide structure and organ-

ization. Your child needs routine—a set time to sit down and complete his homework in a quiet place, away from distraction. Check over your child's work to see not only that it was done correctly but also that all activities are completed. Homework done this way becomes a routine, not a battle, and your child will naturally incorporate it into his life.
—*Beverly Hammond, kindergarten to 4th grade teacher for 31 years, West Point, Virginia*

Some kids walk in the door and don't pick homework up until after supper, and parents find themselves yelling and screaming to get it done when really there's not enough time to finish it. Parents need to set homework guidelines.
—*Susan Draughn, 7th and 8th grade special education teacher for 24 years, Sunman, Indiana*

When homework is an established priority in the home, it makes a world of difference. Your child knows what you expect and will seek other interests or read when there is no other homework.
—*Sharon Stubbs, 5th and 6th grade teacher for 28 years, Hopkins, Michigan*

The homework monster, gasp! We sign homework contracts with our kids that detail the performance we require of them and give a copy to their teachers to let them know our expectations. It lets the teachers know we're working on it, as well. The kids aren't wild about that whole thing because it gave us an ally. The teachers know what we're doing and where the gaps are.
—*Kim Shepherd, mom of Jessica, 17, Jeremy and Josh, 12, and Jennifer, 10, Indianapolis, Indiana*

When it came to homework, I seemed to set my daughter off. I couldn't explain how they did it in school, so I couldn't help her. I asked my husband to make sure he was around, because sometimes it was better when he was. We found out what was available to our daughter at school, and she ended up going in early to get help at the math lab a few mornings a week.
—*Michelle Turpel, mom of Chris, 19, Haley, 15, Brianna, 8, and Anthony, 4, Thousand Oaks, California*

It's Greek to Me—How Can I Help My Child?

◉ Your child may be taking subjects, learning methods, and dealing with information you never learned in school or just can't remember. If you find your child constantly requires help you can't provide, there are still things you can do to assist him.

◉ Start by asking, "Where are you stuck?" and "Show me what you've done so far." Then talk to his teacher and get her advice on how you can best help. Ask her about the methods she uses in the classroom. Teachers often become frustrated when parents teach their children shortcuts and methods that conflict with the approaches they are teaching. By staying consistent with her approach, you avoid possible conflicts.

◉ Consider asking the teacher to borrow a copy of the textbook your child is using for a week or two to understand what he is learning in the classroom. You can also purchase a copy of the textbook by calling the publisher, but publishers usually will not sell the teacher's manual to the public.

◉ You can also go online with your child to look at homework help sites, many of which have online tutors. Together, you may be able to find information to resolve his confusion.

A factor in the homework dilemma is that children are learning differently than their parents did. The parents are trying to teach children math using methods and vocabulary from when they learned it in school, and some of these methods have changed considerably.
—*Kerri Charette, elementary school teacher for 10 years, Ledyard, Connecticut*

Make sure you truly understand what the assignment is asking before you start helping your child. When parents try to bluff their way through it, then my job is twice as hard be-

cause I have to reteach something that's done wrong the first time. If you can't help your child, get help and communicate with the teacher.
—*Lawanna Ford, 5th grade teacher for 25 years, Argonia, Kansas*

I've taught parents basic phonics instruction to help their kids at home and we've also had math sessions and other topical seminars when the parents requested them. All the teachers kept our doors open so Mom and Dad felt comfortable saying if they didn't understand the work their child was doing.
—*Heather Daigle, teacher of all grades, Plymouth, Massachusetts*

There are plenty of good websites with tips for parents. Go to homework help sites and look at the types of questions your child is supposed to be able to answer. Also, if your child runs into trouble, ask him, "Do you have any notes? Have you seen that before?" You don't have to know how to do it to be helpful.
—*Laurie Olmstead, 7th and 8th grade math and science teacher for 4 years, Union, Maine*

If all else fails, attach a note to your child's homework explaining what you and your child tried to do, and the outcome.
—*Amie Parker, 1st and 2nd grade teacher for 7 years, Lynnwood, Washington*

I worry about homework help on tough subjects, especially if I'm not knowledgeable in those particular areas. My son had trouble with chemistry and went after school to talk with a teacher who had extra time to meet with him and help him out. Also, the school set up after-school study groups, so students could get together to do their work. Both of these were really helpful.
—*Debbie McCandless, mom of BC, 18, and Sarah, 13, Knob Lick, Kentucky*

Sometimes it's tempting for frustrated parents to dash off a note saying, "I have a master's degree and I can't even do this assignment!" but that's not going to win you a friend or an ally in the teacher for your child. Last week, I had a parent come in with a very hostile attitude, concerned her child was having difficulty academically. She was very angry with all three of her child's teachers and used very negative body language. To calm her down, I said, "Okay, anytime you're not sure what we're doing, or are concerned your child doesn't understand, please send us a note so we can pull her aside and work with her one-on-one to help her understand her assignment." Teachers and parents get along very well if they keep their tempers in check.

—*Martha Ann Chandler, 3rd to 6th grade teacher for 14 years, Florence, South Carolina*

How Can I Cut Down on Homework Mistakes and Sloppiness?

◉ Not only does neatness make it easier for a teacher to review a child's work, but it also can cut down on critical mistakes in math problems and other written assignments. Emphasize the importance of doing work neatly and legibly. Once kids master the basics of block letters, numbers, and cursive penmanship, their handwriting tends to deteriorate and become sloppier.

◉ Teach your child to pay close attention to minor but important details, such as putting his name on all papers he turns in to the teacher.

◉ If your child rushes through homework too quickly and makes multiple mistakes, ask his teacher for a suggested minimum time he should spend on homework. Create a timetable and have additional work or reading to do for the remaining time so that your child has no incentive to speed through assignments.

◉ Encourage your child to organize his thoughts and, if necessary, create an outline before starting written assignments. This will make his answers more understandable and establish a solid base for more complex papers as he gets older.

◉ Have your child do the first round of proofreading. He should get in the habit of reviewing his work to make sure he's answered the questions, fulfilled the assignment requirements, and checked for legibility, spelling, grammar, and punctuation.

The reason I receive homework that is barely legible and less than top quality is students do it a few minutes before class. Parent help definitely comes in here—when a child comes home, ask what he has for homework and how you can be of help.
—*Angela McNutt, 6th to 12th grade Spanish teacher for 1 year, Glade Spring, Virginia*

Lots of children have messy work. It's a big problem. Watch your child to see if he's going too fast, and tell him to slow down and make him check his work. For messy handwriting, it can be helpful to teach your child to type.
—*Kristyn Mulada, educational director of a Sylvan Learning Center for 2 years and former kindergarten teacher, Hanover, Massachusetts*

Working on the computer is a useful way to check spelling and grammar mistakes and avoid handwriting issues.

◉ Look over homework to make sure your child has completed it correctly. If homework is sloppy, incorrect, or incomplete, circle mistakes and ask him what he thinks is wrong.

How Should I Approach the Dreaded Big Projects?

◉ When embarking on a large project, take the time to clarify exactly what your child's teacher wants the final product to be. If it is something he has to construct, what type of materials can and can't he use? What criteria must the final product meet? How long does he have to complete the assignment?

◉ Find out whether the point of the project is to get you and your child working together on something. For some projects, teachers actually want you to roll up your sleeves and tackle the project as a team with your child.

☺ Group projects do teach children to work collaboratively but they are fraught with perils. Some children almost invariably get left out or neglect their workload, while others get stuck doing all the work or become overly controlling. Kids are surprisingly reluctant to tell the teacher when one or more members of a group aren't pulling their weight. If you feel your child is continuously being taken advantage of in group projects, call the teacher and discuss your concerns.

☺ Create a checklist together so your child can cross off each component as he completes it.

My kids struggle the most with big projects. Suddenly it's Thursday night at 10 P.M., an hour-and-a-half past bedtime, the project's due the next day, and it's not done. Kids don't have the wherewithal to organize their time. When something's due in 30 days, it seems an eternity away to them. Kids need to learn to plan ahead. I help my kids divide their projects into parts and budget their time for the work. For a month-long project that involved reading a book and then making a big poster, we counted up the pages and came up with a plan that by reading two chapters a night for eleven days, would leave two weeks to do the posterboard. I find it helps when I break the project into workable chunks and give them a timeline.
—Priscilla Thibault, mom of Ruzena, 11, Cameron, 10, Eloise, 7, and Clarice, 4, Orange Park, Florida

When it comes to large projects, you need to make sure your child understands the instructions first. Ask questions to help your child generate ideas when he seems stalled. Try to base the topic on your child's interests. Don't throw a project at him because, nine times out of ten, it will wind up in your lap. The point is to pull responses out of your child, not to lead the way. Let him develop a plan. A good project is one in which your child has enough interest to start work independently and take on the tasks himself, but you may need to help him set goals and priorities.
—Kay Symons, special education and kindergarten to 8th grade teacher for 27 years, South Georgia

@ Brainstorm all the materials your child will need for a project. Make a list and take a trip to the store together.

@ If your child starts running into problems, have him contact the teacher early on. The sooner he approaches her, the more likely she will be willing to extend deadlines.

@ For a written report, make sure your child knows the following:

✴ Can the final report be handwritten, or does it have to be typed? If written, does it have to be in cursive? Pencil or pen?

✴ Do the pages have to be numbered, have his name on each, or be stapled together?

✴ Is there a minimum or maximum page length?

@ Keep a collection of assorted magazines on hand. Many big school projects for young children require them to cut out pictures.

How Can I Encourage My Child to Brainstorm Ideas for the Project?

@ Use dinner table discussion to brainstorm ideas for big projects or papers and make creative suggestions. Remind your child that the thought, organization, and research he does before starting to write all determine the final product's quality.

@ Act as your child's secretary and write down his ideas. Don't feed him the concepts, but instead bounce them back and forth to develop his thoughts and find his inspiration.

@ If your child's teacher assigns a topic, encourage him to pick an angle that interests him. The challenge in producing a well-written report is keeping the reader interested. If your child is interested in the topic, he will be much more likely to produce an engaging paper.

The teacher should give your child a list of topics for the project and you should go through the topics together. If your child has another idea that's not on the list, write a note to the teacher to ask if the topic is okay. Ask your child how he wants to do the project and make a list of tools he needs to get it done.
—*Libby Anne Inabinet, kindergarten, 1st grade, reading, and gifted and talented teacher for 15 years, Columbia, South Carolina*

Encourage your children to write about something they know about. Search engines on the Internet are wonderful because you look up one thing and wind up finding something else.
—*Lawanna Ford, 5th grade teacher for 25 years, Argonia, Kansas*

Help your child limit his topic to a manageable scope. As a general rule, the more specific the topic, the easier the book search will be because you'll turn up more relevant materials. But make sure the topic is broad enough for your child to find ample information.

Encourage your child to use the library to gather ideas or find how-to books about constructing his designs.

How Should My Child Structure His Time for a Project?

A main purpose of long-term projects is to teach your child to organize his time and synthesize a number of small tasks into a composite whole.

Break a large task into smaller, manageable parts with self-contained deadlines

If your child flips out over a huge homework assignment at home, find out details about the assignment first. Often, kids have a whole week to work on a larger assignment but leave it to the night before and then feel angry and overwhelmed. Instead of buying into your child's hysteria or anger, try to help him look at the situation rationally. Ask your child questions like, "When did you get the assignment? How have you worked on it so far? May I see the directions? May I see your class notes or workbook?" If a parent immediately gets angry or frustrated in defense of the child, it reinforces his behavior and creates a vicious cycle of the behavior repeating itself. Sit down with your child and a calendar and map out a timeline for getting it done. Create mini-deadlines along the way that you can help enforce, such as completing a rough draft by Friday.
—*Jennifer M., 5th grade teacher for 6 years, Boston, Massachusetts*

Teach your child time management. If he has a paper to write, help him plan to use day 1 to brainstorm, day 2 to write a rough draft, day 3 to revise, day 4 to revise again, and day 5 to have you look at it. As parents, we need to guide our children to develop time-management skills.
—*Libby Anne Inabinet, kindergarten, 1st grade, reading, and gifted and talented teacher for 15 years, Columbia, South Carolina*

I tend to give projects in school and block time into the day for children to work on them in class. Planning, getting materials, and helping their children find resources like library books are important ways for parents to help. I like to have the majority of work on projects done in the classroom because we use projects for assessment, and we are assessing the child, not the parents.
—*Mary Beth Lewison, 2nd and 3rd grade teacher for 15 years in Ludlow, Massachusetts*

to motivate your child to complete the assignment on time. This is especially helpful for book reports or month-long projects.

@ Set up a system to keep track of where your child needs to be as the weeks progress. Some teachers will have checkups for each step in the process: deciding on a topic, creating a bibliography, making an outline, and handing in a rough draft.

If your child's teacher doesn't impose these requirements, have your child set his own deadlines for the completion of each stage.

◉ Write these deadlines on an oversized calendar and hang it near his homework spot to keep him aware of his progress. Periodically check in on his progress, and make sure he's meeting all the necessary deadlines.

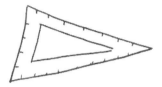

How Can I Best Help with Big Papers?

◉ One of the most useful ways you can get involved with your child's research papers is to guide him through research methods. Teach him to use the Internet and help him navigate the library to find relevant books. Look for age-appropriate material; encyclopedias are great resources, but the language is likely to be beyond your child's understanding.

◉ Your child should know the teacher's rules about resources. Is he allowed to use the computer to type reports or to do research?

◉ It's helpful to describe effective methods of note taking and researching to your child. Explain why he needs to know where he got all of his information and help him organize his sources.

◉ After he has finished researching, have him outline what he wants to say in the report. Framing the topic as a series of questions or smaller subtopics will keep him from taking endless notes or simply amassing a pile of facts.

◉ Help your child organize his research by writing the topic, resource, information, and quotes on index cards. Buy a small card file box to keep all the information together. This task also helps him when organizing a paper into a series of paragraphs or sections by laying them out in order before he begins writing.

◉ Give your child examples of how to restate things in his own words so he clearly understands the difference between researching and plagiarizing.

◉ Urge your child to hand in papers early, especially for longer assignments. Of-

This year my daughter started being assigned book reports. It's been hard getting her time management right. She starts off like a ball of fire and then lags behind, so it becomes a marathon the last couple of days trying to get everything done. A time management plan where she does a little bit of reading every night works much better. Otherwise, I'm going ballistic at her, she's upset, and it's not a good situation for either of us.
—*Laura Doctor, mom of Nicole, 10, Cleveland, Ohio*

tentimes, an early paper sticks out from the crowd and receives extra attention from the teacher, who may be willing to look it over and offer feedback for revisions.

© Your child can practice for an oral presentation by performing it in front of you. Remind him to stand up straight, maintain eye contact, and speak slowly and clearly. Suggest that he avoid swaying back and forth and "umm-ing."

© Encourage your child to use visuals and graphics in his reports to create a more engaging final product.

How Do I Know If I'm Too Involved in My Child's Project?

© When you or your child starts talking about *our project,* you have invested too much time on a project that is supposed to be his. While you are bound to get a bit overinvolved from time to time, recognize when this happens and take a step back.

© You should not be commandeering the project or doing all the work. Becoming overly involved in your child's projects may seem like a great way to ensure high quality, but when you take on the brunt of responsibility, you also take away the satisfaction your child gets from his work. He may not care if his model teepee is lopsided, the stream doesn't have a realistic-looking current, and he gets a B+ instead

Teachers see the children on a daily basis, and we know what they're capable of. When all of a sudden, this amazing project comes along, we think, "This isn't coming from them." It becomes unfair when it comes to grading, because we want to grade students for what they did, not what their parents accomplished.

—*Lawanna Ford, 5th grade teacher for 25 years, Argonia, Kansas*

I've always been involved with my son's projects, but only to a certain extent. I let him know, "OK, this is what we need," and then we get whatever is on the list. I let my son do most of the work and then I give a little feedback. The biggest thing parents can help out with is planning. For example, they can remind their child, "Hey, we have the next three weeks to get this done," or ask, "What kind of materials do we need?" This way the child is learning the thought process to getting the job done one piece at a time.

—*Ruth Anne Manroe, kindergarten to 6th grade teacher for 27 years, Golden, Colorado*

I think it's a parent's place to get supplies, give encouragement, and help cut things out, but kids should do all their own writing and drawing so they know it's theirs. You can tell which kids did the project themselves and which ones didn't. With most teachers, as long as all the components are there, they'll get a good grade for it. I also help them clean up. After all that work, they deserve it!

—*Jennifer O'Gorman, mom of Olivia, 11, Jake, 9, Sam, 7, Annabelle, 4, Luke, 2, and Eleanor, 1, Lebanon, Maine*

Last year, one of my daughters' teachers assigned a big project. There's so much pressure because you want your child to feel proud of herself; you know other kids will be bringing in museum quality work and you don't want your kid bringing in something terrible. I helped my daughter formulate what she wanted to do, and we went online and found instructions for the project. But once the materials were together, it was all up to her. I found it a real challenge to be hands-off and let the project be hers when I wanted her to be proud of it.

—*Pam Fierro, mom of twins Meredith and Lauren, 8, and parenting multiples guide at www.multiples.about.com, Virginia Beach, Virginia* of an A. The pride he takes in his own work is far more important than any of these factors.

◉ Set guidelines before you get involved in the project, and tell your child what you will help him with and what you won't. You can expect to be involved in much of the planning and execution of a big homework project while your child is in grade school, and to become less of a force as your child develops the skills to complete his projects independently. However, chances are your child will still need you to help him budget his time and obtain supplies.

◉ Think ahead of time about how your child is going to get his project to school on the day it is due. He's not going to be able to carry a papier-mâché sculpture mounted on a huge plywood square, so make plans to drive him to school when he needs to transport large projects. Also, avoid fragile materials that can easily smash or can't be fixed quickly and independently.

Mastering Tests

What Are the Different Types of Tests and What Do They Aim to Assess?

⊚ Tests serve myriad purposes, from determining how well a child learns material to comparing students' progress and skills. Testing results help schools judge the need to fine-tune courses or change teaching methods: Assessments identify students' strengths and weaknesses, determine how they have developed over time, and some exams, like standardized tests, may affect your child's placement in school. Despite their intended purposes, however, test results are often more reflective of test-taking skills than subject mastery.

⊚ Given the intensity of testing in today's schools, your child needs to become test-savvy. His ability to succeed on tests follows him throughout life, so he needs to hone these skills early.

⊚ Standardized tests come in many varieties.

✤ *Aptitude tests* assess your child's cognitive ability—how easily he can remember and apply new information. These tests measure skills such as verbal and mechanical ability, creativity, and abstract reasoning. Aptitude tests are especially useful when trying to spot an underachiever, as they highlight a child's cognitive abilities which can then be compared to his actual class tests.

✤ *Achievement tests* assess how well a child has mastered a certain subject, knowledge, or set of skills, and whether he is performing at grade level.

✤ *Criterion-referenced tests* compare a child to objective standards rather than to other students, while norm-referenced tests compare him to a large sample group of students who have taken the test in the past.

✤ A *norm group* is a carefully selected racially and geographically diverse set of students chosen by test creators to serve as a basis of comparison for most children in a certain population (such as third grade). Stanine scores compare your child against a norm group, often within just one school or community. Ratings are as follows: 9–7 is above average, 6–4 is average, and 3–1 is below average.

✤ *Classroom tests* help teachers evaluate a student's knowledge, retention, subject matter understanding, and ability to apply what he's learned to solve or analyze a new problem or situation.

✤ *Performance assessments* measure student achievement using essays, oral presentations, and projects.

✤ *Portfolio assessments* measure a student's achievement through a collection of his work, including papers, drawings, teacher evaluations, and test scores.

✤ Additional forms of assessment include *anecdotal evidence* and *student journals*. Using several of these methods simultaneously offers teachers multiple ways of viewing each student when assigning final grades.

Why All the Controversy Over Standardized Tests?

◉ Standardized tests aim to provide a common measure of children's performances. Because students across the nation and state take the same test, the results aid teachers, schools, and school systems in measuring relative performance. Such standardized tests also can be used to measure how well the teacher is doing, as well as to diagnose learning problems.

◉ Our society emphasizes student evaluation and many schools, counties, and states give children standardized tests on a yearly basis. No Child Left Behind calls for the testing of "every child, every year," and requires nationwide testing in reading and math for all students in third through eighth grade by the 2005–2006 school year.

◉ Despite this national prevalence of standardized testing, required testing for elementary school students remains highly controversial. One parent activist group, the Coalition for Authentic Reform in Education, collected about 15,000 signatures for a petition against the Massachusetts Comprehensive Assessment System (MCAS), which tests children from third grade through high school graduation. In Ohio, parents, students, and  teachers lobbied to strike down a proposed Senate bill that called for proficiency tests to place students in educational tracks starting in kindergarten. Teachers in Florida tore up bonus checks they received for increasing student scores on the Florida Comprehensive Assessment Test, which awards schools letter grades and cash bonuses for student performance.

◉ Standardized tests are often problematic in the primary grades, especially before fourth grade. Children's development is uneven and idiosyncratic during these years, so standardized tests may not accurately represent a child's ability. An early evaluation as a poor student can have consequences for the extent of a child's education, because labeling a child as deficient can become a self-fulfilling prophecy.

◉ Opponents of standardized tests claim preparation and the test's administration take too much time away from the regular curriculum.

© Another major problem with standardized tests is that district, state, and federal authorities assume high scores reflect strong and effective instruction and adjust ranking and even funding accordingly. This pressures educators to teach to the test, often at the expense of a more creative curriculum.

© Despite their controversial flaws, standardized tests serve a number of useful functions for students, parents, administrators, communities, and government agencies alike. They help individual students and parents by identifying strengths and weaknesses the teacher may overlook. They show school administrators and teachers where students lack basic skills and identify ineffective teachers and teaching methods. Standardized tests keep communities aware of how its schools are doing and determine the need for reform. They also raise the bar for underachieving schools and help ensure all students master basic skills before progressing to the next grade.

Standardized tests and grades are all for parents and government officials. Teachers use their own assessments to know what they have and haven't taught well and what kids have and haven't learned. The school and teachers should be accountable for the students' learning, but unfortunately we haven't found a better way to do this other than standardized tests.
—*Kallie Leyba, 1st and 2nd grade teacher for 2 years and mom of Lauren, 11, Lucas, 8, and Samson, 4, Highlands Ranch, Colorado*

Don't get me started about standardized tests! In our state, every child has to pass a test in order to move up to the next grade—it doesn't matter if he has done well all year round. If he has test anxiety or a bad test day and fails that particular test, then it's mandatory summer school in order to take the test again. It's been a big issue.
—*Stephanie Lee, substitute elementary school teacher, Lawrenceville, Georgia*

Standardized testing can definitely hurt kids because it doesn't take into consideration environmental factors. Who knows what's going on in a kid's home that day? Parents put so much pressure on their children because of these tests, and there's so much pressure from the government. I really feel we've lost sight of the purpose of education. Tests can be a great tool for monitoring growth and seeing what the kids are capable of, but there's too much dependence on them.

—Deb Brown, kindergarten to 4th grade special education teacher for 26 years,
   Conyers, Georgia

Standardized tests have good and bad points. The good side is that we need them to find the weaknesses in a child's knowledge. I study independent test results on top of group results. I find it very interesting to look at subcategories to see, "Oh, this child is weak in comprehension, this child needs help with antonyms." We need to be teaching skills that children are not adept in.

—Libby Anne Inabinet, kindergarten, 1st grade, reading, and gifted and talented teacher for
   15 years, Columbia, South Carolina

I'm not a proponent of standardized testing, though it is big right now. In Florida, if a child doesn't pass an achievement test in third grade, he or she can't go on to the next grade. I just feel some kids are test takers and some are not. You spend so much time preparing them for this test that it becomes your sole focus, and there's too much pressure on these kids to perform at such a young age. Now Florida is testing first graders as well. As teachers, we aren't able to be as creative anymore because we have to teach to the test. We're reduced to teaching kids how to answer multiple choice questions, or how to read nonfiction books.

—Joy Pumphrey, 2nd and 3rd grade teacher for 12 years, Clearwater, Florida

Kids aren't standardized, so standardized tests are inherently flawed from the beginning. I particularly dislike the press coverage of them. If the tests and scores were kept in the school it could be quite useful, showing where kids are working well and where they're not. But it shouldn't be quite as high stakes as it is. It's only one day in the life of a child. To predicate their entire high school career on one test is absolutely wrong.

   When our state's standardized test results came out, we tried to ignore them, before finally going into panic mode. Testing skills are in the curriculum now, but we try to incorporate them in a way that impacts the learning as little as possible and fits into the existing curriculum. It isn't all negative: we have seen some positive changes in the way we teach. You want to give students the tools to do the best they can because they will be taking tests for the rest of their lives.

—Sue Abrams, elementary school principal and former 1st to 5th grade teacher for 22 years, Natick, Massachusetts

Standardized tests cause a lot of stress. My kids take a state exam at end of the year and we're instructed to teach "above the exam." This means making the classroom work more difficult than what's on the test, so when our kids sit down to take the state proficiency exam, which they have to pass at the end of 8th grade to go on, we get a 100% passing rate. It puts tremendous pressure on the students.

—Amy Watson, 7th to 12th grade teacher for 5 years, Oyster Bay, New York

So much emphasis is placed on standardized testing, but it doesn't tell you much about how a child learns. Also, a lot of children don't learn or respond in the manner in which they are being tested. But, these tests can give a general idea of a child's strengths and weaknesses, what they've learned, and what they can remember in a certain amount of time.

—Kay Symons, special education and kindergarten to 8th grade teacher for 27 years, South Georgia

They start standardized testing in second grade in California. It seems like the focus of the entire year is on these silly tests taken at the end of the year and you never see the results. In kindergarten and 1st grade my daughter learned phenomenal things. In 2nd grade she just stagnated. It was rote drills and practice testing all the time. There was no art or creative writing, the subjects she liked. I understand the need to review but thought it was excessive. I understand the teachers and school district have no choice and have to do this, but I'm hoping this year the new teacher concentrates on things other than the test.

—Jennifer Clements, mom of Kaitlin, 8, Ian, 3, and Reilly, 1, Murrieta, California

What Should I Know About High-Stakes Testing?

◉ Many states have introduced high-stakes testing in an effort to stop the practice of promoting students with academic deficiencies to the next grade level. Scores on these tests can be the basis for requiring students to attend summer school or remedial classes, denying them access to a preferred high school, and retaining them at the same grade level. The tests also can indicate students for a school's gifted-and-talented program or help teachers identify individual students' strengths and weaknesses.

◉ Because states and districts allow high-stakes testing to determine what and how to teach, many parents worry that it unfairly puts an intense amount of pressure on their children, since children learn in different ways.

◉ Many districts offer pay raises to teachers whose students score well, and some fire teachers whose classes have poor scores. Teachers' fear of losing their jobs if they do not lead their school to testing success results in more rigid curriculums and a larger amount of influence from principals and other administrators. Also, increasing amounts of school funding are being put toward testing, rather than toward programs that help teachers learn how to teach more effectively. Accordingly, 66% of surveyed teachers said they feel forced to concentrate too much on tested material at the expense of other subjects.

◉ Some amount of preparation is appropriate for standardized tests: familiarizing students with the test format, incorporating test-taking skill instruction into the curriculum, and addressing student questions about the purpose and content of the test. However, you should be concerned if your child's school restructures the curriculum, reduces creative or long-term assignments, narrows instruction in core areas, or does away with certain programs to make room for test preparation.

◉ There's no escaping the fact that standardized testing will affect your child, as it determines not only his academic future but also his level of self-confidence.

Accountability is a buzzword in education right now. We want our educational system to be held accountable for learning, and it should be. I would not feel like I was doing a worthwhile job as a teacher if my students weren't learning, on task, and working toward their maximum potential all the time. But, way too much emphasis has been placed on testing. It has reached the point where every day, everything we do in class is supposed to be directed to passing the end-of-the-year high-stakes test. I know we want children to function in a society that tests, but it's not always developmentally appropriate. It's stressing the parents, teachers, and children, and takes a lot of the joy out of school. It's been months since I've been able to play math games with my kids because I think, "Oh my gosh, the test is coming up." Yet any change has to come from the societal level—teachers don't have a say in it at all. As a parent, you may need to lobby state legislatures to get your voice heard. Tell them to put less stress on our poor kids. Let them draw a beautiful picture instead of making them read and answer questions every day. Ten years ago we were able to have a lot more fun, and children truly learn more from engaging activities than from all this drilling and preparation for testing.
—*Martha Ann Chandler, 3rd to 6th grade teacher for 14 years, Florence, South Carolina*

When I teach kids, I pay attention to their learning styles: whether they need manipulative instructions, auditory direction, or a different approach. But when it comes to standardized tests, it is just paper and pencil.
—*Julie Kirkpatrick Carroll, 4th grade teacher for 6 years, Benson, Minnesota*

I have a lot of experience with standardized testing. As a math consultant I would go in and do refresher lessons on areas in which our district historically performed low. I don't think a national curriculum is a bad idea. If the curriculum was standardized across the board, then the standardized test would have a lot more meaning. The way it is now, you can play with the numbers and numbers can be deceiving.
—*Kerri Charette, elementary school teacher for 10 years, Ledyard, Connecticut*

How Can I Help My Child Prepare for Standardized Testing?

๏ Before your child takes a standardized test, discuss with him the importance of putting in his best effort, but remind him that it is only one test and far from the sole determinant of his future.

๏ Early elementary school children are not familiar with the atmosphere of a testing room in which the teacher must refuse to answer questions. Make sure your child is aware of test day rules, such as directions to begin, whether leaving his seat to sharpen a pencil is allowed, and when he must stop writing.

๏ Tell your child not to worry if he does not complete the examination. Many standardized tests are structured so many students will not be able to complete the entire test in the time period allotted.

๏ Tell your child to look back over the test to make it neat and easily correctable. Savvy test takers check for stray marks and bubbles that they have not filled in correctly, as these errors can deduct points.

๏ Tell your child to watch his time carefully, skip questions he doesn't answer right away to come back to later, and not spend too much time on any one question.

๏ Your overachiever who is used to getting the best grades in the class may be in for a rude awakening on standardized tests. Suddenly, he will be competing against students from across the nation, many of whom are the best in their respective classes.

๏ Some classroom tests are graded on a curve and measure your child in relation to the other kids taking the test. Thus, if your child has very smart classmates, he might actually do well on a test but get a low grade based on how others performed.

๏ Children diagnosed with learning disorders often get special treatment for standardized tests. If your child qualifies, he will likely have the opportunity to take his standardized test in a different location with extended time, more breaks, and amid a smaller group of people. Children with certain learning disorders can be excused from parts of, or possibly, the entire standardized test.

The more your child reads, the better he will do in all areas of standardized testing. Reading skills are vitally important, and will be examined on every standardized test your child takes.

It will help your auditory learner to soundlessly read the test questions and answers by moving his mouth and lips as if he is reading, so he can hear the words.

Ask your child's teacher the following questions about standardized testing:

Which tests will my child take during the school year and for what purposes?

What type of practice tests will there be to help my child prepare?

Will a high test score result in a more challenging curriculum for my child?

If my child's test results are poor, will he have access to extra help?

Standardized testing companies make lots of sample books that contain the types of questions that will be asked on the test. Get ahold of one of these for the test your child will be taking or go online to download the different types of questions with which your child will need to be familiar. Seeing the types of questions ahead of time will help your child strategize a way of attacking each variety and get used to the time limits.
—Kristyn Mulada, educational director of a Sylvan Learning Center for 2 years and former kindergarten teacher, Hanover, Massachusetts

There are certain things test scorers are going to be looking for that you can teach the child how to do so he will feel more confident. We need to do a better job teaching higher levels of thinking, as children need to know how to respond to questions which make them use these skills on tests. Basic recall is the lowest level of thinking, so if you ask, "What color is the sky in this story?" that's easy. If you ask, "How would you compare the sky in this story to ice?" children have to think to formulate answers. If your child can develop his own

synthesis when reading a novel or story, then he will know how to answer synthesis questions on a standardized test.
—*Libby Anne Inabinet, kindergarten, 1st grade, reading, and gifted and talented teacher for 15 years, Columbia, South Carolina*

I try to keep my kids excited about standardized testing. I work with a lot of parents who put a lot of pressure on their kids, but kids do their best when they're relaxed. We try to be really laid back about it and not make a big deal out of it. That's all you can do, besides getting them to go to bed early and having them eat a big breakfast.
—*Jennifer O'Gorman, mom of Olivia, 11, Jake, 9, Sam, 7, Annabelle, 4, Luke, 2, and Eleanor, 1, Lebanon, Maine*

What Should I Know About Test Results?

ⓒ A national percentile ranking tells you how well your child did in comparison to the other thousands of children who are in his norm group. This means if your child scores a 50% on the math section, he did better than 49% of the other students who took the test.

ⓒ How you respond to your child and his test scores can significantly impact how he feels about himself. React to lower-than-expected scores in a calm, comforting manner, and remember that having one bad day does not determine the course of his academic career.

ⓒ If you feel your child's test scores inaccurately reflect his skill mastery, set up a meeting with the teacher to figure out where the root of the problem lies: Is it cognitive or organizational? An issue with test taking itself? Did he do poorly compared to the rest of the test takers, or do his scores not match the quality of work he brings home from school? If your child hasn't been doing well in school but brings home high test scores, he may not be working to the best of his ability.

- Talk to your child about how he felt when taking the test. You are likely to discover outside factors that affected his performance and score. Discuss the wrong answers with your child and find out why he chose them. He may have misunderstood or misread a question, or known the correct response but answered unclearly. Also, talk over how your child appropriated his time and whether guessing was a good idea. Evaluating his testing strategies will help him improve them for the next test.

- Remind your child that confusion and mistakes are an inherent part of learning and often the first step in acquiring new knowledge. The key to making mistakes useful is teaching your child to be open-minded and willing to learn from them.

Parents put way too much emphasis on tests, especially standardized tests. It's just one day. There are a billion different reasons why a particular child might not have done well on that specific day. You have to look at the whole picture. If, over a period of time, there's a continuing pattern of low scores, it's time to take a look at what may really be going on.
—*Kathy Carabine, pre-k and 3rd grade teacher for 16 years, Boston Massachusetts*

One parent responded to her child's standardized test scores by saying, "Oh my gosh, my daughter must be in the bottom of the class, failing!" This parent was so worked up and I had to tell her to stop and remember that her daughter was reading, enjoying it, and understanding what she read. I had to reassure her that the test is just one piece of the puzzle. Sometimes, however, the converse occurs, and you have parents who will say, "My kid is a genius! How could he be getting bad grades or having issues? Look at this test score!" I get so scared when parents start calling each other, comparing notes on test scores, and talking about whether I'm doing a good enough job. I've actually had a parent call me and say, "My friend says her child's scores were really good last year, so I want you as a teacher."
—*Julie Kirkpatrick Carroll, 4th grade teacher for 6 years, Benson, Minnesota*

When it comes to your child's tests and grades, adopt this as your mantra: "Your best is all I expect."
—Amie Parker, 1st and 2nd grade teacher for 7 years, Lynnwood, Washington

Too much emphasis is put on test scores, so parents start to freak over the whole testing issue. Teachers and districts need to explain to parents how they use test scores by looking for gaps to make the child stronger. I would get the class scores of the children I taught to make me a better teacher and the children better learners. The weak links are what really need to be addressed. If every child doesn't do well in capitalization on a test, I know I need to do a better job of teaching capitalization.
—Libby Anne Inabinet, kindergarten, 1st grade, reading, and gifted and talented teacher for 15 years, Columbia, South Carolina

How Can I Best Help My Child Study for an Upcoming Classroom Test?

Being a good student requires more than possessing innate intelligence. Studying takes time, effort, organization, and self-discipline.

If your child has difficulty studying, it may be because he doesn't know where to begin. Ask the teacher to give him some extra instruction on how to take notes, identify important information, and prepare for tests. Ask him to share what strategies and memorizations worked for the material and your child's learning style.

Schedule time to study for tests in advance so your child will be able to space out his study periods.

Before you even start reviewing with your child, make sure he is clear on what the test or quiz will cover. Also, find out the test format: multiple choice, true/false, short answer, fill in the blank, or essay.

◉ Lower grade levels usually use short-answer or multiple-choice tests, which measure memorization and recognition skills. Higher grades usually test with essays, which measure a student's ability to articulate analytical and critical responses to problems.

◉ Your child should also review all of his homework for that unit, paying particular attention to any areas with which he struggled or which he did not understand the first time through. Go over these together to ensure he understands his mistakes, what underlying information he needs, and how to solve this type of problem if he encounters it again.

◉ Flashcards are helpful for studying vocabulary words, important dates, or any information that needs to be matched to a person, event, or idea. Your child can shuffle them to make sure he learns each fact separately rather than just memorizing them in order. Index cards make excellent flashcards, and colored index cards are especially good for visual learners and students who need to organize or sort information.

◉ Another great way to memorize definitions or fact lists is using folded study sheets. Fold a sheet of lined paper in half lengthwise. Your child can list words or ideas on the left side of the paper and the definitions or answers on the right side of the fold. By refolding the paper, he can test himself by looking at the left and seeing if he can recall the information on the right.

◉ Teaching information to another person helps your child memorize, organize, and clarify it. Ask him to teach you what he has just learned or make up and answer test questions for himself.

◉ Avoid over-studying: review facts frequently, but remember to end the session before your child becomes frustrated and tired.

◉ Remember that cramming is not learning. Your child truly learns information through studying over a period of time, not the night before the test. Try to have short, frequent drill sessions. Set realistic goals for each drill, such as ten out of fifteen vocabulary words each night.

◉ Effective studying is a skill that develops with practice over time. Use your child's test results as a way to gauge the effectiveness of his review methods. The results should tell you how well prepared he was and give you an idea of what you can help him change for next time.

◉ To ensure your child's studying is progressing, don't review a new set of facts until he has completely memorized or grasped the previous information. It's easier to absorb information in small chunks rather than to look over a number of things at once.

◉ Study with your child right before bedtime. His brain keeps busy during sleep by organizing and reviewing information.

◉ Quiz your child, but not right after learning new information. You want to check long-term rather than short-term memory.

If you give your children the skills to be good self-teachers, they will be successful in life. If they read a story or learn a new math problem, have them make up their own problems or ask their own questions. They will learn the material much better by teaching themselves. Kids love to make up tests. Have them make up their own test questions, and they will understand and recognize the kinds of questions they see on the test. I have found lots of success teaching those strategies.
—*Libby Anne Inabinet, kindergarten, 1st grade, reading, and gifted and talented teacher for 15 years, Columbia, South Carolina*

Kids have a tendency to go into a test unclear on terminology, so they might not understand the directions, which can be more of a problem than not knowing the information. The best thing parents can do for math and science tests is review the questions with their child to make sure he understands the terms.
—*Anne Wonson Curry, 5th to 12th grade math and science teacher for 12 years, Rockport, Massachusetts*

As a parent, if I were helping my child study, I would go right to the teacher and ask, "What should we focus on?" Teachers will give you short cuts and help you focus on what's really important. Once you are home, don't assume your child has read or understood what he's supposed to. Start talking about the stuff; he might nod like he gets it, but you can usually tell when he doesn't. Take it paragraph by paragraph, reading and going through all of it with him. There's no magic short-term answer, just take it a step at a time.

—*Ken Pauly, high school social studies teacher for 13 years, St. Louis Park, Minnesota*

Being prepared and knowing the material reduces test anxiety. Practicing can help, but students are exposed to a great deal of testing as it is and this can get mundane for them. Finding unique ways for students to remember material can be fun and effective. We have used mnemonics, visuals, and key words to help. Don't get discouraged if your child thinks these are silly. My 8th grader couldn't believe I wanted him to visualize me in a pose to remember material on a social studies test, but he later reluctantly admitted it was how he remembered it at test time.

—*Pam Pottorff, 3rd and 4th grade teacher and 8th grade reading teacher for 5 years, Sioux City, Nebraska*

I'm big on flashcards as study aids, even though they might be considered old school. Anything put to musical rhyme helps with memorization. Check educational stores, which have great resources.

—*Joy Pumphrey, 2nd and 3rd grade teacher for 12 years, Clearwater, Florida*

My daughter has a spelling test every week, and she tends to study so when she memorizes the words, she memorizes their order as well. I mix them up when I quiz her to make sure she understands the concept of the words and not just their order.

—*Laura Doctor, mom of Nicole, 10, Cleveland, Ohio*

How Can My Child's Learning Style Affect Testing?

◉ Evaluate how your child learns best before offering advice on how he should study or do homework. If you can figure out the way he best retains information, you will be able to choose effective learning techniques.

◉ The three primary types of learning are:

◉ Visual: He relates best to information he has seen and written down himself.

✤ Visual learners learn most effectively when they can picture the subject matter in their heads.

✤ Flashcards are useful for math basics, dates, and vocabulary words.

✤ Taking notes in class is especially important for visual learners. Your child will memorize information best if he writes notes and creates diagrams as he studies. Tell him to jot down the important parts of what his teacher says and to look over his notes after class to grasp them more fully.

◉ Auditory: He relates best to the spoken word. He may not internalize information until he hears it, so he may need to read written information out loud.

✤ Read directions to him out loud, and ask the teacher to do the same in class.

✤ Auditory learners have trouble concentrating when reading because they cannot process the information as quickly. Tell your child to try reading his homework assignments out loud, or quietly to himself in class by mouthing the words. For longer at-home reading assignments, check with your library to see if they have the book on tape.

◉ Kinesthetic: He comprehends best through touch, movement, and space.

✤ Classroom lessons often do not suit kinesthetic learners, and these students need to learn independently.

✤ Kinesthetic learners often have trouble focusing on written or spoken in-

Become familiar with your child's learning style and help him learn in the way he learns best. Learning style encompasses everything he does while he learns. Some kids learn best while lying on the carpet, some while sitting at a desk, and some while eating. You can be most helpful by knowing his learning style and facilitating his efforts. Some children are incremental and sequential learners; that is, they take all the small pieces and come up with a big picture. Many other children are top-down learners and like to look at the big picture first.
—*Martha Ann Chandler, 3rd to 6th grade teacher for 14 years, Florence, South Carolina*

Schools only cater to visual learners; they only test in a visual, written format. So, while it's fine to encourage different learning styles, your child will likely be penalized if you don't add visual styles to his toolbox.
—*Pat Wyman, former elementary school vice-principal, reading specialist, and founder of*
  www.howtolearn.com, Windsor, California

If your child is a visual learner, use flashcards at home to help him learn. My children don't remember information simply by hearing it; they have to visualize things before they can remember them. If your child is an audio learner, tell him to say things out loud. For kinesthetic learners, help them trace letters with their hands.
—*Nickey Langford, 2nd and 3rd grade teacher for 3 years, Birmingham, Alabama*

formation. They learn through hands-on activities and physically moving themselves and objects. Sitting still causes them to lose concentration instead of focusing on their work.

◉ It is possible to train a physical or auditory learner to translate what he knows into the visual world of test taking by using study and memorization tips. Have your child spell a word out loud, then close his eyes, try to see the word in his mind, and spell it again. Techniques with words include saying them out loud, spelling them in his head (subvocalization), writing them out, and looking at a list to memorize them visually.

@ Convergent thinkers bring different pieces of thought together to make a whole. They tend to do well when asked to extract a single answer from their broader body of knowledge, such as on short answer and multiple choice tests, as well as essays and papers.

@ Divergent thinkers are adept at generating many ideas on one topic, but have trouble putting them together to formulate one larger answer. Rather than following through, they focus on new ideas and options. While this often means they have trouble in writing longer response answers, they are great brainstormers.

@ Logical thinkers can easily follow chains of thought, and do well in math, science, and languages.

@ Creative thinkers excel in fluency, flexibility, originality, and elaboration, but may have trouble concentrating on more straightforward areas of study. They are likely to excel on projects and creative activities, but may have more trouble with everyday assignments and tests.

@ While you can help your child to do his best by understanding how he learns and focusing on those techniques that will help him learn most effectively, you will do him even more good by working to expand his ability to learn in each of the different ways.

How Can Mnemonics Help My Child Remember Facts?

@ Mnemonics (pronounced ne-mon´-ics, from the Greek word *mnemonikos,* which means to be mindful) are tricks or strategies that aid in memorizing information. They assist the memory by using a system of artificial aids—rhymes, rules, phrases, diagrams, acronyms, and other devices—to help recall names, dates, facts, and figures. Mnemonics draw upon the right side of the brain, which is sensitive to visual images, rhymed patterns, and emotional associations.

@ Examples of classic mnemonic techniques include:

© *Acronyms:* Make a word using the first letter from each word that needs to be remembered. This works best when the list is fairly short. Some common acronyms include:

🌸 The Great Lakes: HOMES (Huron, Ontario, Michigan, Erie, Superior),

🌸 The musical notes of the lines in the treble clef: Every Good Boy Deserves Fudge (EGBDF),

🌸 The order of planets in our solar system: My Very Educated Mother Just Served Us Nine Pizzas (Mercury, Venus, Earth, Mars, Jupiter, Saturn, Uranus, Neptune, Pluto),

🌸 The priority of functions in a math equation: My Darling Aunt Sarah (multiplication, division, addition, subtraction),

🌸 Colors of the rainbow: ROY G. BIV (red, orange, yellow, green, blue, indigo, and violet),

🌸 The metric system: Kids Have Dropped Dead Converting Metrics (kilo, hecta, deca, deci, centi, milli),

🌸 The Roman numerals in order: Lucy Can't Drink Milk (LCDM).

© *Sayings:* Rhymes and sayings help with memorization, for anything from names to dates, to facts. For example:

🌸 America discovered: "In fourteen hundred ninety-two, Columbus sailed the ocean blue."

🌸 Celsius scale: "30 is Hot, 20 is Nice, 10 is Cold, 0 is Ice."

🌸 I before E, except after C, or when sounding like A as in neighbor or weigh.

🌸 Words like *oat* or *eat:* When two vowels go walking, the first does the talking.

🌸 Dessert vs. desert: Would you rather have one dessert or two?

🌸 Words like cap/cape and hat/hate: The silent e makes the vowel say its name.

✸ Find the "rim" in "perimeter."

✸ Principle vs. principal: Your principal is your pal.

✸ Days in each month: Hold up two fists together. Starting with January, each knuckle has 31 days and the valleys between the knuckles, except February, have 30 days.

☺ *Imagery:* Humorous or unusual imagery makes it easier for your child to remember vocabulary words. Explain how to do this by thinking about what each word reminds him of, and then create an image that depicts the association. Make connections between new and old information, whether logical or not. Often, the wilder the association, the easier it is to memorize.

I believe in mnemonic devices: making up a rhyme, associating, or linking associations. There's no substitute for them to help with memorization. Retrieval cues definitely help. I can't tell you the number of tests I've gotten back where the kids have whatever mnemonic device they're using written at the top of their papers, and I know they might not have gotten the answers if they hadn't done that.
—Ken Pauly, high school social studies teacher for 13 years, St. Louis Park, Minnesota

How Can I Teach My Child to Take Better Notes in Class?

ⓒ Even though teachers don't spend time teaching note taking, it is one of the most important skills for success, especially as your child progresses to middle school and high school.

ⓒ The most important component of taking good notes is listening closely. Most teachers give cues, as they lecture, to help students identify key information. Any time the teacher calls information important, it is. Suggest that your child pay special attention to and write down all definitions and examples the teacher gives in class, things she repeats, the subjects on which she spends a significant portion of time, and the material reviewed right before a test.

ⓒ Your child's class notes should not be a complete summary of what the teacher said. Rather, the notes should be a concise review of the most important information. If your child struggles with identifying information likely to be on a test, tell him to take his notes to the teacher for suggestions on improving his skills.

ⓒ Teach your child shorthand methods for recording information during fast-paced lectures, such as using abbreviations (w/, +, ~) and breaking sentences into shorter phrases.

ⓒ Your child should organize and elaborate on his class notes as he reviews them. Tell him to pick out vocabulary words and key phrases or dates and relate new information from the textbook or current lessons to things learned in previous classes.

ⓒ A good technique for reorganizing notes during review is to draw a line on a piece of paper, leaving more space on the right than the left. Your child can write main ideas, concepts, and vocabulary words on one side, and the definitions or supporting details on the other. This technique makes for easy self-testing.

ⓒ When reading a textbook, have your child first skim the headings and table of contents to get an overall idea of where the text is heading, as well as what the author considered important enough to feature in his headers and subheadings.

◉ If your child owns the book, he can use a highlighter, underline, or jot down notes in the margins to aid concentration.

◉ Show your child how to use diagrams for tasks from mapping out a math problem to keeping track of all the key characters in a book.

Which Test-Taking Tips Should I Reinforce with My Child?

◉ Even when your child is well prepared, he can make costly mistakes by moving too quickly or misreading directions. By going through these test-taking steps with your child, you'll ensure he conserves time and improves accuracy.

◉ During a math test, your child should:

✴ Try to guess answers through estimation,

✴ Consider how each individual step affects the whole solution,

✴ Complete arithmetic problems using straight lines,

✴ Use a European seven with a line through the base if he confuses ones and sevens,

✴ Consider constructing a drawing or diagram to understand the problem or find the answer, and

✴ Look at the phrasing of word problems to figure out what type of math function he needs to use: *sum* means addition, while a problem that asks about *difference* calls for subtraction.

◉ Sometimes questions build upon each other. By reading them all first, your child will start to unconsciously think about later questions while working on the earlier ones, and may recall additional relevant information.

Make sure your child knows the following basics well in advance of a test:

✴ Is the test timed? If so, how much time will I have to complete it?

✴ What kind of test will it be?

✴ Is there a particular order in which the questions must be answered?

✴ Is there a penalty for not answering a question? Even on tests that penalize for guessing by taking away points for wrong answers, it's usually in your child's best interest to make the most educated guess he can.

Teach your child to read test directions carefully! Children need to read the directions at least twice before trying to answer any questions. Also, help your child learn how to pinpoint distracters—unneeded information put into a test question to create confusion. Another thing to work on is learning to eliminate answers that cannot be correct, and then choosing from the remaining options. This takes a lot of practice and should be happening in the classroom with consistent follow-up at home.
—*Beverly Hammond, kindergarten to 4th grade teacher for 31 years, West Point, Virginia*

Teach your child to read directions carefully, check back over his work, listen well, stay focused, and breathe deeply during a test.
—*Keith Averell, 3rd grade teacher for 27 years, Pleasanton, California*

Teach your child vocabulary for the test he will be taking. For example, he might not know what the word *synonym* means and won't be able to answer vocabulary questions. I also found students needed work with math vocabulary, like knowing the difference between parallel and perpendicular lines.
—*Libby Anne Inabinet, kindergarten, 1st grade, reading, and gifted and talented teacher for 15 years, Columbia, South Carolina*

◎ If your child is particularly diligent or meticulous, he may have trouble abandoning a question with which he is struggling. Reinforce the importance of answering all questions he finds easy first so he doesn't run out of time working on the harder ones, and that it is perfectly okay to change an answer to a question if another answer seems like the best one.

◎ Neat and organized writing counts a great deal in the elementary and middle school years. Correct grammar, paragraph indentations, and good penmanship make it easier for a teacher to read your child's answer and predispose her in favor of the content itself.

◎ Tell your child if he is unsure how to answer a question fully, he should attempt at least part of it in order to get partial credit.

◎ If the test uses a Scantron answer sheet, remind your child to repeatedly double-check to make sure he fills in the correct bubbles on the scoring sheet.

◎ Discuss with your child the importance of using all time available. Many children feel peer pressure to turn in their tests as soon as they finish in an effort to be among the first done or to avoid being the last. Assure him the best students use extra time left at the end of the test to double-check their answers, grammar, spelling, and math to catch any mistakes. Encourage him to take all the time allotted, even if that means he's among the last to turn a test in.

What About Writing Test Essays?

◎ Essay questions test not only your child's ability to remember information, but also his skills in analyzing and formulating creative, organized, well thought-out answers. Essay questions are often more subjective than other types of tests, but whether or not there is a right and wrong answer, there is always a correct setup for the argument. Essays should have an introduction, development of ideas, and a conclusion.

◎ Your child should:

✹ Quickly determine what his teacher wants: comparison and contrast, an argument for or against a point, and so forth. Underline key words in the instructions. Verbs used in the essay question give powerful clues about how the answer should be structured.

✸ Start by jotting down thoughts and points to cover on scrap paper, then form these into a quick outline to help structure the answer.

✸ Make the opening sentence strong by clearly spelling out the thesis. Follow the opening with supporting statements of fact.

✸ Have each paragraph express a distinct point. The beginning of the paper should include an introduction to the topic and his opinion on it. The middle paragraphs should contain reasons for the opinion, supported by examples from the texts that the test covers. The conclusion should summarize opinions and arguments. Unlike in math problems, the conclusion reached in an essay answer does not matter as much as the reasoning your child gives to support his conclusion.

❂ Some basic essay verbs, and what the teacher is looking for in response:

Analyze:	Break down a whole into the parts that make it up.
Compare:	Emphasize the similarities between two or more things.
Contrast:	Describe the differences between two or more things.
Criticize:	Give your thoughts, perspective, and judgment on an issue.
Defend:	Argue one side of an issue.
Define:	Explain what a word or words stand for.
Describe:	Tell what happened using details in the correct order.
Diagram:	Create a clearly labeled drawing that explains an object or concept.
Discuss:	Analyze all parts of an event or topic.
Evaluate:	Make a judgment about the topic.
Explain:	Give the reasons behind a situation or position.
Interpret:	Share your opinion about the meaning of a statement.
Relate:	Show how two or more things are connected.
Summarize:	Put a large amount of information into fewer words.
Trace:	Go through a development or process.

What Are Good Multiple-Choice Strategies?

◉ Multiple-choice questions often test your child's ability to recognize and recall facts. These types of questions usually feature the correct answer surrounded by other true facts your child remembers and recognizes from class.

◉ Your child should always guess an answer before looking at the options offered. Multiple-choice questions are designed to be tricky, so guessing first will help him avoid falling into the trap of enticing trick answers. However, even if his guess appears, it's important to read all the choices to see if any options seem more precise than the guess he came up with. Remind your child there will be potential answers that are very close to correct, but aren't quite right. Distracters—answers that are almost the right ones—often pop up in multiple-choice questions. He will need to think carefully and reread the question or text to weed these answers out.

◉ If your child's guess does not appear among the answers, then he should start using the process of elimination to narrow his choices down to the correct answer. It is sometimes easier to spot the wrong answers than the right ones.

◉ If your child encounters answer choices that contain unfamiliar explanations or vocabulary words he has never seen before, they are likely wrong, as few students will draw a correct answer from something not discussed in class or the materials.

◉ Remind your child to stay focused on choices that answer the question posed. Many answers, while correct in what they say, do not relate to the key part of the question.

◉ As in true-false questions, watch out for absolute words such as *all, none, always,* and *never* in the answers to multiple-choice questions. If the answers to a multiple choice question are numbers, most likely the largest and smallest numbers will not be correct. Instead, it will be one of the middle two answers, which are often similar to each other in an attempt to confuse.

◉ Tell your child that if two answers are either very similar or complete opposites, then one of the pair is most likely the right answer, and if one of the choices is *all of the above,* he should pick this if two of the answers seem correct.

I tell my students: For multiple-choice questions, read the question and don't even look at the answers. Cover them up with your hand or a piece of paper and think of the answer in your head before looking. Otherwise, they do not look at the question that they're being asked and will jump straight to the answers without really reading it. If they're in a bind, then they can use process of elimination.

—*Libby Anne Inabinet, kindergarten, 1st grade, reading, and gifted and talented teacher for 15 years, Columbia, South Carolina*

Are There Tricks to True-False Questions?

@   On true-false tests, it is likely there will be more true answers because false ones are harder to write. If your child has to guess, he should choose true.

@   The wording of true-false questions can be tricky, so make sure your child pays extra attention to it. Also, he needs to make sure *all* parts of the answer he chooses are correct.

@   Negatives make a statement false, and can easily trick your child if he is not paying enough attention. Tell him to take out the negative to see if the statement is true without it, then answer the opposite.

We've worked with our kids to spot giveaway words on tests such as *always* or *never*.

—*Stephanie Lee, substitute elementary school teacher, Lawrenceville, Georgia*

Your child also needs to watch for statements that offer only one reason for something. Most statements of this kind will be false.

Advise your child to ignore any answer patterns that seem to emerge, and just answer each question with his best guess.

What About Reading Comprehension Questions?

Reading comprehension questions test your child's knowledge of vocabulary words, his ability to identify the main idea and recall facts and details in the reading passage, and how well he can draw inferential conclusions based on information not specifically mentioned in the paragraph.

Tell your child to read the questions that follow the passage before the passage itself so he can keep an eye out for critical information.

Encourage your child to take notes or underline as he reads.

Tell your child to be wary of answer choices that paraphrase part of the passage, yet do not answer the question and eliminate answer choices that include information not found in the passage and reject answer choices that contrast with the main point of the passage.

For reading comprehension questions on tests, highlight answers in passages. Discuss chapter books. With your child, summarize events you experience together, like a trip to zoo or a movie you watched.

—Jennifer Rodman, 3rd grade teacher for 6 years, Fulton County, Georgia

What Are Strategies for Matching Items in Two Lists?

@   Advise your child to read both columns carefully before answering any of the questions. He should match the ones he is sure of the first time through to narrow the choices for tougher pairs.

@   Your child should start with the first question in column A, find its answer in column B, and circle or cross out the letter of the answer he has chosen so he knows not to match it with another answer. If he doesn't find a match right away, he should come back to the question later. If he thinks two answers could be correct for a question, he should lightly pencil both next to the question, fill out the rest as best he can, and see if one of the answers fits another one of the questions.

@   If one column being matched has longer statements than the other, your child should work his way down the longer one, as he will then be reading through the shorter list multiple times.

How Can I Help My Child Overcome Test-Taking Jitters?

@   Often, your child can freeze in a moment of test anxiety and forget everything he has been studying for the past week. Test anxiety may be due to self-doubt about not knowing the material well enough, or intense pressure from a parent, teacher, or the child himself to perform well.

@   Students who suffer from test anxiety tend to believe their success in school depends on how they perform on tests. They worry about the future, are extremely self-critical, and become afraid of failure. This makes them anxious about tests and their own abilities.

@   Students with test anxiety often perform below ability. Their nervousness is debilitating, they are more easily distracted, and they encounter mental stumbling blocks on answers to questions they know because they blank out or have racing thoughts during the exam. Statistically, children who suffer from severe test anxiety are more likely to perform poorly in school and repeat grades.

@ Test anxiety appears with physical symptoms such as headaches, nausea, faintness, and feeling overheated or chilled. It can affect emotions as well, causing children to feel angry, helpless, upset, or even giggly during a test.

@ The night before the exam, help your child collect any supplies he may need to avoid any last-minute panic.

@ Ease your child's nerves by using praise, enthusiasm, and small rewards for his accomplishments. Avoid excessive gushing and reassurance. By doling out praise and encouragement only when it is necessary, you will keep him from discrediting your opinion.

@ Help your child feel good about himself as he walks into the test room. Be positive and encouraging and build up his self-esteem. Discourage negative talk, such as, "I'm terrible at math," by producing evidence to the contrary, such as a math quiz on which he received a high score. If he seems nervous at breakfast about a test later in the day, take a few minutes to sit down with him and help him visualize getting an A or reaching his test goal.

@ Teach him how during the test he can relieve stress by taking deep breaths, thinking about something happy, or stretching his legs.

@ Confidence enhances memory. If a student is stuck for an answer during a test, have him give himself a confidence booster, "I know this, it will come to me." Skipping the question may give him the time and space to figure it out when he comes back to it, without wasting valuable time for other questions.

@ Fatigue and hunger are two major distractions in a student's test-taking experience. Make sure your child is well rested and eats a hearty breakfast on test day.

@ If your child will have lunch or a snack at school before the test, make sure it is a healthy choice. Fast food, snack bars, carbonated drinks, and candy are full of processed ingredients, artificial colorings, caffeine, salt, fat, and sugar. The initial boost of energy your child will feel ends quickly, leaving him exhausted and unable to concentrate. Pack fruit and raw vegetables for snacks, instead. Raw foods increase the rate at which brain cells use oxygen, so children learn faster after eating them.

When it comes to taking tests, reinforce the idea that everyone makes mistakes and it is okay if your child does not have all the answers all the time. Allow him to take risks and fail. It is good for his character and self-esteem when he works diligently on something until he does succeed. Don't allow your child to say, " I can't." Say to him, "You can try."
—Amy Shaver, kindergarten and 1st grade teacher for 10 years, Bondurant, Iowa

I tell parents not to put a lot of emphasis on tests because I'm just giving it to see how they're doing and how much they've learned so far. I tell them not to focus on the word test, but to make it more casual. For my students, I put little notes on each of their desks that say things like, "Good luck," "You'll do fine," or "I believe in you," and then go around the room to whisper in their ear what each one says. I try to make each note different and specifically for them. That helps a little bit, too. I'm not the big, bad test-giving teacher; it helps them realize I'm on their side.
—Alison Gowers, kindergarten teacher for 5 years, West Point, Virginia

Oftentimes, children don't understand what's going on, and that can make them anxious or even affect the accuracy of test results. Parents need to sit down with their kids and de-escalate this fear. Say, "We want you to just be you."
—Lynn M., high school, deaf students, and middle school special education teacher for 21 years, Boston, Massachusetts

My advice before your child takes a test would be to downplay anything stressful, enforce healthy eating habits and sleeping schedules, and then forget about it.
—Deborah Berris, 3rd, 5th, and 8th grade teacher for 5 years

There are some strategies you can give a nervous test taker, such as taking deep breaths, studying ahead of time to feel prepared, and knowing what types of questions will be on the test. Also, tell your child to jot down any memorized information right as the test begins so he doesn't have to recall it later on. With certain types of tests, your child can memorize the directions ahead of time to save time during the test.

—*Kristyn Mulada, educational director of a Sylvan Learning Center for 2 years and former kindergarten teacher, Hanover, Massachusetts*

School Transitions

Which Factors Should I Consider When Choosing a School for My Child?

◉ You have to be an informed consumer when choosing the right school for your child. With so many options, this can prove to be a daunting task. Public or private, parochial or secular, or public charter? A school may have great academics, a beautiful campus, and a sound reputation and still not be the right fit for your child. Decide whether the school can address his needs and learning style fully. Be sure the school has a philosophy that reflects the educational approach that you feel will be best for your child.

◉ Begin your search by checking out the opportunities available to you. In some cases, districts allow for a choice between public schools. If one elementary school in town has a far stronger reputation, investigate whether you are allowed to enroll your child in your preferred school.

◉ Look at your child's social skills carefully and determine whether he makes friends easily. This may affect whether he should attend a school with a large, impersonal environment, or one with a more familial feel.

◉ Consider whether you'd prefer your child to attend a single-sex or coeducational institution and whether you'd prefer the school to be religiously affiliated or nondenominational.

◉ Though boarding schools offer many advantages, don't assume this option is best for your child. Some high school kids thrive on independence and discipline, while others benefit from the structure of a home environment.

◉ Another option to explore is charter schools, which are autonomous public schools set up by parents and teachers with the help of foundations, private donations, and corporate sponsors to achieve educational innovation in a smaller classroom setting.

◉ When considering your child's options, keep in mind private school is not always better than public school. The quality of the education your child receives at a school depends on many factors besides the school's price and reputation. Your decision to send your child to a particular school should be based upon the school's ability to accommodate your child's learning style and contribute to his academic, emotional, social, and behavioral development.

◉ A school's personality should be a critical factor in your assessment of whether the school will be a good fit for your child. The best way to get a feel for a school is to spend a day there and meet the teachers and students. Have your child come with you to see if he thinks he will be happy there.

◉ Make your child an integral part of the decision-making process, and allow him to discuss his needs and other issues important to him. Find common ground and go from there.

◉ Questions to ask when evaluating a school:

✹ Does the school philosophy and approach to education mesh with your values and goals?

✹ How does the school measure individual achievement and progress?

✴ How rigorous are the classes? Is the academic environment competitive or struggling?

✴ Does the school feel like a community? Are students interacting with teachers both inside and outside the classroom?

✴ How diverse are the student body and faculty?

✴ Are the faculty and staff involved in decision-making and curriculum development?

✴ What are the average standardized test scores?

✴ What is the rate of teacher turnover?

✴ Do teachers modify their lesson plans to cater to the children in the classroom?

✴ What is the tuition? Are scholarships available?

What Can I Learn from the Faculty I Meet While Visiting the School?

◉ You can tell a lot about a school from the behavior of its administrators. A welcoming environment is the first thing you should sense when visiting a prospective school. If the students and teachers do not appear friendly and inviting, this may not be the place for your child.

◉ Consider the attitude of the teachers and administration. Are they enthusiastic about their roles in children's lives? Do they make you feel as if you are disrupting their daily routine?

◉ Classroom atmosphere matters tremendously. If your child is part of a caring, supportive environment, he will participate more fully in the learning process.

◉ Low student-teacher ratios are important. Try to pick a school where the class-rooms have twenty or fewer kids. A smaller class size will give the teacher more time and energy to be responsive to your needs and those of your child.

◉ Sit in on a class and watch how the teacher divides up class time. Is she lecturing, administering tests, letting the class do homework, or involving the group in open discussion and debate? Observe the ways in which she interacts with students and watch how involved they are in the classroom, noting whether they ask questions or appear bored.

◉ Schedule a meeting with the principal to learn his opinion of the school's strengths and weaknesses. He benefits from promoting the school, so avoid questions that allow generalized answers. Instead, ask questions more specific to his school:

✦ How do you feel about the staff's authority over educational concerns, like teacher evaluations, budgeting, and curriculum?

✦ How much do you interact with students and parents?

✦ To what extent does the school incorporate outside resources?

✦ In what kinds of off-campus academic alliances does it participate?

✦ How does the school deal with high-risk students who disrupt normal classroom and school activities? What are the policies on retention, suspension, and dismissal?

◉ Request that the school arrange a few teacher interviews for you. Some great questions to ask include:

✦ How long have you been at the school? How many classes do you teach? Do you supervise any extracurricular activities?

✦ What are the school's biggest problems, and what is being done to address those concerns?

✦ What do you consider to be your most serious challenges at the school?

✦ How much input do you have in structuring the curriculum and designing lesson plans?

What Special Programs, Services, and Facilities Should I Consider?

◉ When visiting a potential school, ask the administration about extracurricular activities and check out the facilities. Check out the gym, newspaper and yearbook offices, drama and music centers, stages, art and photography facilities, and radio and television stations. Pay attention to the variety and condition of materials available.

◉ Find out if there is an after-school program; if there is, ask about its location and structure.

◉ Inquire about administrative services such as a full-time nurse on staff, transportation options, guidance and psychological counseling, and learning specialists.

◉ Visit the school library and ask how often students use the library and how many books they are allowed to take out at one time.

◉ Ask how the school integrates technology into the curriculum. Find out if computers are available to all students and whether they are wired for the Internet.

◉ Get information about programs for gifted students, like enrichment classes, independent study, or classes with older students.

If your child has special needs to consider, interview schools just like you would a daycare center. Weigh your options. Find out what they offer. When Joey started at public school, I was really direct and said, " My child is very bright but has these special needs. What do you want me to do and what are my options?" We met with the school social worker, the counselor, the principal, and the special education team. The overarching question was, " What does Joey need to be successful in his education?" Once you know what your child needs, the schools offer services to help him succeed.
—Kathleen Tucker, mom of Joey, 9, Jordan, 7, and Abigayle, 4, Lansing, Michigan

@ If you have a child with special needs, evaluate the school's resource department thoroughly and meet with the special education teachers.

What Are the Pros of Private School?

@ More and more parents are choosing to send their children to private schools because of dissatisfaction with public school quality. This shift is increasing as overcrowding and poor testing results at some public schools receive more publicity.

@ Private schools are, on average, half the size of public schools. Smaller private school class sizes enable teachers to give more individual attention to students. They also tend to foster a greater sense of community among students, teachers, and parents.

@ Private school principals and teachers exercise much more control over the curriculum than their public school counterparts; the State Department of Education dictates the curriculum to public school educators. Principals and teachers in private schools also have more control over school policy and discipline.

@ Private schools have the right to admit students and decide who is allowed to stay in the school after admission. This means schools can choose not to admit troublesome students or can kick them out if they become too disruptive.

@ Despite factors like lower pay, private school teachers often voice more satisfaction with their working conditions, expressing a greater feeling of community and more independence regarding policy, curriculum, and discipline. Tenure is either nonexistent or more difficult to attain in private schools, which means that your complaints about a teacher will carry more weight, and the school will be more likely to remove a poor teacher.

@ If your child struggles in the public school system and seems to be progressively losing interest, curiosity, or behavioral control, then consider alternative private schools that will accommodate his individual learning style. Allowing children to move at their own pace can take away the pressure a fast-paced classroom environment instills.

What Are the Cons of Private School?

When your child changes from public to private school, the curriculum and academic demands can shift dramatically. He will have to adjust to a new and different social world as well.

On average, public school teachers have higher salaries and more benefits than private school teachers. This often gives public schools more power to lure the best teachers.

Private schools often offer less religiously, ethnically, and economically diverse student bodies than public schools.

There can be intense competition among motivated children (and their driven parents) for academic success in private schools, so it can be more difficult to get remedial help for your child. Private schools are also less likely to have in-house resources for diagnosing and dealing with learning disorders.

In my experience, private schools are not necessarily better than public. It all has to do with parent involvement. I want my daughter to know the kids who are her neighbors and really feel part of her community.
—Amy Kamm, mom of Ava, 5, and Lily, 2, Burbank, California

I really believe in public education if at all possible. I wanted my daughter to experience both racial and economic diversity. At the same time, I didn't want to compromise her academic development just to accomplish this. We decided the best thing was to go to another school still within the city.
—Charisse Carney-Nunes, mom of a 5-year-old, Washington, D.C.

How Can I Prevent Academic Regression During Summer Vacation?

© For most students, summer is a three-month-long vacation for the brain, with little or no time with books. As a result, summer learning loss is a common problem. Teachers often have to spend the first six to eight weeks of the school year reviewing material that has been forgotten during the summer months.

© Students who do not review and learn during the summer months struggle to get back into the swing of things and often score lower on tests in September than they did before vacation began.

© Especially if your child has struggled academically, it's a good idea to have an end-of-the-year conference with the teacher to discuss his situation and ask for suggestions of enriching summer activities and tutors who can help your child during the vacation.

© Some fun ways to keep your child intellectually engaged throughout the summer:

✸ Go on a nature hike at a park and bring a library book to spot plants, birds, and local wildlife.

✸ Plant a vegetable garden in the backyard and have your child take photos or keep a journal about how the plants grow over the months.

✸ Play weatherman outside. Keep a thermometer outdoors, observe weather patterns and predict how the weather will be for the day.

✸ Visit local museums and historic sites.

✸ Register your child in summer reading programs at the local library.

Summer is not the time to put everything away and go to the pool every day. Take a bunch of books with you. Academic regression is huge in the summer, and parents need to help prevent it. Teachers often say they work from September to December just to get the kids back to where they were the last year. Read books together or turn on closed-captioning on your TV and make your child read it. Cook together, double recipes, and figure out fractions. Turn everything into a learning experience instead of watching *SpongeBob* all summer long.
—*Holly Parker, teacher of deaf students for 10 years, Colorado Springs, Colorado*

The same stigma exists for summer school as for special education. A lot of kids think school's out, summer's here, don't bore me with schoolwork, but I have to plug the Sylvan Learning Center. A lot of parents enroll their kids just so they don't lose those basic skills over the summer. Lots of teachers also send home summer reading lists and math packets. Make it fun so your child's not bored and saying "I just did this yesterday." Give him a goal. Tell him if he works on this he can have some kind of reward. There are some awesome books I've used that tell you what your child needs to know as a basis in each grade. These are great for both inside and outside the classroom because they give a core of what the average kid needs throughout the year. Do different things just so your child keeps thinking, and it can be as silly as building a house out of cards or toothpicks. Who knows—your child may use one of his summer experiences in the classroom!
—*Heather Daigle, teacher of all grades, Plymouth, Massachusetts*

Technology has afforded incredible opportunities for kids to stay active during the summer. Have your kids on the computer a lot and give them monitored Internet use. Even with my four-year-old, I have found so many science projects to do at home online, along with tons of crafts and ideas. Parents need to make a concerted effort so kids don't turn into lumps. Not only can children lose what they learned but they can also become completely unfocused. Take them to museums and stimulating events—even sporting events—to get them out of the house and keep their brains working.
—*Chris Grimm, 7th grade social studies teacher for 3 years, Ventura, California*

How Should I Approach the Beginning of a New School Year?

◉ The beginning of the school year increases a child's anxiety levels as he familiarizes himself with new teachers, classmates, and subjects. Get your child to open up about his expectations for school. Ask him if he feels excited, anxious, or a little bit of both. Talk with him about specific worries he has for the upcoming year.

◉ In the weeks before school starts, resume a school schedule with your child. Explain the upcoming school routine in detail. Go over your child's schedule, including the times he'll need to wake up, eat breakfast, and be ready to leave the house. Have him go to sleep earlier at night and get up early in the morning. After breakfast, have him engage in productive activities, such as reading, writing, or solving math problems.

◉ Emphasize the importance of schoolwork and how he must be considerate of classmates, listen to and cooperate with his teachers, and give classes and other activities his best effort.

◉ Type up generic permission slips (field trip, going home with another child, being picked up by someone other than you) and excuse notes (doctor's appointment, out of town, sick). Make copies of them that you can fill in, date, and sign as the need arises.

◉ Wait until the first week of school to buy supplies; by then you will know what the teacher expects your child to have.

◉ Label everything your child takes to school since you can bet a dozen kids will have something that looks very similar to what your child brings to school, especially for items like coats and lunchboxes. Better yet, get a lunchbox and backpack with your child's initials written or sewn onto them.

◉ If your child will walk to school, go over the route with him during other trips. Talk about landmarks, places to rest, and dangerous intersections.

◉ With your child's help, brainstorm a list of his favorite school lunches and snacks to make grocery shopping easier.

© Make sure your calendar includes important back-to-school dates, and be aware that babysitters will be in high demand for events like PTA meetings.

I start my kids going to bed fifteen minutes earlier each night about two weeks before school, with no more staying up until ten or eleven o'clock at night. On the first day of school each year, we encourage the kids to invite new friends over after school to have hot dogs and play outside in the sprinklers.
—*Sarah Essick, mom of Lauren, 12, and Parker, 7, Johnson City, Tennessee*

At the beginning of the school year, I make index cards for all of the tasks they need to do in the morning. No one is allowed downstairs to the kitchen until he is dressed, done, and ready to go. We start our school day routine about a week before school actually begins. This helps to start the habit before the big day and gets them back on school time before they need to be. It sounds like a lot, and in August and September it is, but once it becomes a habit and everyone knows the rules and what to expect, it makes life so much easier.
—*Amy Boyle McCarthy, mom of Dylan, 9, and Shawn, 8, Pittsburgh, Pennsylvania*

In the summer, we go to my daughter's classroom so she can see the room and get comfortable. Sometimes the teacher is there, which is a great time for a first meeting, but if she's not we go into the classroom on the first or second day and introduce ourselves. Getting your face in there is important, so if you have a choice, don't wait until back-to-school night.
—*Ellen Cameron, mom of Alison, 8, and Hilary, 4, Lexington, Massachusetts*

Send a letter at the beginning of the year to alert teachers to specific concerns or issues. For example, as a parent, I send a letter to my children's teachers about our Native American traditions and holidays, and I find that this sets a cooperative tone during school.
—*Claudia Fox Tree, 7th grade special education teacher for 15 years, Lincoln, Massachusetts*

I always let teachers know in the beginning of the year that I appreciate them, and I want to know how my kids are doing—if they're slacking off, as well as when things are going well. I check to see if the teacher allows parents to drop by the classroom from time to time, and I send lots of notes.

—Pam Fierro, mom of twins Meredith and Lauren, 8, and parenting multiples guide at
    www.multiples.about.com, Virginia Beach, Virginia

How Can I Make the First Day of School Exciting Instead of Anxious?

◉ Ease jitters on the first day of school by having a group of neighborhood kids meet at the bus stop for juice and cookies one afternoon before school starts. Or, gather them together for a "Kick-off" party complete with hats, noisemakers, and a cake.

◉ Start the school year off right by making the first day something to celebrate. Have a big breakfast, decorate the kitchen, serve a favorite meal, and hand out new lunchboxes or school supplies.

◉ Bake your child a batch of his favorite cookies as something to look forward to after the stress of the first day.

◉ Take pictures each year in a specific memorable spot, such as the front porch or steps.

◉ Make a big sit-down dinner the night before or on the first day. As a family, talk through some of the summer's highlights and state goals for the coming school year.

◉ Plan with neighborhood parents to meet at the bus stop for breakfast on the first day.

◉ Let your child pick out his favorite outfit to wear.

◉ Pack something familiar in your child's backpack to make him feel more comfortable, and something new to make him feel special.

◉ Go over the after school arrangements with your child, designating a time and place for pickup and ensure that he knows where to go.

◉ Remind your child it is not unusual to suffer from first-day jitters—everyone feels nervous on the first day.

Bryce starts kindergarten this year. A packet of information came for me in the mail and with it came a mystery snack coupon he has take to class the first day in order to redeem his snack. That's all Bryce thinks about for now—not if he'll take the bus, or how he'll find his teacher, or all the million other things I've told him that might make him worry. That word *mystery* is magic.
—*Rosemarie Turner, mom of Bryce, 5, and Margot, 3, Wayland, Massachusetts*

We used to have a get-together with all the moms in my neighborhood. We'd have ice cream parties so our kids would know who was going to be on the bus to reduce that scare factor.
—*Heather Daigle, teacher of all grades, Plymouth, Massachusetts*

Every day at the bus stop I tell my son, "I love you, have fun, and learn a lot." I say those three things in order of importance for me. My son relies on that every morning, and one day, when I forgot to say it, he came running back up the steps of the house to get me.
—*Angie Pederson, mom of James, 6, and Joann, 2, Lee's Summit, Missouri*

How Can I Ease My Child's Transition to a New School?

If your child is attending a new school, help him become familiar with the school grounds and people he will be meeting before the first day. Attend any open houses or orientations, but also consider taking your own tour. Look at the bathrooms, playground, library, and specialist rooms for music, art, and physical education.

When you visit, focus on an activity, game, or toy your child does not have at home, such as Tempera paints or a sandbox, and make that a particular thing for him to look forward to on the first day. Try to stop by the classroom he will be in and meet his teacher, if possible.

Invite another child who's in the same class to play with your child so he will know someone on his first day.

Find out if the school needs written permission from you or a note from your pediatrician for your child to take medication during school hours. Inform the school nurse about your child's allergies or illnesses and ask if your child should keep the following or leave them with the nurse: asthma inhaler, prescription medicine, over-the-counter medicine, cough drops, and throat lozenges.

If your child struggled with social problems at his old school, understand they will not necessarily disappear just because he is immersed in a new group of peers. Some social problems are a function of emotional or psychological struggles and run deep within the individual despite his surroundings.

Schedule meetings with people who will impact your child's education, including administrators, teachers, special education personnel, and guidance counselors.

Do your best to reassure your child. The prospect of making new friends can be a daunting and frightening experience. Encourage your child to get involved with sports or extracurricular activities to help him get to know classmates.

Your child may be hesitant to share his feelings with you, but let him know that the anxiety he feels is perfectly normal. Listen carefully when he talks about his day, his new friends, or other children in his class.

◉ Share with your child a time when you faced a similar situation. Let him know what you do when facing an unknown experience—just think about the cocktail hour you attended where you didn't know anyone. Remind him that feeling secure again may take a little while and friendships need time to develop.

◉ You may consider having the teacher arrange for another child to show him around for a day, or make sure that he has a buddy when having children work in pairs. Feeling like the only one left out is a painful and humiliating experience for a child, while working together on a project is fodder for a new friendship.

It's definitely beneficial to visit the school so you and your child know where things are. If a child knows his parents are familiar with the school, it makes it a more comfortable place for him.
—*Alison Gowers, kindergarten teacher for 5 years, West Point, Virginia*

Go and check out the school before the first day. Meet with the teacher prior to your child going by himself. If you move to a new home, meet friends down the street and tell them you're going to the same school. Do everything you can to keep your child from feeling like an outsider looking in. Don't hide the fact that your child needs services from the new school. Instead, admit that you need help. Have a meeting with the principal and don't be afraid to say, "Hey, I have a concern because my child is new to this school, and he may have difficulty adjusting." There will be hurdles you have to jump over, but get involved.
—*Heather Daigle, teacher of all grades, Plymouth, Massachusetts*

When we moved, my son had a hard time. He is not flexible in new situations and there were two straight weeks of crying just getting him to the school. After that, there were two weeks where he wouldn't play at recess and would cry in the cafeteria because he wasn't used to that many people and the loud noises. Miraculously, after that month, he was fine. I don't think it was because of anything I did, but I talked to him and the teachers a lot during this period. The teachers were very patient and kept me informed of what was happening.
—*Stacy Henry, mom of Nicolas, 6, and Sarah, 3, Nashville, Tennessee*

How Can I Help Change My Child's Bad Reputation?

☢ The teachers' lounge is often a place for airing concerns about students, administrators, parents, and schedules. If a bad reputation follows a child, then teachers dread getting him after having heard gossip about him. The discussions about students can mean long-term damage for your child.

☢ If you think your child has an undeserved negative reputation, talk to his teacher at the beginning of the academic year. Explain the issues that may have led to that reputation and what has changed about him.

☢ If your younger child gets a teacher with whom an older sibling didn't get along, inform the teacher that you are aware of your past differences but would like to start fresh this year. Also, express concerns over sibling comparisons to her. It is especially important to talk to the teacher if your two children are radically different from one another.

If you know that your child's teacher is hearing bad things from prior years, sit her down, and maybe even bring your child, and address the issue with her. Start the meeting off by saying something along the lines of: "My child has had behavior issues in the past, but we've discussed this as a family at home, and this is the plan we've come up with for this year." Stress that you want to make a new start; it's a new year, and you feel that your child should get a clean slate. Make a plan for the year so the teacher knows not to hesitate to call you, and you will both be on the same page.
—*Florence Michel, middle school teacher for 8 years, New York, New York, and Baltimore, Maryland*

Of course we teachers talk, so when we're sitting at a table and someone says something about a child I'm getting in the new school year, that's going to be my first impression of him. I try not to bring any biases into the classroom—but of course I do as I come into the classroom with some warning. As I start to see behaviors emerge, I might go to a student's previous teacher and say, "What works with this kid? Rewards? Keeping him in from lunch? Putting a hand on his shoulder to get him to listen?" But then I might go and get an earful, "Oh, golly . . . let me tell you all about him." So in all honesty you do have to be concerned about your child's reputation among the teachers.

—*Kallie Leyba, 1st and 2nd grade teacher for 2 years and mom of Lauren, 11, Lucas, 8, and Samson, 4, Highlands Ranch, Colorado*

We all talk about kids coming into our classroom because it gives us more information about them, but I seldom hear one teacher telling another, "Oh no, you've got to deal with this child?!" That's not the way we think in the teaching profession. We think this is the year that will really make a difference. What didn't work one year may work the next. A different class makeup and different teacher interactions can make all the difference; there's no way of knowing what might end up being effective without trying all the options. Even if there is a long history of behavioral issues, part of teaching is being convinced that you can make a difference in the life of a child. It's a challenge to see if you can work that out. Every child comes in to school in September with a new opportunity, a new chance.

—*Sue Abrams, elementary school principal and former 1st to 5th grade teacher for 22 years, Natick, Massachusetts*

Reputations particularly follow siblings. An older brother or sister could have exhibited poor behavior and then the younger one has to prove himself in the school. If you encounter this problem, having a face-to-face talk with the teacher is very important.

—*Paul O'Brien, 7th to 12th grade math and science teacher for 27 years, Sheffield, Massachusetts*

What Should I Be Looking for in a Preschool Experience?

The overall aim of a preschool program is to provide your child with the tools and experiences he needs to grow, thrive, and prepare for kindergarten. Preschool helps him learn the basics of proper classroom behavior, like following directions and waiting for his turn. Communication skills play a central role in preschool as your child learns how to participate in conversations, ask questions, and, most important, articulate and control his emotions.

Young children are incredibly curious about the way the world works, and preschools are wonderful environments to provide them with hands-on opportunities to explore the world around them through games and activities. This play is crucial because it gives children the opportunity to challenge themselves without risk, maintain concentration, and look at learning as fun.

Children learn just as much from other children as they do from adults, particularly when it comes to taking turns, sharing, and the basic give-and-take essential

So much of preschool is about socialization—being with other children and learning how to follow rules and participate in activities. Our kids really looked forward to it as a time to be social.
—*Vinca LaFleur, mom of Jackson, 6, and Evan, 4, Washington, D.C.*

When looking at preschool, I found one in which my son thrived. The teachers were fantastic—one was warm and fuzzy, and the other was a very cut-to-the-chase kind of person, so they balanced perfectly. The classroom was small and all the kids were within four months of each other so there were no large age gaps. It was a nice, cohesive little group, a very tight-knit class. My son loved it.
—*Danielle Cohen, mom of Sam, 3, Westford, Massachusetts*

to peer dynamics. Many children don't receive this opportunity to learn from peers until preschool.

◉ Experiencing love and care from someone other than a parent helps a child view the world as a safe and nurturing place.

How Do I Find the Right Preschool for My Child?

◉ During the preschool selection process, focus on what works best for you and your child. You may come across a school that seems absolutely perfect, but may not be right for your family.

◉ Location is often an important consideration. Will it fit better into your family's routine for the preschool to be close to your home or workplace? Also, many preschool programs offer the flexibility for parents to choose the number of school days each week and whether those days are half or whole, so look for a program that best suits your family's needs.

◉ The school and staff should be committed to communication among parents, teachers, and the school, as a whole. The school should spell out its goals and focus on the entire range of young children's needs—social skills, emotional growth, communication, and physical development. Find one that applies your own philosophies.

◉ Preschool teachers should have training in early education, and be able to give individual attention to each child and balance supporting children's efforts with fostering their independence. A low student-teacher ratio is a good sign that teachers will be able to fully interact with students and deal with conflict.

◉ Don't choose a preschool without first making a visit and bringing your child along, if possible.

When I was looking for preschools, I walked through the classrooms and observed the kids. Did they seem to be happy? How did they respond to the teacher? Was the teacher approachable? Would we get weekly progress reports? I was concerned with the teacher-student ratio and how the class was structured. I wanted to make sure the children were encouraged to be creative and experience all types of different things.
—*Pat Hanuman, mom of Matthew, 4, Jacksonville, Florida*

Diversity was our primary concern. My husband and I wanted the school to represent the world around our daughter as well it could, while providing a good education, challenging her, and attending to her individual needs. We also chose a preschool that was not overly concerned with preparing our child to have a leg up, but rather focused more on giving her social experience. I really wanted Olivia to experience the classroom atmosphere and learn to deal with other children. I was less concerned with her grasping academic concepts. I wanted preschool to be fun for her, and if she learned something along the way, then that was just a bonus.
—*Patty Potter, mom of Olivia Logan, 6, and Isabel Logan, 3, Ft. Worth, Texas*

There are two highly thought of preschools in our area, and one reason I chose one over the other was the teachers' low turnover rate. This speaks volumes about contentment: Do the teachers like being there? If they do, it comes through in the way they teach.
—*Molly Schaffner, mom of Monty, 3, and Lila, 1, Louisville, Kentucky*

My daughter has juvenile diabetes, so I had to find a preschool that was able and willing to do regular blood sugar checks and notice if she was acting differently. Some places said they were willing to do it but then I would check out their resources, like their capability to make an alternate menu, and find out the kitchen wasn't equipped for that. If my daughter didn't have diabetes, I wouldn't have known to dig a little deeper.
—*Kendra French, mom of Parker, 2, Fairfax, Virginia*

Ask the following questions before choosing a preschool:

✽ Are the teachers happy? Are they willing to talk with you and answer your questions? Does it seem like they will be a good match for your child's needs?

✽ How much experience do the teachers have? What is their educational background? How long have they been with the school?

✽ Do the kids look busy and happy?

✽ What is the basic daily routine? Does it include nap time, snack time, or lunch?

✽ Do the teachers emphasize structure, or do the children have opportunities for creativity and initiative? How often do children work in groups, and how often by themselves?

✽ How do the teachers respond to problems? What is the school's policy on discipline?

✽ Does the school emphasize academics or early enrichment?

✽ How are the rooms organized and decorated? Is there enough space for creative play? Do the rooms have certain areas set aside for different activities?

✽ Do the teachers display children's artwork?

✽ Does the school have an adequate supply of creative materials, such as dress-up clothes and art supplies?

✽ To what extent does the school expect and allow parents to get involved? How does this coordinate with your own needs and schedule?

✽ Are there conferences during the year for you and the teacher to discuss your child? Does the school send home periodic performance reports and keep a file?

✽ How often do the kids go outdoors? Does the school have a designated playground area?

✽ How does the school take care of sick or injured children? Do they have a nurse on staff? What are her hours? What is the procedure if you can't pick your child up if he gets sick at school?

✳ How often do the kids go on field trips?

✳ What is the vacation and holiday schedule?

✳ What is the policy on toilet training? Be clear on the school's policy because even though many 3-year-olds are still in diapers, most preschools won't admit your child unless he is fully potty trained.

How Can I Help My Child Make the Preschool Transition?

◎ Getting your child started at school is an emotional milestone for parents and kids alike. Your child will take his cue from you, so extend a warm, positive attitude about his upcoming school experience.

◎ Ease your child into preschool gradually. Arrange playdates with other children to get him used to socializing before putting him into a situation with twenty peers.

◎ Young children do best with routine and repetition, so developing a personal ritual for saying good-bye will ease the separation from you each day. Practice the good-bye ritual with your child beforehand.

◎ Don't drag out good-byes. After you leave, it will be easier for your child to find something to distract himself. Tell him when you'll be back, referring to the structure of his day instead of giving him the exact pickup time, such as after nap time, instead of telling him you'll see him at 1:30 P.M.

◎ Give your child a photo of you to look at during the day or pack a note with his lunch.

◎ Separation anxiety is normal, but listen to your child to make sure he isn't having other problems at school. If your child still isn't adjusting well after a month or two to being away from you and he can't get used to the daily activities it may be time to check out other options. Children with extreme separation anxiety may not do well if they're pushed too far too early.

When my son was going to start a new preschool, I took pictures of the rooms, the playground, and the teachers. At the center's open house, I took pictures of him there. I created a New School scrapbook. We looked at it every day in the few weeks leading up to school. By the time he started, the school felt totally familiar to my son.
—*Amy Schaefer, mom of Drew, 3, Needham, Massachusetts*

When my daughter was nervous about starting preschool, I took her to the school beforehand. We peeked in the windows and played on the playground. This way she felt more comfortable on the first day. It only takes a little bit of preplanning to help with the familiarity of the school. For my son, who sometimes has separation anxiety and will enter preschool this fall, we have been going to his preschool classroom for the past 6 months. Just that little bit makes a big difference.
—*Jennifer Clements, mom of Kaitlin, 8, Ian, 3, and Reilly, 1, Murrieta, California*

My youngest son had a tough time adjusting to preschool, as he's really shy. So every morning when I left the preschool, I put something in his pocket: stickers, a fake tattoo, a candy corn around Halloween, and once in while I would forget and have to rummage through my purse for a quarter. I did that for a couple of months, along with a kiss folded in his hand to save for later. He started wanting me to leave already so he could get the surprise. One day I turned back to watch him through the window as I walked. He reached into his pocket for the sticker, and then unfolded his palm with the kiss and put it on his cheek. It really worked for him.
—*Suzanne Morris, mom of Jackson, 8, and Devin, 5, Belmont, Massachusetts*

My daughter is entering preschool this fall. A few parents took it upon themselves to organize a pre-first-day playdate for all the kids in the class at a local playground. One mom

brought juice boxes and another made phone calls. It's great for all the parents to meet and the kids to break down fears and realize, "Everyone else in the class is three, too!"
—*Rosemarie Turner, mom of Bryce, 5, and Margot, 3, Wayland, Massachusetts*

Don't prolong the morning transition. It sounds so cruel, but don't linger long, or your child will have more trouble transitioning into the classroom. So many books will tell you to stay with your child for the beginning of the morning and then leave, but you've got to let him make the break. If you send him off confidently, he'll get the message that everything is okay. If you linger, he'll think, "Why isn't she going? What's wrong here?" and may cry because he knows Mom will stay with him if he does. If he's crying when you drop him off, it usually only lasts for five minutes and then he finds a friend or gets distracted.
—*Kathy Carabine, pre-k and 3rd grade teacher for 16 years, Boston Massachusetts*

My daughter didn't want to go to preschool at first, and she cried every day and wouldn't let me leave. So I finally decided to take her out and try again a couple months later. I talked it up and when she went again, she was more ready and things went fine.
—*Julie Jones, mom of Mikaela, 4, Brandon, 3, and Allison, 1, Carmichael, California*

Is My Child Thriving in Preschool?

Preschool age is a crucial and delicate time because your child is developing faster than he ever will again. Even though his skills will not be tested formally the way they will be in later grades, talk to his teacher and take note of his progress in the following areas:

* How is his motor development? Can he handle basic physical activities like running and climbing? How is his fine motor development in areas like drawing?

* Does he take an interest in other kids? Does he get along with them, or do

they scare him or make him hostile? How does he handle himself when he gets into conflicts with other students?

✸ Can he pay attention?

✸ Does he feel comfortable approaching the teacher and asking for help?

✸ Are transitions, like moving from one activity to another, challenging?

☺ Children, especially at the preschool age, develop more quickly in some areas than in others, so don't worry if assessment shows an imbalance. Use your child's strengths to work on his weaknesses. For example, if he's physically coordinated and likes sports but is not doing so well socially, try building his social skills through concepts like teamwork.

How Do I Know If My Child Is Ready for Kindergarten?

☺ In the past, a child's age was the sole factor in determining when he would start kindergarten. Today, parents have significantly more input and kindergarten readiness is an important factor to consider. With the ever-increasing size of kindergarten classes, the growing demands on teachers, and the trend toward pushing accelerated academics in earlier years, it is in your child's best interest to have all the advantages on his side when he begins formal schooling.

☺ Kindergarten readiness also depends on the child's overall development, not just his academic ability. Children who believe in themselves, are curious, have some degree of independence, and can finish what they start will do well in kindergarten. A child who's ready for kindergarten should also be able to get along with others, share, and refrain from acting out physically.

☺ Ask your child's preschool teachers whether they think he is ready to start kindergarten. Find out how he socializes with other kids and whether he made friends in his group. Ask how adept he is at following directions and how he compares to the rest of his class.

◎ Find out the specifics of the kindergarten program. How is the classroom organized and how formal is the instruction? How big is the class size? For a shy child, a large class size can be intimidating and keep him from getting the individual attention he needs.

◎ Research shows that any advantage children gain by waiting an extra year to attend kindergarten disappears by third grade. Studies also show, however, that children, especially boys, who start kindergarten before they're ready often have academic problems, perform poorly on standardized tests, and are more likely to fail grades. If the evaluation suggests holding your child back a year, take the following steps:

✿ Ask for the specific reasons the school found for holding your child back the extra year. Did they base the decision on his age, maturity, motor skills, or social abilities?

✿ Investigate your school's screening procedures to get an idea of how they evaluated your child. Find out whether your school tracks students and if so, when.

✿ Find out what skills the school expects of kindergarteners, what the curriculum will draw on during the year, and how best to prepare your child for the demands of school. A school may also consider a child more or less ready for kindergarten based on its particular expectations and requirements; a child who would need to stay back at one school may be perfectly fine at another.

◎ If your child is not quite ready for kindergarten, it is a good idea to enroll him in a prekindergarten or transition class to help him prepare for kindergarten the following year.

The biggest indicator of kindergarten readiness is being able to separate from the parents—that's the hardest transition. The kids need to have a little bit of independence and be willing to try things on their own or do things they haven't done before. It's also helpful if they know some basic skills, such as recognizing shapes and numbers, going to the bath-

room on their own, and writing their names. If they don't have the skills going in, it's beneficial to wait that extra year.
—Alison Gowers, kindergarten teacher for 5 years, West Point, Virginia

Children who are prepared when they enter kindergarten are talkative, but able to sit and listen, and have good fine motor skills. Kids who excel are willing to try anything and are not afraid to fail.
—Amy Shaver, kindergarten and 1st grade teacher for 10 years, Bondurant, Iowa

My oldest child turned five in July, and my husband and I spent many months deliberating the question, "Do we send him to kindergarten or wait another year?" Thus far, it's been our biggest parenting decision. We decided to send him and he enjoyed every second. I do, however, wonder if I will continually worry about his success as the years pass and, if there are stumbles, blame it on our decision to send him.
—Leslie Nicholson, mom of Kyle, 6, Emma, 4, and Julia, 2, Edina, Minnesota

When I was a kid, preschool wasn't a concern. Now it's almost like you need to be reading before kindergarten . . . the whole system is definitely more accelerated than it was.
—Amy Kamm, mom of Ava, 5, and Lily, 2, Burbank, California

The most important factor in deciding whether or not a child is ready to go to kindergarten is the ability to separate. If they separate easily from their families and are secure enough in themselves to form relationships with people other than their parents, they are probably ready for kindergarten. But it depends a lot on parental attitude, as well. If the parents are uneasy, the child will pick up on that. I've seen kids at 6 who are not ready and kids at 4 who are just rarin' to go. It's not based on age, but the personality of the child and the attitude of the family.
—Kathy Carabine, pre-k and 3rd grade teacher for 16 years, Boston Massachusetts

When Does Academic Redshirting Make Sense?

© Academic redshirting—a concept adapted from the practice of benching sports players for a year so they can gain experience—refers to the practice of holding back age-eligible children from entering kindergarten to allow them extra time for social, emotional, intellectual, and physical development. This happens most often with children whose birthdays fall close to the grade cut-off dates.

© In part, redshirting is a response to the increased focus on academics and higher demands placed on students at increasingly early levels. Teachers report that 48% of their students are ill prepared for kindergarten because they lack crucial communication and academic skills and the ability to work independently and follow directions.

© Studies have found that in the short-term redshirting is an effective technique for raising a child's academic achievement and conduct to be on par with his classmates' and increases his social skills, confidence, and even popularity as well. It's also believed redshirting can reduce or even eliminate the need for special education in cases it would otherwise be necessary.

© According to the National Center for Education Statistics, redshirting occurs at a rate of about 10% among kindergarten-age children, with this practice of delaying entrance more common in affluent communities and private schools, and more frequently used for boys than girls.

© Parents who are anxious to have their kids be the best both academically and athletically keep their five-year-olds, especially boys, in preschool for an extra year. This trend has become an epidemic in many suburbs. Thirty years ago, only 5.8% of all kindergartners were 6 or older, while today this statistic has risen to more than 13.2%, according to the U.S. Department of Education.

© The trend continues into the early elementary school years, with more principals getting flooded with requests for children to repeat a grade. Parents believe their children will have a competitive edge over their peers if they are the oldest in the class. By doing this, however, you risk making your child feel bored and unchallenged, awkward around smaller and younger classmates, and worried about letting you down if he doesn't live up to high expectations.

So many of my daughter's friends are doing an extra preschool year, it's unbelievable! Parents want to give their kids an extra edge, so their child will be the best, brightest, and most athletic in the class.
—*Jill Brack, mom of Stella, 6, Newton, Massachusetts*

The question you need to ask is whether your child is cognitively and socially ready to move on. My son is one of the youngest boys in his class and is not as emotionally ready as the older kids. The effects won't really show up until middle school, but he already doesn't feel comfortable with some of the other kids, and while he's gained acceptance through playing sports, he's not the most popular boy in the grade and he's uncomfortable talking to girls. If you are looking at a child who struggles with making friends, is withdrawn or is not cognitively ready—which may have nothing to do with intelligence—then yes, you need to hold your child back. I have never heard a parent say she regrets holding her child back, but I have heard many parents say they regret sending their children on.
—*Libby Anne Inabinet, kindergarten, 1st grade, reading, and gifted and talented teacher for 15 years, Columbia, South Carolina*

How Can I Help My Child Feel Confident About Starting Kindergarten?

Almost every child feels nervous about starting kindergarten, even if he has attended preschool or day care. Start preparing for his first day in advance.

Talk to your child in a positive, upbeat way about starting kindergarten. Tell him fun stories about your first year of school and read him books on the topic to make him more comfortable. Encourage your child to use language frequently and talk to you instead of passively listening.

Sometimes parents set their kids up to be afraid of going to school. We had a child with a huge case of school phobia, and the teachers recommended that her mother walk her to school. Every day we would peel the screaming child away from her mother, and one day I heard her mother telling her, "Don't worry honey, if Mommy dies today you will have your brothers and sisters to take care of you." No wonder the child was so scared! I recommend doing a lot of talking and being really straightforward with your child, saying something like "Mommy and Daddy know it's not easy, but can you tell us why you don't like school?" Try role playing at home about what's going on at school.
—*Claudia Flanders, kindergarten to 8th grade teacher for 34 years, Santa Monica, California*

Have your child ride the bus! So many parents want to bring their child to school the first day, but it's very hard to separate when you're at the building. If you put them on the bus and get the separation over with, it's easier on both you and your children. Also, before you send your children to kindergarten, concentrate on working with them so they can sit down and work on something for ten solid minutes without getting up and running around. Explain to them what the school will expect and how it might be different than what they are used to so the new environment isn't a total shock to them.
—*Alison Gowers, kindergarten teacher for 5 years, West Point, Virginia*

A visit to the school and a meeting with the teacher can calm some of the child's fears. A lot of children come to my room when I'm setting it up, and I show them some of the things on the walls and tell them some of the activities we're going to be doing. It makes it a little more comfortable; when they come on the first day, I'm a familiar face and they know I've spoken with their family members.
—*Kathy Carabine, pre-k and 3rd grade teacher for 16 years, Boston Massachusetts*

◉ Attend activities the school hosts for your child's class before the start of the year. Many schools have some sort of open house just for the kindergarteners so they can become familiar with the building and teachers before their first day. Show your child where the bathrooms, gym, playground, and lunchroom are.

◉ Create small rituals that make starting kindergarten an adventure, such as making a calendar that counts down to the first day of school. Make choosing a lunchbox and picking out a first-day-of-school outfit exciting.

◉ Find out if anyone from your child's preschool or neighborhood will be attending the same school, and arrange playdates so they can get to know each other better. Seeing a familiar face on the first day will be very comforting.

◉ If your child will be taking the bus for the first time, find out if you can do a trial run together.

◉ Stay in the classroom for a little while or introduce your child to some of his classmates before the teacher takes charge.

◉ First separations from your child can be poignant, but keep a brave face. Your child's enthusiasm will wilt as your anxiety increases. Talk with other parents for reassurance and anticipate that once the opening few weeks pass and your child happily settles in you will feel more comfortable yourself.

◉ Make up a good-bye ritual your child can count on. Give him a hug, a kiss, and a warm but firm good-bye.

What Can I Expect from the Move to Middle School?

◉ Middle school can be overwhelming for any child. He suddenly jumps to six or seven different classes, each with a different teacher, and faces a major increase in homework responsibilities. Even the sheer size of a new building can be intimidating. In the middle grades, students wrestle with issues of authority, independence, and increased visibility in the community, in addition to coping with increased extracurricular choices.

☺ Children develop a stronger sense of self and exercise more of their own judgment in problem solving after entering middle school. They naturally refuse guidance from parents in a quest to assert their independence and establish personal privacy and ownership. Your adolescent child will ask for your opinion less frequently when he makes a decision and will want to spend more time with friends and less at home. Do not abandon him during this tumultuous period of his life, but expect that he will require more space and freedom.

☺ If your child suddenly exhibits a major change in behavior or grades in the beginning of the year, recognize that he is going through a difficult transition and that it may take him a little while to adjust.

☺ Middle school can also be a big shift for you. Many middle schools put less energy into keeping you informed, extending the independence they require of their students into the autonomy they ask of parents. Now, the job of staying involved becomes more your responsibility.

☺ Transition and uncertainty often surround the middle school years, with your child wanting to feel autonomous but still needing your involvement.

☺ Your child's adolescence can be just as turbulent for you as it is for him. Many parents experience feelings of helplessness and depression when dealing with a rebellious, angry, or disobedient child struggling for independence. Your child's small rebellions don't mean you've failed; at the same time, when you absorb your child's anger and glares, you still serve as the anchoring influence in his life. Keep discipline methods constant and continue to expect high standards for schoolwork and interactions with family members.

☺ Middle school years are the prime time for you to set a new standard of involvement in your child's education. By then you should be easing your way into the position of guide, promoter, and mentor.

Middle school is hard for parents because kids care so much about what peers think and start shutting out Mom and Dad, but they still really care about the messages their parents send. It's kind of a tightrope walk for parents. Students and parents alike need to let go of elementary school expectations. Deadlines are really deadlines. If a student does not turn in his work and fails or gets a zero, parents will frequently ask what their child can do for extra credit or how he can make it up. Starting in middle school, kids need to learn the choices they make have consequences.

Stay connected by showing an interest in what your child is working on. When your child says, "I've done my homework," say, " Can you show it to me?" just to let him know you're still interested and still care how he's doing in school. Sometimes a kid can't do it and is too scared to say so.

—*Laurie Olmstead, 7th and 8th grade math and science teacher for 4 years, Union, Maine*

When kids come into middle school, they must leave behind the security of a smaller class size and the familiarity of friends for a much more rigorous school experience. Kids have to adjust to core classes and several different teachers with whom they must interact every day. Going from having a personal relationship with one teacher 75% of the time to flip-flopping between 6 individuals with drastically different teaching styles can be very difficult.

—*Amy Watson, 7th to 12th grade teacher for 5 years, Oyster Bay, New York*

Parents are often very involved in elementary school, but by the time their children get to eighth grade they think, "My child is now old enough to manage things on his own." They overestimate their children's independence and underestimate their own roles in their children's education. Even as their kids get older, parents need to check in with their children: "Did you do your homework? Where are your tests? What's in your book bag or binder?" That's the biggest thing I saw with parents of middle schoolers. They say to their kids, "Oh, it's up to you," and then when they get to the conference they are surprised to learn that their children haven't been doing homework or have done poorly on their classroom tests.

Don't try to be friends with your middle school kids—they have enough! It doesn't help them—they need you to be their parent!

—*Florence Michel, middle school teacher for 8 years, New York, New York, and Baltimore, Maryland*

The level of organization and double-checking necessary in middle school is much higher. Parents need to help their kids come up with strategies, like using a daily planner or assignment notebook and making sure they write the assignments down properly.

—*Anne Wonson Curry, 5th to 12th grade math and science teacher for 12 years, Rockport, Massachusetts*

Appendix A

Sample Letters Praising Teachers

Letter to the Principal 1

I wanted to write to you to share some effusive feedback about Stephanie H., my daughter Kyle's fourth grade teacher. She is, simply put, one of the most compassionate, inspiring, intellectual, challenging, and nurturing teachers I have ever seen in action. From childhood, every one of us has one teacher who profoundly and dramatically shapes our lives, and for Kyle, I believe that teacher is Mrs. H.

Mrs. H. brings to fourth grade Literature and Studies an intellectual level that many college professors in my major at Brown aspired to but never achieved! She manages to have fourth graders spellbound as they study works such as *The Fledgling,* and discusses everything from the use of imagery as symbolism and alliteration to personification and allegories. She turned Kyle from a competent but reluctant reader to a passionate devourer of books, a poet, and a nonstop creative writer (including writing fiction throughout the year with a fellow classmate who will be moving at the end of the year). In each of her students, Mrs. H. draws out a passion for study, a thoughtful reflectiveness about the materials being discussed, a sensitivity to nuances, and a view of language as something that can be crafted, enhanced, and reworked until it glows.

Moreover, Mrs. H. achieves all this with an extraordinary level of empathy, warmth, patience, and genuine interest in how each of her students individually fares and feels. She takes a deep, personal interest in helping each of them grow, mature, and become passionate about learning. She sets high expectations and her students feel inspired to reach deep down to achieve their best for her. In her soft-spoken, unassuming way, she inspires them to shine.

The students have secretly nicknamed her Miss Honey after the teacher from the movie *Matilda,* which is surely their highest form of a loving tribute to a teacher they all adore. She is so universally worshipped and admired by her fourth graders that they even dispose of their cool personas to gush about her and seek out her attention. And they're right—she is simply the best.

Warmest,

Stacy DeBroff

Letter to the Principal 2

I am writing to you to share enthusiastic feedback for Jennifer M., who, simply put, is an outstanding fifth grade teacher. Her excellent math teaching skills, warmth, maturity, concern for each of her students, and calm composure make her stand out in a school that is packed with an exceptional and seasoned teaching staff.

My daughter Kyle, who is currently in her class, constantly raves about her and has become a math enthusiast this year largely in response to Ms. M.'s inspiration. Jennifer's combination of being incredibly organized and poised while being kind and humorous has all the fifth graders looking to her as a role model.

Jennifer has also excelled in a team teaching model, forming a tight, cohesive, and amazing team with her two other fifth grade teachers. Together, they seem to be able to tackle seamlessly any classroom or curriculum issue that comes up, and support each other's efforts to meet the individual needs of all seventy students whom they teach. The ability to work so well with these two teachers is in large part reflective of Jennifer's collaborative approach and the lack of ego issues she brings to her work.

Simply put, I think she's a star, and deserves to be commended for a job so well done!

With warm regards,

Stacy DeBroff

Sample Letter for a Teacher Award

Dear Committee Members,

I write to offer my strongest recommendation for Dawn M. for your Teacher of the Year award. Dawn has taught first grade for more than twenty years. My daughter had Dawn three years ago, and last year my son was in her class. Simply put, Dawn is an absolutely amazing teacher. She embodies the outstanding qualities that one expects of the recipient of National Teacher of the Year.

Dawn embraces her students as if they were her own children, and brings an astonishing depth of passion to her work. She challenges the children academically, infusing them with a love of learning, reading, and figuring things out on their own. As an African-American teacher in a school with incredible diversity (over 35 native languages spoken in a school of only 500 children), she imparts to the children a sense of embracing each other's differences and learning to celebrate each other's unique strengths. Dawn is at once joyous, protective, patient, inspiring, thoughtful, and reflective. She hones in on each child in a way that makes the children feel incredibly special. She continually refreshes her teaching material and puts in hours of preparation into every class. She even photographs the children throughout the year and creates for each a first-grade album.

I literally could go on and on, as could hundreds of other parents who view Dawn as our resident Teacher Goddess. She has launched at least two generations of students with whom she continues to stay in touch, even attending their graduation ceremonies! She is so warm, gracious, and inspiring to be around, I could imagine no finer person serving as an ambassador for the profession.

I called parents whose children are in Dawn M.'s class currently or have had her in the past to gather the enclosed quotes. The conversations I have had with parents from all different walks of life about how much they admire, respect, and adore Dawn have been astounding. Even more remarkable has been the repetitive nature of the superlatives in these conversations, with phrases like "quintessential teacher" and "wonderful example for educators everywhere" echoing from parent to parent.

I have also enclosed some photos from Dawn's in-class Valentine's Day celebration, which capture the vibrant spirit of her classroom.

I passionately believe that no teacher could better embody the spirit of your award, or serve as a better ambassador for the profession than Dawn. She is, simply put, the best.

With warm regards,

Stacy DeBroff

Appendix B

Parent Resources

American Federation of Teachers (AFT)
555 New Jersey Avenue, NW
Washington, DC 20001
(202) 879-4400
http://www.aft.org/parents/index.htm

The American Federation of Teachers (AFT) focuses on representing the economic, social, and professional interests of classroom teachers. The AFT advocates sound, commonsense public education policies, including high academic and conduct standards for students and greater professionalism for teachers and school staff, excellence in public service through cooperative problem-solving and workplace innovations, and high-quality healthcare provided by qualified professionals. The organization's five divisions denote its broad membership spectrum: teachers; paraprofessionals and school-related personnel (PSRP); local, state, and federal employees; higher education faculty and staff; and nurses and other health care professionals. The AFT also hosts the Quality Educational Standards in Teaching (QuEST) conference, a professional issues meeting that attracts nearly 3,000 educators from around the country.

Family Education Network
http://www.fen.com

Family Education Network offers a tremendous wealth of educational content and resources for parents, teachers, and kids. The website provides parents with practical guidance, grade-specific information about their children's school experience, strategies to get involved with their children's learning, free email newsletters, and fun and entertaining family activities. The network brings together leading organizations from both the public and private sectors to help parents, teachers, schools, and community organizations use online tools and other media resources to positively affect children's education and overall development.

National Association for the Education of Young Children (NAEYC)
1509 16th Street, NW
Washington, DC 20036-1426
(800) 424-2460
http://www.naeyc.org

The National Association for the Education of Young Children (NAEYC) is the nation's largest and most influential organization of early childhood educators and others dedicated to improving the quality of programs for children from birth through third grade. NAEYC leads and consolidates the efforts of individuals and groups working to achieve healthy development and constructive education for all young children. Primary attention is devoted to assuring the provision of high-quality early childhood programs for young children. NAEYC currently has a national network of 100,000 members working to improve professional practice and working conditions in early childhood education and to build public support for high-quality early childhood programs.

National Coalition for Parent Involvement in Education (NCPIE)
Sue Ferguson, Chair
3929 Old Lee Highway, Suite 91-A
Fairfax, VA 22030-2401
(703) 359-8973
www.ncpie.org

The National Coalition for Parent Involvement (NCPIE) advocates for the involvement of parents and families in their children's education, and promotes fostering relationships between home, school, and community to enhance the education of all our nation's young people. NCPIE seeks to serve as a visible representative for strong parent and family involvement initiatives at the national level and to conduct activities that involve the coalition's member organizations and their affiliates. The coalition also provides resources and legislative information that can help member organizations promote parent and family involvement.

National Dissemination Center for Children with Disabilities (NDCCD)
P.O. Box 1492
Washington, DC 20013
(800) 695-0285
nichcy@aed.org
www.nichcy.org

The National Dissemination Center for Children with Disabilities (NDCCD) is a center that provides information to the nation on child disabilities, services available to children with disabilities, and effective practices for children with disabilities. NDCCD is also a great resource for information on IDEA, the nation's special education law, and No Child Left Behind.

National Education Association (NEA)
1201 16th Street, NW
Washington, DC 20036-3290
(202) 833-4000
http://www.nea.org

NEA is the nation's leading organization committed to advancing and restoring public confidence in public education. NEA has 2.7 million members who work at every level of education, from preschool to university graduate programs. NEA has affiliates in every state, as well as in more than 13,000 local communities across the United States. NEA currently focuses its energy and resources on the restoration of public confidence in public education.

National PTA
330 N. Wabash Avenue
Suite 2100
Chicago, IL 60611
(312) 670-6782
(800) 307-4782
www.pta.org

The National PTA is the largest volunteer child advocacy organization in the United States. A nonprofit association of parents, educators, students, and other citizens active in their schools and communities, the National PTA is a leader in reminding our nation of its obligations to children. With over 6 million members, the organization has an amazing impact on families, schools, and communities throughout our nation. The National PTA offers a powerful voice for children, a relevant resource for parents, and a strong advocate for public education. The PTA is the catalyst for effective parent involvement, safe and nurturing communities, and quality public education for children in this country. The organization is currently working to address challenges that include parents' time constraints, cultural differences, and school budget shortfalls.

Parents Advocacy Coalition for Educational Rights (PACER)
8161 Normandale Blvd.
Minneapolis, Minnesota 55437
(952) 838-9000
pacer@pacer.org
www.pacer.org

PACER Center was created by parents of children with disabilities to help other families facing similar challenges. PACER is staffed primarily by parents of children with disabilities and works in coalition with 18 disability organizations. The center focuses on expanding opportunities and enhancing the quality of life of children and young adults with disabilities and their families.

U.S. Department of Education (DOE)
400 Maryland Avenue, SW
Washington, DC 20202
(800) 872-5327
customerservice@inet.ed.gov
http://www.ed.gov/index.jsp

The U.S. Department of Education promotes equal access to education and educational excellence throughout the nation. The department promotes improvements in the quality of education through federally supported research, evaluation, and information sharing. The DOE is dedicated to establishing policies on federal financial aid for education, prohibiting discrimination, and ensuring equal access to education. The department supplements and complements the efforts of states, local school systems, public and private nonprofit educational research institutions, and community-based organizations, parents, and students to improve the quality of education.

Bibliography

Anderson, Winifred, Stephen Chitwood, and Deidre Hayden. *Negotiating the Special Education Maze: A Guide for Parents and Teachers.* Bethesda, MD: Woodbine House, 1997.

Andre, Lynda, Mary Hawkley, and Robert Rockwell. *Parents and Teachers as Partners: Issues and Challenges.* Fort Worth, TX: Harcourt Brace, 1996.

Armstrong, Thomas. *In Their Own Way: Discovering and Encouraging Your Child's Multiple Intelligences.* New York: Penguin Putnam, 2000.

Beaulieu, John, Alex Granzin, and Deborah Romaine. *Working Parents Can Raise Smart Kids.* Tacoma, WA: Parkland Press, 1999.

Bellino, Lydia, and Lucy Calkins. *Raising Lifelong Learners: A Parent's Guide.* Boston: Addison-Wesley, 1997.

Bempechat, Janine. *Getting Our Kids Back on Track: Educating Children for the Future.* San Francisco: Jossey-Bass Publishers, 2000.

Berger, Kristina, Peter Cookson, Joshua Halberstam, and Susan Mescavage. *A Parent's Guide to Standardized Tests in School.* New York: Learning Express, 1998.

Cartwright, Nancy, Denis Gleeson, and Derek Glover. *Towards Bully-free Schools.* Buckingham: Open University Press, 1998.

Chase, Bob, and Bob Katz. *The New Public School Parent: How to Get the Best Education for Your Child.* New York: Penguin Books, 2002.

Clark, Rosemarie, Donna Hawkins, and Beth Vachon. *The School-Savvy Parent: 365 Insider Tips to Help You Help Your Child.* Minneapolis: Free Spirit Publishing, 1999.

Coloroso, Barbara. *The Bully, the Bullied, and the Bystander.* New York: Harper Resource, 2003.

Cooper, Harris. *The Battle Over Homework: Common Ground for Administrators, Teachers, and Parents.* Thousand Oaks, CA: Corwin Press, 2001.

Dellabough, Robin, and Roberta Kirshbaum. *Parent Power: 90 Winning Ways to Be Involved and Help Your Child Get the Most Out of School.* New York: Hyperion, 1998.

Elliot, Michele, ed. *Bullying: A Practical Guide to Coping for Schools.* London: Pearson Education Limited, 2002.

Epstein, Joyce. *School, Family, and Community Partnerships.* Boulder, CO: Westview Press, 2001.

Fujawa, Judy. *(Almost) Everything You Need to Know About Early Childhood Education: The Book of Lists for Teachers and Parents.* Beltsville, MD: Gryphon House, 1998.

Giannetti, Charlene, and Margaret Sagarese. *The Roller Coaster Years: Raising Your Child Through the Maddening Yet Magical Middle School Years.* New York: Broadway Books, 1997.

————. *Cliques: 8 Ways to Help Your Child Survive the Social Jungle.* New York: Broadway Books, 2001.

Golant, Mitch, and Susan Golant. *Kindergarten Isn't What It Used to Be.* Los Angeles: Lowell House, 1997.

Goldstein, Sam, and Nancy Mather. *Overcoming Underachieving: An Action Guide to Helping Your Child Succeed in School.* New York: John Wiley, 1998.

Greene, Lawrence. *Finding Help When Your Child Is Struggling in School.* New York: Golden Books, 1998.

Hall, Susan, and Louisa Moats. *Straight Talk about Reading: How Parents Can Make a Difference During the Early Years.* Chicago: NTC Publishing Group, 1998.

Hirsch, Gretchen, and Carol Strip. *Helping Gifted Children Soar.* Scottsdale, AZ: Great Potential Press, 2000.

Jackson, Shirley Babilya. *Children First: ABC's of School Success. A Guide for Parents.* Lanham, MD: Scarecrow Press, 2001.

Kline, Peter. *The Everyday Genius: Restoring Children's Natural Joy of Learning—And Yours Too.* Arlington, VA: Great Ocean Publishers, 1997.

LaForge, Ann E. *What Really Happens in School: A Guide to Your Child's Emotional, Social, and Intellectual Development, Grades K–5.* New York: Hyperion, 1999.

Leonhardt, Mary. *Parents Who Love Reading, Kids Who Don't.* New York: Crown Publishing, 1995.

Levine, Karen. *What to Do When Your Child Has Trouble in School.* Pleasantville, NY: Reader's Digest, 1997.

Mack, Adrienne. *A+ Parents: Help Your Child Learn and Succeed in School.* Ithaca, NY: McBooks Press, 1998.

Ramey, Craig, and Sharon Ramey. *Going to School: How to Help Your Child Succeed.* New York: Goddard Press, 1999.

Ramsey, Robert. *501 Ways to Boost Your Child's Success in School.* Columbus, OH: McGraw-Hill, 2000.

Rathvon, Natalie. *The Unmotivated Child: Helping Your Underachiever Become a Successful Student.* New York: Simon & Schuster, 1996.

Reichardt, Veronica, and Mary Wolf. *Crosswalk Connection: A Parent's Guide to*

Bridging the Gap Between Home and School. Tempe, AZ: DDJ Enterprises, 2000.

Rimm, Sylvia. *Why Bright Kids Get Poor Grades: And What You Can Do About It.* New York: Crown Publishers, 1995.

Sanchez, Benjamin, and Susan Sanchez. *Should I Go to the Teacher?: Developing a Co-operative Relationship with Your Child's School Community.* Portsmouth, NH: Heinemann, 1996.

Seal, Kathy, and Deborah Stipek. *Motivated Minds: Raising Children to Love Learning.* New York: Owl Books, 2001.

Simmons, Rachel. *Odd Girl Out: The Hidden Culture of Aggression in Girls.* New York: Harcourt, 2002.

Smutny, Joan Franklin. *Stand Up for Your Gifted Child: How to Make the Most of Kids' Strengths at School and at Home.* Downsview, Ontario: Free Spirit Publishing, 2001.

Springate, Kay Wright, and Dolores Stegelin. *Building School and Community Partnerships through Parent Involvement.* Upper Saddle River, NJ: Merrill/Prentice Hall, 1999.

Stepp, Laura Sessions. *Our Last Best Shot: Guiding Our Children Through Early Adolescence.* New York: Riverhead Books, 2000.

Strickland, Guy. *Bad Teachers: The Essential Guide for Concerned Parents.* New York: Pocket Books, 1998.

Unger, Harlow. *School Choice: How to Select the Best Schools for Your Children.* New York: Facts On File, 1999.

Weyhmuller, Jr., Robert. *Beyond the Bus Stop: 180 Ways to Help Your Child Succeed in School.* Portsmouth, NH: Heinemann, 1999.

Whale, David. *The Parent's School Action Guide: Making the Education System Work for Your Child.* Greensboro, NC: Avisson Press, 1999.

Whitley, Michael. *Bright Minds, Poor Grades: Understanding and Motivating Your Underachieving Child.* New York: Penguin Putnam, 2001.

Wiseman, Rosalind. *Queen Bees and Wannabes.* New York: Crown Publishers, 2002.

Wyman, Pat. *Learning vs. Testing.* Chicago: Zephyr Press, 2001.

Index

N

About the Author

STACY DEBROFF is a nationally acclaimed parenting expert and bestselling author of *The Mom Book: 4,278 of Mom Central's Tips for Moms,* from *Moms; Sign Me Up! The Parents' Complete Guide to Sports, Activities, Music Lessons, Dance Classes, and Other Extracurriculars;* and *Mom Central: The Ultimate Family Organizer* .

A media-savvy interviewee, Stacy has appeared on network television as a Mom Expert with guest spots on the CBS *Early Show* and NBC's *Today,* as well as over 300 television affiliates in every major market. From 2003 to 2004, Stacy shared her advice weekly on the New England Cable News as their parenting expert and produced her own live segment for the morning news. She has been a guest on over 500 radio shows, and is frequently heard on both national and local radio programs including *Daybreak USA* and *Dateline Washington,* in addition to independent stations throughout the country. Stacy is regularly featured and quoted in diverse national publications such as *USA Today, New York Times, Washington Post, Christian Science Monitor, Washington Times, Chicago Tribune, Boston Globe, Parenting, Parents, Child, Better Homes & Gardens, First for Women, Good Housekeeping, Woman's Day, Working Mother, Woman's World, Redbook,* and *Entrepreneur Magazine.*

Stacy has also served as the corporate spokeswoman for a number of companies, including most recently Whirlpool, Glad, General Mills, and Kimberly Clark. She is also CEO and founder of Mom Central, Inc., with over 300,000 moms around the world visiting the Mom Central website at www.momcentral.com every month to arm themselves with smart household and parenting solutions, and Stacy's monthly newsletter reaches over tens of thousands of moms worldwide.

As a dynamic, funny, and energized public speaker, Stacy gets invited as a feature speaker for parenting and women's groups, as well as corporations. Her talks include Getting Organized!

Stacy holds a B.A. in Psychology and Comparative Literature from Brown University, magna cum laude and Phi Beta Kappa; and a J.D. from Georgetown University, magna cum laude. Prior to launching Mom Central, Inc., Stacy founded Harvard Law School's Office of Public Interest Advising, launching a generation of law students into public interest work by heading an office staffed with seasoned public interest attorneys. *The American Lawyer* recognized Stacy for her entrepreneurial contribution to law with an in-depth profile in their issue on the Top Forty Lawyers Under Forty in 1997. The *Massachusetts Lawyers Weekly* also chose her as one of the Top Ten Lawyers of 1998.

She lives in Chestnut Hill, Massachusetts, with her husband and two children, ages 12 and 10.

For more helpful tips, articles and updates, visit: www.momcentral.com.

LaVergne, TN USA
16 August 2010
193533LV00002B/8/P